CRITICAL PERSPECTIVES ON RURAL CHANGE

Volume 2

TECHNOLOGICAL CHANGE AND THE RURAL ENVIRONMENT

TECHNOLOGICAL CHANGE AND THE RURAL ENVIRONMENT

Edited by
PHILIP LOWE,
TERRY MARSDEN
AND
SARAH WHATMORE

LONDON AND NEW YORK

First published in 1990 by David Fulton Publishers Ltd.

This edition first published in 2023
by Routledge
4 Park Square, Milton Park, Abingdon, Oxon OX14 4RN

and by Routledge
605 Third Avenue, New York, NY 10158

Routledge is an imprint of the Taylor & Francis Group, an informa business

British Library Cataloguing in Publication Data
A catalogue record for this book is available from the British Library

ISBN: 978-1-032-49781-5 (Set)
ISBN: 978-1-032-49610-8 (Volume 2) (hbk)
ISBN: 978-1-032-49612-2 (Volume 2) (pbk)
ISBN: 978-1-003-39462-4 (Volume 2) (ebk)

DOI: 10.4324/9781003394624

Publisher's Note
The publisher has gone to great lengths to ensure the quality of this reprint but points out that some imperfections in the original copies may be apparent.

Disclaimer
The publisher has made every effort to trace copyright holders and would welcome correspondence from those they have been unable to trace.

CRITICAL PERSPECTIVES
ON
RURAL CHANGE SERIES

TECHNOLOGICAL CHANGE AND THE RURAL ENVIRONMENT

EDITED BY

PHILIP LOWE
TERRY MARSDEN
SARAH WHATMORE

David Fulton Publishers

London

David Fulton Publishers Ltd
2 Barbon Close, Great Ormond Street, London WC1N 3JX

First published in Great Britain by
David Fulton Publishers, 1990

Note: The right of the contributors to be identified as the authors of their work
has been asserted by them in accordance with the Copyright, Designs and Patents
Act 1988.

© David Fulton Publishers Ltd

British Library Cataloguing in Publication Data

Technological change and the rural environment.
 – (Critical perspectives on rural change).
 1. Rural regions. Environment. Rural environment. Effects of technological
change
 I. Lowe, Philip   II. Marsden, Terry   III. Whatmore, Sarah
 IV. Series.
 333.76

ISBN 1-85346-112-1

Typeset by Chapterhouse, Formby L37 3PX
Printed in Great Britain by
Biddles Ltd, Guildford & Kings Lynn

Contents

Contributors

W. Jos Byman — Department of International Relations and International Public Law, University of Amsterdam, The Netherlands

Graham Cox — School of Social Sciences and Humanities, University of Bath, UK

Margaret FitzSimmons — Graduate School of Architecture and Urban Planning, University of California, Los Angeles, USA

David Goodman — Board of Environmental Studies, University of California, Santa Cruz, USA

Philip Lowe — Bartlett School of Architecture and Planning, University College, London, UK

Terry Marsden — Department of Planning, Housing and Development, South Bank Polytechnic, London, UK

Richard Munton — Department of Geography, University College, London, UK

Miklós Persányi	Senior Advisor Hungarian Ministry of Environment and Water Management Budapest Hungary
Michael Redclift	Environment Division Wye College University of London UK
Joyce Tait	Centre for Technology Strategy Open University Milton Keynes UK
Sarah Whatmore	Department of Geography University of Bristol UK
John Wilkinson	Postgraduate Programme in Agricultural Development Federal University of Rio de Janeiro (CPDA/UFRJ) Brazil
Michael Winter	Centre for Rural Studies Royal Agricultural College Cirencester UK

Acknowledgements

Chapters 3, 5 and 6 relate to research sponsored by the Economic and Social Research Council under the Joint Agriculture and Environment Programme; and Chapter 8 to a research project on Risks of Biotechnology and their Regulation, also sponsored by the ESRC.

Editorial Advisors

Helga Repassy	University of Budapest, Hungary.
Geoff Lawrence	Centre for Rural Welfare Research, New South Wales, Australia
Patrick Mooney	University of Kentucky, United States
Maria Delors Garcia-Ramon	Autonomous University Barcelona, Spain.

PREFACE

Critical Perspectives on Rural Change Series

This series aims to promote international debate and dissemination of current empirical and theoretical research relevant to rural areas in advanced societies. Rural areas, their residents and agencies, face considerable change and uncertainty. The balance between production, consumption and conservation is being adjusted as economic activities are relocated and primary production is transformed. Similarly the values placed upon rural living and participation are altering. Local and external political forces structure choices within rural areas, not only for those concerned with agriculture, but also with regard to rural development, general economic and social policy, and regional and fiscal arrangements. To understand contemporary rural change, therefore, demands a critical and holistic perspective able to transcend traditional disciplinary boundaries and to encompass different spatial and institutional levels of analysis. The series is intended to contribute to the development of such a perspective, and the volumes are designed to attract a wide audience associated with international comparative research. Each provides a review of current research within its subject. This, the second volume, focuses on the relationships between technological change and the rural environment. It is intended that contributions should be prospective in character, by identifying new research agenda and the likely consequences of contemporary changes in policy and economy. The overall focus upon 'rural change' should not encourage the 'ghettoisation' of these particular strands of social scientific endeavour. The editors are committed to providing a vehicle for the application of a wide range of social science approaches relating to theory and practice and, particularly, to exploring abstract social concepts and their 'grounding' through empirical investigation.

Philip Lowe
Terry Marsden
Sarah Whatmore
London 1990

INTRODUCTION:

Technological Change and the Rural Environment

Philip Lowe, Terry Marsden and Sarah Whatmore

This volume brings together key themes usually neglected by social scientists, but nevertheless of pressing social relevance. While there has always been considerable interest in the socio-economic consequences of technological change, technology itself has tended to be treated as an independent and external force to which society and various social groups are obliged to adapt. Equally, the rural environment has traditionally been treated as vestigial on the assumption that urban-industrial society effectively concentrates processes of economic and social innovation. Indeed, the physical environment in general has been neglected or discounted by social theorists as a significant determinant of human action.

The subject of the volume juxtaposes, therefore, one factor traditionally regarded by social theorists as exogenous and another regarded as residual. The pressure to bring them from the background to the foreground of attention stems initially not from social scientists but from mounting popular disquiet. Technological change has come to be seen as neither neutral nor benign. With growing alarm over various global ecological changes, there are increasing doubts about the continued sustainability of present patterns of urbanisation and industrialisation. In this context, the complex dependency of urban society on the rural environment has become more apparent, leading to a re-valuation of the latter's social and ecological importance. At the same time, the rural environments of most developed and many developing countries have been transformed by a quite unprecedented technological revolution. This simultaneously challenges the notion that these are somehow still backward zones but also provokes increasing concern over the destruction of traditional landscapes and cultures as well as the widespread environmental degradation that has ensued (see Figure A and chapters 1–4 below).

Figure A Environmental problems arising from the intensification of agricultural production

- The human health effects of pesticide and fertiliser residues, heavy metals, feed supplements and other contaminants in soil, water bodies, food products and the food chain;
- The diminution and partition of biotopes valued for nature conservation;
- The contamination of ground and surface waters and the eutrophication of surface waters by nitrates and phosphates leading to local health risks, decline in the quality of aquatic resources, losses in recreation values and increased water supply costs;
- Agricultural pollution problems associated with the growth of intensive animal husbandry;
- Air pollution from intensive animal production, manure spreading and crop spraying;
- The salinisation of soils, which is contaminating water supplies and causing losses in soil productivity and landscape amenity values;
- Losses in landscape amenity and wildlife habitat caused by the amalgamation of farms, the growing emergence of monocultures, the removal of hedges, walls and terraces, the draining of wetlands and the deterioration and destruction of traditional farm buildings; and
- Soil compaction, erosion and pollution which have led to productivity losses, declines in the quality of water resources and reduction in the capacity of water storages.

(Source: OECD 1989, pp. 13–4).

These issues raise certain analytical problems. Central to contemporary debates about the impact of technological change is the notion of control. On the one hand, technological mastery connotes control over nature but also social and economic power. On the other hand, chronic ecological problems and novel technological hazards speak of a technology that is out of control.

This conundrum is nowhere more apparent than in agriculture which, as the most extensive user of land, is thereby the primary social and economic activity creating and recreating the physical environment. Modern farmers have available to them an unprecedented battery of chemical and mechanical aids to boost production. Yet individual farmers may know very little about the wider and often harmful effects which can accompany the use of these products. Even those who do appreciate the consequences may feel that they have little alternative but to take environmental risks. By their very sophistication and potency, agricultural technologies have cast the ordinary farmer into the role of the sorcerer's apprentice. But how has this come about?

As a result of technological change and the provision of production incentives, agricultural output has quadrupled this century. Yet, in most developed countries, apart from the collectivised agriculture of the Socialist economies (Persányi: chapter 2), farming remains a form of economic activity based largely on family labour and family-based units of production. The full penetration and development of capitalism in agriculture has been constrained by the individual ownership of land and the refractory nature of the biological and ecological processes which agricultural production harnesses and which still require the individual attention of the farmer.

Against these limitations of organic nature and land, the industrial innovation that has occurred has been fragmented. Capital has been forced to pursue partial appropriations of the rural labour processes which are then re-incorporated in agriculture as valorised inputs or produced means of production, i.e. as bought-in fertilisers, pesticides, seed, feed and machinery. In this way, capital has progressively but discontinuously appropriated activities and value once regarded as essential to farming. As constraints to subsumption have been overcome through technological change, so farming has been increasingly penetrated by capital (Goodman and Redclift, 1986).

The dynamic of technological advance in farming thus lies outside of agriculture. It arises from the independent research and development (R&D) strategies of firms in the supply industries each involved in the continual update of its products to hold its market share (see Goodman and Wilkinson: chapter 6). Farmers may have little real influence over this process or its consequences. For most of them, choice over the adoption and use of technology is constrained (Lowe *et al.*: chapter 3). The condition of perfect competition in agricultural production makes them very susceptible to new techniques that lower production costs and enhance productivity. Increasingly, they have to rely on external advice in selecting and using particular products, and the esoteric and interlocking nature of many agricultural techniques and practices creates its own form of technological dependence at the farm level (see Munton, Marsden and Whatmore: chapter 5).

A specific example is provided by the American insecticide industry (Perkins, 1984). In spite of a twelve-fold increase in insecticide use between 1945 and 1977, US crop losses from insect pests almost doubled, and America still lost about as much of its crops before harvest as any other country. There are three basic reasons why the wall of chemical controls has kept falling in: first, since most insecticides kill both the pest and its predators, surviving pests rebound quickly in a world without natural enemies; secondly, these broad-based strategies often elevate insect species once of little significance, to major pest status; and, thirdly, the genetic elasticity of insects means that most pests develop resistance to any given chemical within five years, sometimes in a single season. Most farmers, though, are locked into the insecticide treadmill; and the expanding volume of sales has suited the agribusiness corporations. Alternative and potentially more effective strategies would be possible, particularly integrated pest management (IPM) drawing on various biological controls. These, however, would require co-ordinated regional action and they have little appeal to the corporations, as they do not come in a commoditised and patentable form. Much depends, therefore, on the organisation, funding and priorities for agricultural R&D, and the way these are influenced and determined by different interests (see Munton, Marsden and Whatmore: chapter 5).

The context for technological change in centrally planned economies has been very different, though the outcome has often been similar (Persányi: chapter 2). The enforced collectivisation of agriculture allowed for the rationalisation and industrialisation of production on a large scale. Here again, though, the dynamic of technological change lay elsewhere; in this case, with central ministries which prescribed usually very rigid economic and industrial goals with little regard for the variability or sensitivity of the rural environment. Since the over-throw of Communist regimes in Eastern Europe, moves to reprivatise agriculture have begun, though the consequences are as yet unclear. Undoubtedly, the technological pressures will not abate. Under market conditions, indeed, pressures in addition to those from the input industries may arise as already happens in the capitalist countries.

From the big, commercial food processors and retailers, for example, farmers face increasingly more exacting specifications on the type and quality of their produce. The food industry, in general, has increased its R&D expenditure boosting it from a 'low-tech' to a 'medium-tech' sector (OECD, 1986). Some developments could have radical implications. Biotechnology, for example, opens up a multitude of new substitution possibilities which promise to break down traditional food sector and industrial boundaries (see Goodman and Wilkinson: chapter 6). The most well known example involves new sweeteners which bring into competition sugar, grain (the source of iso-glucose) and synthetic low calorie sweeteners (such as aspartame), with major implications for European and North American agriculture and for third world sugar producers. Transnational chemical and pharmaceutical firms now dominate biotechnology research and increasingly are involved in producing intermediate and final products for the food industry. Concomitantly, leading food processors are diversifying into non-food outlets for agricultural produce. These developments foreshadow the growth of a generic bio-industry (see Goodman and Wilkinson: chapter 6; Byman: chapter 7).

One consequence, already emerging, is a restructuring of the traditional relationship between agriculture and industry as the farmer becomes squeezed between the big chemical manufacturers and the food conglomerates. Established agricultural policy which is built on that former relationship is seriously challenged too, with wider political and ecological implications. The productivist agricultural policies pursued by most industrialised countries since the 1930s and 1940s have been oriented towards the support of nationally or regionally (eco-system) based commodity systems and related input and processing sectors. They have often incorporated a certain political settlement between such interests. The international reorganisation of agriculture-industry relations and the movement from a resource-oriented to a science-based agriculture are undermining these regional and national coalitions. Some of the implications for the viability of US agricultural regions (FitzSimmons: chapter 1), for international trade and especially US/EC trade relations (Byman: chapter 7) and for agriculture in developing countries (Redclift: chapter 4) are explored further below.

The interaction between technological and social and environmental change is intrinsically uneven (Smith, 1984). In this respect, rural areas can be understood as those geographical spaces which traditionally have been given over predominantly to the extraction of the natural resources – food, fibre, minerals and water – required either for subsistence or for industrial production and urban consumption. But technological change and capital concentration in the food, fibre and other production systems are profoundly altering these relationships, intensifying the exploitation of some areas and marginalising others, and, in either instance, often undermining long-term sustainability (Redclift: chapter 4).

These processes of spatial unevenness have their counterparts in conceptual boundaries which distinguish urban from rural, society from nature, technology from the environment. Such dualisms, though, often obscure wider relationships which, in reality, transcend these divisions. For example, we see technologies as artefacts, such as a piece of machinery or a chemical compound, and thus divest them of the asymmetrical social relationships surrounding their production and use. Likewise, technological change is often portrayed as an autonomous process deterministically driven by scientific advance and with social and environmental effects analytically separate from rather than integral to the process.

The partitioning of scientific research in relation to technological change reproduces and reinforces this artificial separation with engineering and the physical sciences seen as sources of innovation, and social and environmental sciences as furnishing analyses of 'up-take' and 'impacts'. Clearly, this divide needs to be overcome if social and environmental factors are to be incorporated in the design, execution and regulation of agricultural and other technology. As it is, the prevailing tendency to reify technology underpins a perpetual spiral in which successive cycles of innovation, needed to maintain capital accumulation, are repeatedly justified as providing the solutions to problems which have arisen in part from previous cycles. Thus, though post-war technological change has been a major factor in agriculture's oversupply and ecological problems, new technologies are put forward as the panacea. And information technology and biotechnology, in particular, are now heralded as part of a prospective generation of 'clean' technologies, as if, apart from their manifold benefits, they will be devoid of their own particular risks, unwanted consequences and disruptive potential (Tait: chapter 8).

These developments, indeed, pose considerable challenges for agriculture, rural communities and the environment. They raise the question of the regulation of technological change and its political economy. There is now considerable evidence of the social and environmental costs both of the green revolution in developing countries and of the 'high-tech' agriculture pursued equally in the industrialised countries (Redclift: chapter 4; Lowe et al.: chapter 3). Nevertheless, until recently, there has been little effort to counteract or prevent these consequences, and the steps that have been taken have been largely ineffective. In the developed countries, environmental controls over farming practices tend to be weak and reactive (OECD 1989); and in many developing countries even these are non-existent (Redclift,

6

Figure B Contribution of agriculture to total production of globally important gases

Product	Proportion produced by agriculture	Agricultural source activities	Major impacts
Methane	40–60%	Anaerobic decompositon in paddy fields and in the guts of cattle and other ruminants. Biomass burning.	A 'greenhouse' gas which increases atmospheric warming.
Nitrous oxide	10–25%	Bacterial action on nitrogenous fertilisers. Biomass burning.	A 'greenhouse gas'. Also reduces the ozone layer.
Ammonia	80–90%	The volatilisation of nitrogen in fertilisers and animal wastes.	Contributes to acid rain.
Other combustion gases	60–65%	Biomass burning: forest clearance and the burning of crop wastes and residues.	'Greenhouse' gases. Acid rain.

(Adapted from Pretty and Conway, 1989)

chapter 4). No longer, though, are such matters confined within national boundaries, as the promotion and diffusion of new techniques is increasingly controlled by international agribusiness firms, and existing agricultural practices already have a significant impact on global pollution (see Figure B).

Moreover, the prospect of the agricultural use of genetically modified organisms poses quite novel environmental risks and has provoked calls for stringent controls, linked to a pro-active regulatory strategy (Tait: chapter 8). Such moves towards a more rational regulation of technological change and the management of the rural environment demand an integrated understanding of the processes involved, and it is to this objective that the present volume seeks to contribute.

References

Goodman, D.E. and Redclift, M. (1986) Capitalism, petty commodity production and the farm enterprise, pp. 20–40 of G. Cox, P. Lowe and M. Winter (eds) *Agriculture: People and Policies*. London, Allen and Unwin.

OECD, Science and Technology Indicators, no. 2 (1986) *R and D, Invention and Competitiveness*. Paris, OECD.

OECD (1989) *Agricultural and Environmental Policies: Opportunities for Integration.* Paris, OECD.

Perkins, J. H. (1984) *Insects, Experts and the Insecticide Crisis.* US, Plenum Press.

Pretty, J. N. and Conway, G. R. (1989) *Agriculture as a Global Polluter.* London, International Institute for Environment and Development.

Smith, N. (1984) *Uneven Development.* Oxford, Blackwells.

CHAPTER 1

The Social and Environmental Relations of US Agricultural Regions

Margaret FitzSimmons

In recent years rural sociologists concerned with the sociology of agriculture have taken up analysis of agricultural class relations. They have investigated the circumstances of the ownership of capital and of labour on the assumption that these will be effective points of entry into an understanding of the dynamic social processes of capitalist agriculture, as they were for Marx's analysis of manufacturing. This theoretical project has been complicated by the observation that most farm enterprises, even in the 'advanced societies', do not display the full separation of capital and labour which characterises manufacturing: in most enterprises the farm is owned and the work performed by members of a family, and wage labour contributes only a small fraction to the farm activities. This absence of universal 'advanced-capitalist' class forms in agriculture has stimulated on-going discussion about whether agriculture differs from manufacturing in some essential way, such that petty commodity production can be seen as structurally stable (Friedmann, 1978a; Davis, 1980), or whether agriculture is merely backward, and will be inevitably transformed by technological change in agricultural production and the increasing commoditisation of agricultural inputs (de Janvry, 1980; Goodman, Sorj & Wilkinson, 1987). Investigation of the 'subsumption' of farming to manufacturing capital and to capital in general begins with the family farm as the unit of analysis (Marsden, 1984; Marsden *et al.*, 1986 a&b; Whatmore *et al.*, 1987 a&b).

The new sociology of agriculture has thus taken up this question at two distinct scales: the household; and the over-arching tendencies of capitalist production as they constrain and construct agricultural activities. But it has been largely silent on intervening social relationships and institutions. The apparent contradictions between continuing family-based production and

8

the pressures of the dominant capitalist system need to be better understood, however, by attention to the forces and institutions which structure and sustain agricultural systems at an intermediate, often regional scale. In other words, *class relationships are constituted and defended in particular localities and cannot be fully understood in terms of the internal relationships and tensions of the particular enterprise nor universally derived from pure forms*. Because these regional systems are relatively stable expressions of the historical resolution of particular political struggles, I refer to them (following Clark, 1986) as *regional class contracts*. These relate agriculture to manufacturing and to capital in general through a whole set of complex social institutions: labour markets, input and product markets, capital markets, and political forms.

The chapter develops this theoretical argument, supported with evidence from the United States, a country which provides an opportunity to examine the spatial tendencies of capitalist agriculture in a relatively direct way, for the following reasons. The institutional and geographical patterns of American agriculture arise under circumstances of general commodity production and are not constrained by the geographies of earlier historical periods. The dominant sectors of US agriculture have always been influenced by production for national and international, not local, markets and, at least until the 1980s, have dominated world markets for these commodities. Finally, the federal structure of the US state has provided opportunities to institutionalise political struggles effectively at the regional (sub-national) scale. What has occurred in the US may anticipate similar developments elsewhere in the industrial countries, particularly as pressures for the international integration of capital and labour markets (as with the European Community and 1992) and for the eradication of agricultural subsidies and protective tariffs (as in the GATT talks) continue.

Furthermore, American agriculture is currently in crisis, and this crisis is largely geographical in nature. It is geographical not just in that it is expressed as a regional (as well as a sectoral) crisis but, more importantly, because it presents an abrupt and catastrophic restructuring of a complex set of social *and* spatial relations – within and among the commodity subsectors which define agricultural regions, between agriculture and manufacturing, between the 'urban' and the 'rural'.

To pursue these questions, it is necessary to address the theoretical intersections and lacunae between recent work in rural sociology and in geography. My purpose here is to propose a theory of agricultural change, drawing together the insights of these two disciplines.

Regions in geography

In their introduction to *The Rural Sociology of the Advanced Societies*, Newby and Buttel suggested that rural sociology has been hampered by its inability to resolve certain fundamental conceptual problems, most importantly the theoretical meaning of the term 'rural.' Referring to Copp's statement that 'There is no *rural* society and there is no *rural* economy. It is merely *our* analytical distinction, our rhetorical device', Newby and Buttel wrote

> There has been an ultimate[ly] futile search for a *sociological* definition of 'rural,' a reluctance to recognize that the term 'rural' is an empirical category rather than a sociological one, *that it is merely a 'geographical expression.'* (1980, p. 4, emphasis added)

Geographers (not surprisingly) rarely see geography as merely empirical. But most would agree with the authors' suggestion: that 'rural sociology demands a theory which links the spatial with the social' (1980, p. 5). Recent theoretical developments in geography may provide a foundation for this common theoretical project.

A more effective theory of the rural (in sociology and elsewhere) depends, as does the parallel and convergent theory of the urban , on the recognition that the differentiation between urban and rural society is one case of the general question of the region. Over the last hundred years geographers have taken up, relinquished, and are now again engaged in the formal analysis of regions. In part this is because geographers, as an intellectual community, have not agreed on the crux of our own project: Should we set out to understand what creates geography (as spatial organisation) or what geography creates? Is geography (and its regional expression) to be treated as the cause or the consequence of human action? Debate on these questions has strongly affected what we mean by 'region'.

Early geographers took regions for granted, as phenomenal wholes – appropriate units of analysis in themselves. Where they sought broader generalisations, they most often saw geography as cause, making use of environmental variation (or, occasionally, cultural heritage) to explain inter-regional commonalities and differences. From this, we get two concepts of the region: the *physiographic region* (where spatial pattern results from varying climate and geology) (see Baker, 1929; 1927–33) and the first type of *functional region* (the culture area, territorially based and self-contained) (see Grigg, 1974; Spencer & Horvath, 1963). But this concept of the organic region could not withstand the increasing economic integration of these *a priori* regions, an integration which broke down the appearance of regional autonomy and encouraged a more systematic examination of the differentiating processes by which regions were (re)formed.

This new systematic analysis challenged the earlier ontological presumption of regions as functional wholes. When the various formative linkages within and among regions became themselves the objects of analysis, the integrity of the region itself dissolved, since social processes formed complex spatial patterns without coterminous boundaries. This led many geographers to abandon regional study in favour of analysis of a whole congeries of abstracted geographies – economic geography, social geography, political geography, cultural geography – each of which isolated a particular aspect of everyday life from the multi-dimensional geographical lifespace within which it was embedded (and drew, for its theoretical base, on a different collateral discipline). Where regions appear in this literature, it is as functional regions in a second sense, in which regions express a necessary division of labour which differentiates but simultaneously integrates them into a social whole. Hidden in this second functionalism is a continuing assumption that the efficiencies of market exchange establish regions on the basis of comparative advantage[1] (the neo-classical argument). In such systematic studies the sense of geography as *significantly* causal, (or even as context-forming) disappears; geography is merely consequence, a spatial epiphenomenon of the social processes which make up human activity (see Garrison & Marble, 1957).

Recently, some geographers have suggested that geography must be seen as simultaneously consequence and cause and that regions are' best understood relationally (Harvey, 1982; Gilbert, 1988; Soja, 1989). The *relational region* arises out of the necessary dynamics of capitalism, which

> must negotiate a knife-edge between preserving the values of past commitments made at a particular place and time, or devaluing them to open up fresh room for accumulation... The inner contradictions of capitalism are expressed through the restless formation and reformation of geographical landscapes. (Harvey, 1983, p. 150)

The relational region expresses neither the environmental determinism of the physiographic region nor the balanced equilibrium of the functional region. Ann Gilbert suggests that, in this new work in geography, the region is understood in three ways: as a local response to capitalist processes, as a focus of identification, and as a medium for social interaction (Gilbert, 1988).

Though Gilbert discovers these conceptions of the region among distinct (and differing) communities of geographers, they can be integrated as aspects of a common conception. The region then appears as a coalescence of three moments of contemporary life in capitalist societies, which I will refer to as **regionalisation, regionalism** and **regionality**.[2] Regionalisation results from the dynamic and chaotic process of spatial integration and differentiation within capitalism which Harvey describes; regionalism appears in the politics and the political culture of response; and regionality refers to the concrete spatial history of place and its constructing and constricting effects. These phenomena become regional, not just spatial, where they require a complex pattern of relatively-orderly social interactions (such as economic linkages) and institutions (such as state forms, regional labour markets, or patterns of the reproduction of labour) for their establishment and continuation.

Most of the theoretical development of this approach in geography has been directed to manufacturing and other urban activities (see Clark, 1986; Scott, 1988; Scott & Storper, 1986; Soja, 1989; Storper & Walker, 1989; Walker, 1985). Scott and Storper emphasise the importance of economic linkages among firms, through production subcontracting and other forms of economic integration; Storper and Walker address the continuously dynamic geography of capitalist manufacturing. Of these authors, only Clark (1986) and Walker (1985) explicitly link geography and class, and only Soja connects his analysis of the space-forming dynamics of capitalism with broad questions of politics and culture, though primarily at the urban scale. But this strategy can also be used to examine agriculture (FitzSimmons, 1986).

What is an agricultural region?

Urbanisation as a process constructs both the urban and the rural, the city and the countryside, as the differentiated and segregated geography consequent to this space-forming process. In this sense Buttel and Newby fell into error; the term rural is manifestly a social category (and should be a sociological one), a categorical abstraction constructed by the complex historical social process of the segregation of agriculture and manufacturing, the centralisation of commercial and political life, and the coordination and concentration of circulation and consumption in urban space.

Capital in agiculture faces particular constraints on production and profit (Mann & Dickinson, 1978, 1980; FitzSimmons, 1986), which have stimulated the spatial differentiation of agriculture in the US (as they have in international trade) into a set of commodity subsectors. The basic outlines of this spatial differentiation appear very early (Baker, 1927-33; Murray, 1977; Cochrane, 1980) and, in contrast with Europe, the separate commodity systems extend over large areas. This patterning arises out of the integration of the national economy and export production, an integration which begins early in American history and carries forward as a kind of regional commodity inertia (Spencer & Horvath, 1963). The importance of commodity specialisation in US agriculture cannot be overemphasised (see Friedland, 1980; Friedland et al., 1981); investigations which address agriculture in general (such as Gregor, 1982) are necessarily limited in their analytic power by the problem of comparing apples and cows. The particular relationships and tendencies which characterise the dynamic processes of competition and restructuring in agriculture occur first within particular commodity subsectors, since value is measured in the exchange of particular commodities before it appears as a phenomenal characteristic of commodities in general (Elson, 1979).

The geographical pattern of commodity specialisation in American agriculture, out of which current agricultural regions are derived, results in part from the particular historical moments of settlement of particular territories, in regard to laws regulating land distribution but also in relationship to the particular commodity economies of the agriculture of the time, of market patterns regionally, nationally and internationally. So, the South reflects not just the preference of cotton for warm summers and abundant water but also the relationship between the US and the UK after American Independence and before the Civil War. The wheat farms of the Great Plains result not just from climate and soil but also from the growing demand for wheat for urban (at first European urban) markets (Morgan, 1977). And it is not the commodity, specificially, but the social relationships of production which are persistent: California agriculture has shifted from cattle, to wheat, to speciality crops (intensification) but has remained dominated by the patterns of land-ownership and labour control which characterised its early development (FitzSimmons, 1983).

These social relationships of production take the form of characteristic regional social contracts – accepted norms and forms of social organisation built around distinct labour processes and relationships between labour and capital, and particular regional multipliers and marketing structures. These regional social contracts relate farming to other regional activities and embed agriculture regionally, nationally and internationally, within a structure of capital-in-general. They appear, in their initial forms, out of commodity-specific attempts to overcome particular problems of capital accumulation in agriculture, problems which arise out of the continuing role of nature in agricultural production.

Nature in agriculture

Capital in agriculture encounters problems which capital in manufacturing is not subject to. These result from the continuing role of nature, that is, from the only-partial dominion of capital over the production process in agriculture.

The first relative difficulty arises from the fact that agricultural economies must support a labour force throughout the year, though in modern, specialised production systems the workers may be needed only episodically, at planting and harvest. Marx identified this as the difference between production time (the period required from first investment in the production of a commodity to its completion) and socially necessary labour time. Traditional farming systems addressed this problem in different ways from modern capitalist systems: they combined a diversity of tasks on the farm or in the farming community to make use of labour throughout the year; and they were not driven so fiercely by competition to maximise production relative to the costs of reproduction of the labour force. Modern regional systems have found various resolutions of this problem. In the wheat regions most farms depend primarily on household labour (Friedmann, 1978 a&b); rising equity in land has allowed the purchase of complex and specialised combine harvesters and huge planting rigs, so that farm enterprises can employ wage workers only at particular points in the life-cycle of the farm family. In speciality-crop production, in contrast, farmers have long relied on huge numbers of temporary seasonal workers, drawn from the poor of the US and the Third World, provided in gangs by labour contractors, and sent home when the crop is picked. The first system remains family farming, while the second is clearly industrial in form.

Secondly, it has been more difficult to increase the productivity of labour in agriculture than in manufacturing. This is true despite statistics which suggest that only a small portion of the labour force in the advanced countries now works on farms; much of this reduction in direct labour has resulted from the hiving off, or capture, of many activities once performed on the farm but not captured by industry, including agricultural inputs and processing and a whole complex of artisanal activities (Buttel & Gillespie,

1989; Goodman, Sorj & Wilkinson, 1987). In terms of the tasks of the farm itself, the impediments to increasing the productivity of labour in ways that manufacturing has discovered are clear: it is difficult to work at night (so no 24-hour shifts to make the most effective use of capital invested in machinery and land); the worker must, for the most part, go to the work, not the work to the worker, thus precluding the rationalisation and managerial control of an assembly line; and finally, agriculture is still dependent on ongoing natural processes, which have their own rhythms and, sometimes catastrophic, variability.

Third, agriculture faces particular problems in what Marx called circulation and the realisation of value. The easiest example to give for this (though it is a subtler and more complicated concept than the example would suggest) refers to the inexorable rhythms of agriculture as a constraint on the rate of circulation of capital within the enterprise itself. If an entrepreneur makes a particular investment in manufacturing, and is able to make and sell a product 20 times a year from that investment, his rate of profit compounds and accelerates through that regular realisation of value in exchange; but a farmer, bound by the rhythms of nature, makes an investment in winter wheat in the autumn and then cannot receive a return until spring harvest, or reinvest his earnings in wheat production until the following autumn. Given the role of nature in agriculture, this circulation (and the realisation of value through the sale of the product) is difficult to accelerate. Moreover, the farmer cannot easily respond to market signals to expand or shrink production; if cattle prices begin to rise, it takes two years for a farmer to increase his herd of heifers and begin to sell more feeder calves.

Finally, agriculture faces particular limits because of its extraordinary dependence on land. In an expanding economy, land to support expanded production is likely to be scarce; in an economy in which technological packages (combines, heavy tractors) imply certain production scales, the farmer may find it difficult to use this machinery efficiently; land markets tend to be sticky in comparison to other factor markets; in many areas land varies in effective fertility – it is a highly differentiated, not a standardised, factor of production. When the 1973 Russian grain sale (which doubled average farm incomes in that year) encouraged American farmers to anticipate an expanding market, they invested in expansion, buying new and larger farm machinery and seeking out additional land. Land prices in the grain areas tripled in the next several years in response to competition for what was suddenly a very scarce production factor.

Different strategies for accommodating these difficulties have served to segregate commodity subsectors in particular ways. Some production systems become heavily mechanised (as in grain production), depending on substantial investment in land to provide equity against which to borrow for operating costs from year to year. Other systems depend on seasonal, migrant labour, and are integrated into the structures of finance capital not through their own assets and loans from local banks but by loans from processors and marketers to which they have pre-contracted their crops, or – where they are very large firms, often agricultural multinationals – by

Figure 1.1 Generalised commodity regions

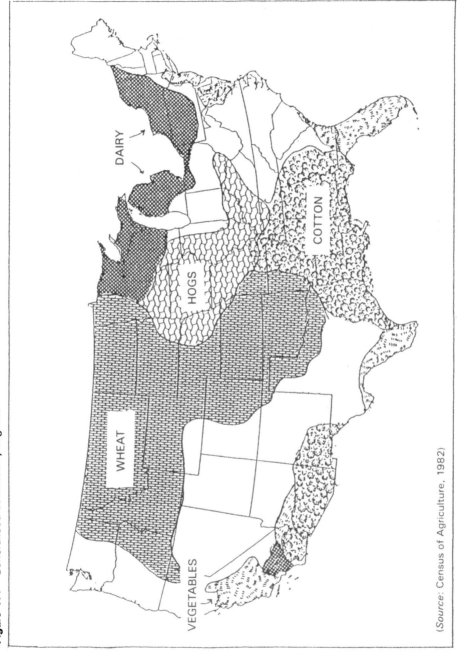

DAIRY

HOGS

COTTON

WHEAT

VEGETABLES

(*Source:* Census of Agriculture, 1982)

Figure 1.2 Long-term wage labour

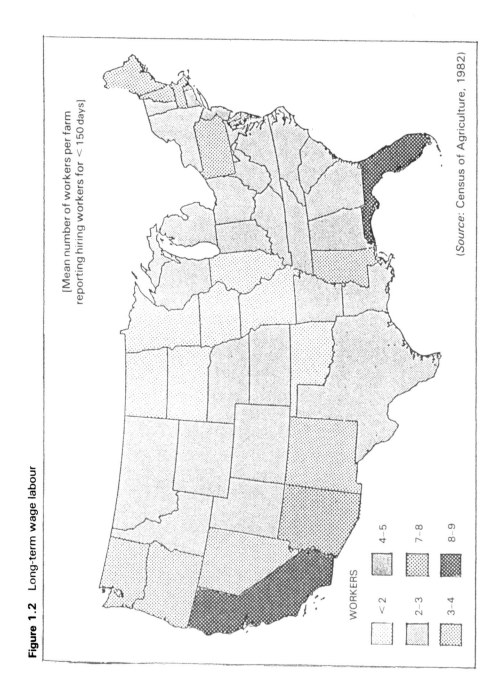

[Mean number of workers per farm
reporting hiring workers for < 150 days]

WORKERS

< 2

2–3

3–4

4–5

7–8

8–9

(*Source*: Census of Agriculture, 1982)

internal self-financing supplemented by participation in national and international capital markets. From this process of institutional development and differentiation arises a complex of agricultural regions. (See Figure 1.1)

Winter wheat is the dominant crop of the High Plains and upper Great Plains, and the source of substantial foreign trade. Wheat production has come to require huge acreages and substantial investment to support farm operators and their families under conditions of continuous surplus production, sustained in part by government price supports through Commodity Credit Corporation loans and other Federal programs. Though the number of wheat farmers is relatively large (436,250 in 1982)[3] and the aggregate value of the crop is great (almost eight billion dollars in 1982), international trade (which sets national prices as well) is largely controlled by six firms (Morgan, 1977). The permanent wage labour force per farm is quite low (one to three workers – see Figure 1.2) and there is little seasonal variation in the labour force. Farmer cooperatives provide inputs and marketing for smaller and medium-sized farms, but the larger enterprises deal directly with suppliers and markets (Klohn, 1988); only 38 per cent of all grain and soy beans was sold through farmer cooperatives in 1983 (Marion, 1986).

Cotton is the traditional export crop of the South from the time of American Independence (Daniel, 1985). The problem of over-production, combined with the general economic plight of the South and the power of Southern senators and congressmen, has made this crop both more subsidised and more regulated than any other except tobacco. Since World War II the mechanisation of the labour process in this crop has ended the sharecropping system and displaced immense numbers of rural people to the industrial cities of the North. But in this same period cotton culture has shifted toward the Southwest, drawn by cheap irrigation and large industrial enterprises and pushed by continuing pest problems in the old cotton areas. This crop is relatively-tightly regionally organised, with ownership of the few commercial gins which serve each major production area becoming increasingly concentrated; cotton marketing cooperatives handled only 19 per cent of product sales in 1983, reduced from 23 per cent ten years earlier (Klohn, 1988).

Beef cattle tie together the open government-owned lands of the West with the grainfields and industrial cities of the Middle West and East. Beef cattle production articulates the activities and investments of Western ranchers, urban speculators, an organised and angry industrial workforce in the slaughterhouses and packing plants still clustered around the railheads of the Midwest and their competition, low-waged unorganised workers in the *maquila* system.[4] Though there were 618,555 farms producing beef cattle in the United States in 1982 (and 84,961 feedlots) 76 per cent of feed cattle were slaughtered by the largest 20 (of 417) packers nationally and in each of the 21 major fed-cattle states the four leading slaughtering firms accounted for an average of 81 per cent of the cattle slaughtered in that state (Marion and Geithman, 1986).

Speciality crops are a dominant form in the West and Southwest, and occur in Florida, the Great Lakes states and New England. Speciality crop production requires a large and migrant labour force for harvest and some pre-harvest activity. Speciality crop systems are integrated and dominated by marketing firms (some of them in the form of producers' cooperatives) (FitzSimmons, 1985; Pfeffer, n.d.), and forward contracting is the primary form of market arrangement. Within this category, permanent (orchard, vineyard) and temporary (fresh market produce) crops also can be theoretically distinguished as a result of their differing logics of investment and accumulation and the influence of the tax incentives of the Federal laws (Vogeler, 1981). Though cooperatives are important in the marketing of certain crops in this subsector, their structural effects must be examined on a case-by-case basis; some (like Sunkist) appear to small and medium grower members much like external marketing monopolies.

The corn/hogs complex, like dairying, has retained the family-farm form with some persistence. Spread throughout the north-central states – Iowa, Ohio, Indiana, Illinois and surrounding areas – this complex retains the social organisation of the agricultural heartland, but encounters the market concentration of the packing industry which also dominates beef cattle production. The old pattern of integrated production of hogs and corn within the same enterprise is breaking down, as factory farming of hogs using purchased feed becomes more common (Hayenga *et al.*, 1985). Cooperatives are important in the provision of farm inputs in this area, and in the sale of corn for feed (Klohn, 1988).

Dairy cattle are the primary commodity of the 'old Northwest' – Wisconsin, Minnesota, parts of Michigan and Ohio, and the rural Northeast. They also are important in the agriculture of the Pacific Northwest and in California. The importance of the dairy industry to these regions has stimulated direct Federal policies of price support and regulation, which have encouraged the differentiation of the product into fluid milk, intermediate-term (ice-cream and cottage cheese), and long-term (cheeses, butter, dried milk) products. Fluid-milk production appears around major urban markets, but the longer term products are more regionally organised, often through farmer-cooperatives. Seventy-seven per cent of all milk and dairy products were sold through cooperatives in 1983 (Marion, 1986). At present, dairying is organised into two production forms: the 'Wisconsin' form, where family farming and household production, small herds, and on-farm production of feed is characteristic; and the 'California' form, with large enterprises, wage labour, huge herds and purchased feed (Gilbert & Akor, 1988). The sector may be substantially restructured with the threatened withdrawal of Federal supports which had sustained the smaller operators.

The differentiation of agriculture into specialised commodity subsectors in response to the four problems outlined above has proceeded far enough to make it less-than-useful to begin by comparing cotton farms with cattle operations or dairying with speciality crop production. Competition occurs among the producers of particular commodities. Any similarities across commodities are due to the general structuring tendencies of a capitalist economy, which moves towards the concentration of capital but not necessarily towards the concentration of firms; and the institutional forms capital constructs around production – specifically patterns of transport, marketing and finance and particular legal rights and political structures.

The structure of agriculture

The role of direct labour in agriculture has been significantly reduced as a result of the reworking of the structure of the agricultural sector, broadly defined. The manufacture of agricultural inputs and the centralisation of processing and marketing make up much of this reworking, trapping on-farm production between a concentrated and agglomerated sector of input manufacturers and an equally agglomerated sector of processor and marketing firms. Farmers encounter monopolies at both ends, and the degree of concentration in input and output markets can be quite extraordinary. In the US, in most regions the compounding of bulk fertilisers is controlled by one or two firms (Liebenluft, 1981); and nine (of 286) companies own 45 per cent of all agricultural chemical plants (US *Industrial Outlook*, 1987). The marketing of both processed and raw products is highly concentrated (Marion, 1986) and, because of the bulk or perishability of agricultural products, markets are strongly spatially organised. This means that within particular commodity regions and subregions, farmers usually have little choice about whom to buy from or sell to. Regional monopolies may thus be much tighter than national data would suggest, and the differential market power of input and output firms that are important national, as well as regional, actors is even further intensified, both generally and specifically.

This puts many farmers in a vulnerable position, caught between monopolistic input and output industries and therefore forced to absorb the risks of production. The regional integration of input, production, and markets makes it difficult for individual farmers to manage risks by diversification, since they cannot find the institutional framework such diversification would require. Furthermore, agriculture faces production risks different from those in industry, since here demand is relatively inelastic while supply is likely to fluctuate wildly (given the effect of natural processes – such as climate, disease, pests – on large numbers of farmers within a concentrated commodity region). Spatial concentration of production of particular commodities intensifies this risk for the enterprise, the farm household, and the regional economy.

The relationships between farm enterprises and input suppliers and marketing firms are complex. They involve various institutional patterns of flows of materials and credit and, in some regions, intricate overlapping patterns of ownership. Though full vertical integration in agriculture is relatively rare (even where an agribusiness firm – such as Tenneco – owns land it is likely to lease that land to tenants who manage the actual farm-level production), farm and off-farm enterprises are linked through cooperatives (in certain commodities), through farmer participation in the Federal Farm

Credit system (a farmer-owned cooperative banking system) and through the increasing role of off-farm work and contract work. These linkages appear in both the ownership of particular enterprises and in the complex patterns of labour market participation: farmers often do specialised contract work for other farmers; farm families often have some family members working in town; and off-farm labour (particularly women's) may link farming with agricultural and non-agricultural interests. Such pluriactivity is not necessarily a source of security. In the Midwest, the social effects of the farm crisis after 1980 were immensely intensified by the consequent collapse of the farm implements industry, which led to the loss of 60,000 jobs (50 per cent of all production jobs) in the regionally-concentrated industry between 1979 and 1987 and which forced the restructuring of the industry from seven to two firms (US *Industrial Outlook*, 1980–88).

This process of commodity differentiation and regional linkage has stimulated two moments of politicial response, two distinct 'social contracts' within particular agricultural regions and between agriculture and capital in general.

Agricultural regions as social contracts: populism and 'commodityism'

Agricultural regions are thus constituted by the complex relationship between farmers and the other institutions of the agricultural sector, and between agriculture and capital-in-general. This relationship between capital in agriculture and capital in manufacturing has tended, as it has developed over time, to subordinate agriculture to manufacturing, the countryside to the city, through a complex sectoral transfer of value which arises out of the different structural positions of the two sectors and the necessity of exchange between them. The subordination has not occurred without struggle.

In this century, the struggle has led to the development of a set of particular political and governmental forms, forged in attempts to protect agriculture from the domination of manufacturing and finance capital. These forms have been spatial in their structure, have appeared out of an already differentiated agricultural space, and have served to defend the different regional agricultural systems in different ways. The struggle of farmers to protect themselves against the pressures imposed by an increasingly dominant urban manufacturing (and finance capital) economy have been particularly intense at times of agricultural crisis (see Figure 1.3).

The first phase of this struggle – the rise of farmers' movements in the late nineteenth century – appeared in the confrontation between agriculture and the manufacturing and finance capital of the Eastern seaboard. It led to the development of the Grange and Farmers' Alliance and of the Populist Party, which briefly challenged the two-party hegemony of the Democrats and Republicans (McConnell, 1969). The purpose of this movement was explicit: its leaders and adherents were committed to direct democracy not only in terms of political representation but also in full and open economic participation, with opportunities for ordinary people. One consequence of

Figure 1.3 Major moments of struggle in agriculture

AGRICULTURAL DEPRESSION	INSTITUTIONAL CHANGE
1866–1890	Rise of farmers' movements – opposition between agriculture and other sectors of capitalism (Grange, Farmers' Alliance, Populist Party) Land Grant College Acts (Hatch Act 1887, Smith-Lever Act 1914) Reclamation Act (1902)
1920 – Great Depression	Regionally organised sectoral/subsectoral institutions: Farm Credit System (Farm Loan Act – 1916, System development – 1920s) Capper-Volstead Act (1922) Soil Conservation Service Commodity-based institutions: Agricultural Adjustment Act of 1933 (and subsequent price-support legislation)
1949–1950	Regionally organised sectoral/subsectoral institutions: Bracero Program (c. 1943–1964)
Crisis of Overproduction 1952–	Commodity-based institutions: PL 480 – Agricultural aid Food Stamp Program Commodity Price Support programs

this movement was the set of state 'unit-banking' laws, which restricted banks in most of the Midwest and Great Plains states to a single branch, thereby tying them closely to their home communities (Kaufman, 1983). In other agricultural areas, banks were allowed limited branching and it was only in the coastal states of the East and West that banking capital remained unfettered by this movement.

Major Federal legislation enacted in response to these populist claims included the laws setting up free public higher education (through the Land Grant College system) and the 1902 Reclamation Act, which mandated Federal investment in irrigation to support small-holder agriculture in the more arid west and which explicitly limited the beneficiaries of this investment to small-holders (160 acres) resident on these farmlands.[5]

The agricultural depression of the 1920s, which foreshadowed and continued through the Great Depression, led to additional attempts to protect agriculture from the power of marketing, finance, and manufacturing capital. The Farm Credit System set up a system of farmer-owned cooperative banks, organised into twelve regional districts, and guaranteed (though not capitalised) by Federal funds. The Capper-Volstead Act of 1922 specifically exempted agricultural cooperatives from certain restrictions of the anti-trust legislation, making it legal for farmers to join together to purchase inputs and to market their products, and to agree among themselves about how much of any particular product to produce. The Soil Conservation Service provided technical support, and some Federal subsidies for reclamation, in those areas where erosion and other forms of land degradation were beginning to affect local environments severely.

Though permitted (and to some degree financially supported) by Federal action, the basic organisational form of all of these institutions was that of the populist vision: locally- and regionally-based direct democracy with full economic participation. And they served, in various ways, to minimise competition among the producers of any given commodity – by allowing general access to credit, to inputs, and to markets, thus mitigating differences in production scale and discouraging rapid innovation in production technology (which would otherwise rapidly devalue the fixed capital investments of marginal producers). But one further major Federal initiative of this period signalled a significant change in the composition and political agenda of those who spoke for agriculture.

In 1933, in the early years of the Great Depression, Congress enacted the Agricultural Adjustment Act as part of the New Deal package of social-economic legislation. Though the Act was eventually overturned by the Supreme Court, in the two years it was in effect it established a different pattern of Federal intervention in support of agriculture – a shift from farmer-owned or directed institutions intended to support the democratic structure of agriculture and to defend it against the increasingly concentrated power of other sectors of capital, towards intervention only at the end point, in the price of agricultural commodities – with the assumption that in other ways agriculture was an economic form just like manufacturing. McConnell (1969) traces this shift to the rising power of the Farm Bureau, which represented the interests of the wealthier farmers as the interests of farming in general, with growing political effectiveness.

Nevertheless, all of these struggles were strongly regional, and led primarily to institutions with specific regional forms (Farm Credit System, Federal Land Banks, Production Credit Association, etc; Reclamation Act, and even, after the Second World War, the Bracero program). Even where the Federal programs were commodity-based rather than regionally-based, their immediate effects were still regional, given the regional specialisation in commodities. These regional forms were fixed in the social relations of farm communities before they were extended into (and protected by) the State. Moreover, they served not only to relate farmers to each other, but also to establish a stable regional relationship between city and countryside, so that farm communities and farmers themselves could live, locally, in peace. This allowed the regional integration (and, in some cases, a shared labour force) of the related (manufacturing) sectors – farm implements in the Midwest, seed companies in the grain region (often initially owned by production cooperatives), dairy marketing and processing in the Great Lakes States, fresh produce marketing in the West and Southwest, cotton ginning (and fabric mills) in the South (and later the Southwest), and so on.

This is what Gordon Clark, in his work on the Midwest auto industry

(1986), has called a 'regional social contract', arising out of crisis and restructured when crisis occurs again.

[T]he theory of regional crisis must allow for knowledge of the economic system, continuous change, and discontinuous economic transformation. It should also allow for local control of events; classes must be able to grasp their history.

Regional crises are resolved by the development of a new, 'intricate class bargain,' involving 'class relations of community,' 'social cum spatial organization of production,' and intimate relationships between managers and workers or (in this case) also between farmers themselves and the industrial structure within which they are embedded.

What we see in the current crisis of American agriculture, however, is a breakdown of these social compacts, within subsectors, among subsectors, and between the agricultural sector and the general political economy. The crisis is deepest in the Midwest and there the relative political position of family farming has been substantially weakened; for the time being, the industrial producers of the speciality crop regions have been able to maintain their special relationship with the State.

In part this arises as a result of the working-out of the second moment of farm politics, the rise of 'commodityism' (as McConnell, 1969, has termed it). As markets for agricultural products become further extended, the production systems of different, previously separated regions become measured against each other in this exchange. In the United States, this has involved a collison between the family-farming systems of the Midwest and the industrial agricultural forms of the Western states. Landownership and agricultural production in the West have been highly concentrated since the initial European settlement of the region, which led to large-scale investment in and control of land and associated resources and which established not only a class of capitalist farmers but an extensive class of wage labourers in agriculture. Though the early outlook of these regions was towards international export, they now compete with the farmers of the Midwest in both national and international markets for particular commodities.

Western agriculture is significantly more concentrated than that of the remainder of the country (including the South) (see Figure 1.4). Though the percentage of large farms with sales greater than $250,000 in 1982 does not vary that greatly (making up 12.6 per cent of all farms in California and Arizona, and less than one per cent in Kentucky, Tennessee, and West Virginia), the proportional share of their product within each state economy varies quite substantially, from more than 80 per cent of all sales in California and Arizona to less than 30 per cent in Wisconsin, Minnesota, Ohio, and other central states. Such farms have the resources to manage necessary transformations of both the social and technical conditions of production, which makes them, and the states where they predominate, more powerful and better protected in times of uncertainty and rapid technological innovation. In a sense, this development marginalises the farming sector of whole regions, if the products of industrial and family

24

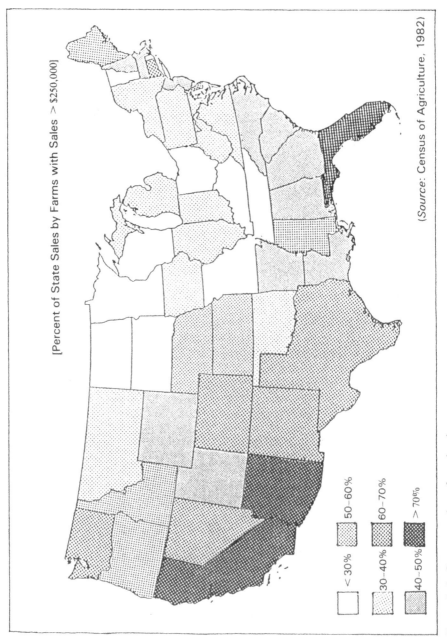

[Percent of State Sales by Farms with Sales > $250,000]

(*Source*: Census of Agriculture, 1982)

< 30%

30–40%

40–50%

50–60%

60–70%

> 70%

Figure 1.4 Concentration of production

forms compete in the market and the current pattern of social subsidy of industrial agriculture (through tax benefits and water subsidies) continues unchecked.

The long term implications for the structure and form of commodity production (and hence, for the class structure of agiculture) may be profound. In every commodity system reviewed here, the average per-farm income of the industrial agricultural states is three or four times the national average. In some commodities (vegetables, cotton) these states have captured the major share of total national production from former commodity regions. In others (dairy, for example) the competition between the cooperative, family-based production forms of the populist Midwest and the industrial, capital-intensive, wage labour forms of the West is not yet resolved.

We can see the crisis before us, but the structures of its resolution are still unclear. The claims agriculture, and agricultural regions, might make on the State are currently under debate. If Federal policy continues to treat agriculture as 'just another industry' with price uncertainties but with no other structural distinctions, the process of industrialisation (and of the development of a fully-capitalist class structure in American agriculture) is likely to continue. However, if the farmers of the Midwest and their regional supporters can successfully challenge this 'business as usual' conception of agriculture, as they have in the past, family forms of enterprise may be preserved.

Successful pursuit of this agenda is likely to require returning to some, at least, of the old populist insights. 'Commodityism' allows capital to move freely to the regions of greatest production efficiency, supporting the uncertainties and defraying the risks of industrial concentration with price support and aggressive Federal export policies. 'Populism', with its emphasis on the social relations of agriculture and of integrated agricultural and manufacturing communities, offers a legitimate alternative, but requires a conscious attention to the geography, as well as the class structure, of agricultural production. In the absence of a successful renaissance of regional populism, it is likely that agriculture in general, and in the East, South and Midwest in particular, will be further subordinated to capital-in-general and further induced to take up its class forms.

Agricultural regions as social contracts: technology and environment

It is in this context of restructuring and intense competition that industrial and populist debates about the environmental implications of agricultural technologies must be examined. Public concern about the environmental effects of current agricultural processes and about the wholesomeness of food is increasing (EPA, 1987). Many farmers, who are after all even more exposed to the hazards these technologies pose, also express this concern; in many agricultural regions some farmers are now experimenting with less-hazardous alternatives (National Research Council, 1989). At the same time, as Goodman, Sorj and Wilkinson (1987) suggest, industrial capital continues to seek to appropriate the tasks of the farm sector into non-land-based, manufacturing forms. Whatever the final outcome, the intermediate stages of this struggle connect questions of technology and environment intimately and at a regional (as well as national) political scale.

These conflicts take regional forms for several reasons: they arise out of the regionalised and still-regionalist political spaces of commodity systems; they often focus on the appropriate role of regional institutions first established in response to previous moments of agrarian populism; and their adherents find local and state struggles more feasible than conflict with the distant (and captured) federal agencies.

The manifestations of regionalism embedded in the new counter-institutions of the populist farmers' movement have attracted little scholarly attention to date. Since 1980 there has been a proliferation of rural self-help and self-defence non-governmental organisations throughout the regions most strongly affected by the current crisis. Many associate appropriate technology, environmental well-being, and agricultural sustainability, challenging the subsumption (or appropriation) of the farm by the agribusiness industry in all its manifestations simultaneously. They find their political legitimacy in references to the traditions of American populism, and are finding allies among urban populist movements as well (Boyte, 1989). One developing alliance is with environmentalists concerned with the growing importance of biotechnology as a corporate strategy for extending the market for agricultural chemicals and resistant seed varieties (see Goldburg *et al.*, 1990).

These alliances also support regional populist agricultural movements in attempts to recapture various regionally-structured state institutions which were initially formed as a result of populist programs. The 1902 Reclamation Act and the Land Grant College Acts (see Figure 1.3) both have been foci of such conflict. The 1902 Reclamation Act permitted Federal investment in irrigation systems to allow the settlement of the arid Western states, but required that the subsidised water delivered by such public water systems be available only to small-holders by imposing an acreage limitation (160 acres per family member, to a maximum of 480 acres per household) on the enterprises to which such water would be delivered. Despite the populist intent of the act, the acreage limitations the act required were never enforced by the Federal Department of the Interior; instead, federally-subsidised water has been used to sustain intensive cropping of speciality crops under the control of large corporate enterprises (FitzSimmons, 1983; Gottlieb and FitzSimmons, forthcoming 1991). From the mid-1960s, this subsidy to corporate agriculture has been a focus of popular struggles, bringing together the United Farm Workers with urban environmentalists seeking to stop water development to control urban land speculation and growth.

The connection that Western water politics makes between the city and the countryside has been augmented by new concerns over pesticides and water quality. Contamination of water by agricultural chemicals is a growing problem. Both fertilisers and pesticides (insecticides and herbicides) are a focus of increasing concern. Here again, responses tend to be regional: California's more stringent regulation of pesticides already regulated by the Federal Government; attempts in Midwest states to tax nitrogen fertilisers to discourage their over-use and the concentration of nitrates in the groundwater which provides domestic water for most human uses (Roberts & Lighthall, 1988). These challenges often take on the research efforts of the land grant colleges and the testing and dissemination programs of the county agricultural extension program, which have tended to promote 'modern' chemical agriculture and to support innovations which transform agricultural production systems into closer symmetry with manufacturing forms (Hightower, 1973; Browne, 1988).

Though these struggles may be regionally based, they may also reflect competition between regions producing the same commodity through different production structures. The campaign to limit the use of bovine growth hormone in the dairy states of Minnesota, Wisconsin, and Michigan has its roots in the competitive pressure dairy farmers in those states already face from industrial dairy operations supported by subsidised water (and thus subsidised alfalfa) in the West. Here an alliance is building between smaller farmers and consumer activitists concerned about hormone use in agriculture.

There are limits to this discourse about populist, sustainable agriculture, however. The report *Alternative Agriculture* prepared by the National Research Council demonstrates these limits clearly. The Council finds the origins of the environmental problems of agriculture in two areas: in heretofore inadequate scientific (and technological) understanding of the nature of agricultural activities; and in the distorting effect of Federal commodity policies. Science, they say, has overlooked the necessary complexity of agriculture, but the real root of the problem is in federal subsidies to agriculture, which (i) encourage farmers towards monoculture (to protect their acreage allocations); (ii) encourage over-production of particular commodities; and (iii) militate against mixed farming systems. This analysis is silent on the social relationships within which these choices are made – on the institutions (private and public) which seek to develop those technologies in which they anticipate profits and on the institutional constraints within which farmers' choices are embedded. Effective intervention must be based on a more sophisticated understanding of the political economy and geography of which farming is a part.

Conclusion

The subsumption of farming to capital in general occurs through complex processes and involves restructuring of relations both internal and external to the farm and to the farming sector *sensu strictu* (Marsden, Whatmore, and Munton, 1987). It also occurs in specific places organised by regional and spatial processes: those of regionalisation (as an economic process), of regionalism (as a political and cultural response), and of regionality (as the constructive and limiting historical geography of place). Analysis of class relations in agriculture benefits from attention to this relational geography, which connects the dynamics of the household to the world-space economy of capitalism-in-general.

Notes

1. Of natural resource location in the primary sector and of market efficiencies and labour force characteristics in manufacturing.
2. Berman (1982) makes this distinction in his differentiation of modernisation, modernism, and modernity, and Soja (1989) demonstrates that it can be usefully applied to the understanding of space.
3. All specific data is from the 1982 Census of Agriculture unless otherwise noted.
4. The twin-plant or in-bond system which allows US firms to export labour-intensive moments of the production process to plants employing Mexican labour. Slaughtering and packing of American-raised beef in Mexico offers US packinghouses freedom from both the labour and environmental regulations which they would face in US operations.
5. The actual history of this investment, however, runs entirely counter to the intent of the original Reclamation law. Though Federal funds constructed most of the major irrigation facilities in the Western States, the acreage limitation provisions and residency provisions of the original legislation have never been enforced, and the benefits of this public investment have been almost entirely diverted to large corporate landholdings.

References

Baker, O. E. (1929) The increasing importance of the physical conditions in determining the utilization of land for agricultural and forest production in the United States, *Annals of the Association of American Geographers*, XI, 17–46.

Baker, O. E. (1927–1933) Agricultural regions of North America, *Economic Geography, seriatim.*

Berman, M. (1982) *All That Is Solid Melts Into Air.* New York, Simon and Schuster.

Boyte, H. (1989) *CommonWealth: A Return to Citizen Politics.* New York, Free Press.

Browne, W. P. (1988) *Private Interests, Public Policy, and American Agriculture.* Lawrence, KA, University of Kansas Press.

Buttel, F. H. and Newby, H. (eds) (1980) *The Rural Sociology of the Advanced Societies: Critical Perspectives.* Montclair, New Jersey, Allanheld, Osmun.

Buttel, F. H. and Gillespie Jr., G. W. (1989) Rural policy in political-historical perspective: The rise, fall and uncertain future of the American rural welfare-state. Unpublished paper, Department of Rural Sociology, Cornell University.

Clark, G. L. (1986) The crisis of the midwest auto industry, in Scott, A. J. and Storper, M. (eds) *Production, Work, Territory: The Geographical Anatomy of Industrial Capitalism*. London, Allen & Unwin, 127–147.

Cochrane, W. W. (1980) *The Development of American Agriculture: A Historical Analysis*. Minneapolis, University of Minnesota.

Daniel, Pete (1985) *Breaking the Land: The Transformation of Cotton, Tobacco, and Rice Cultures since 1880*. Urbana, University of Illinois.

Davis, J. E. (1980) Capitalist agricultural development and the exploitation of the propertied laborer, in Buttel, F. and Newby, H. (eds) *The Rural Sociology of the Advanced Societies: Critical Perspectives*. Montclair, New Jersey, Allanheld, Osmun, 133–154.

De Janvry, A. (1980) Social differentiation in agriculture and the ideology of neopopulism, in Buttel, F. and Newby, H. (eds) *The Rural Sociology of the Advanced Societies: Critical Perspectives*. Montclair, New Jersey, Allanheld, Osmun, 155–170.

Elson, D. (1979) The value theory of labour, in Elson, D. (ed) *Value: The Representation of Labour in Capital*. London, C.S.E. Books.

EPA (Environmental Protection Agency) (1987) *Unfinished Business: A Comparative Assessment of Environmental Problems*. Washington, DC, Government Publications Office.

FitzSimmons, M. (1983) The Industrialization of Agriculture: Environmental and Social Consequences in the Salinas Valley. Unpublished doctoral dissertation (Geography), UCLA.

FitzSimmons, M. I. (1985) Hidden Philosophies: How Geographical Thought is Limited by its Theoretical Models, *GeoForum*, 16 (2), 139–149.

FitzSimmons, M. I. (1986) The new industrial agriculture: The regional integration of specialty crop production, *Economic Geography*, 62 (3), 334–451.

Friedland, W. H. (1980) Technology in agriculture: Labor and the rate of accumulation, in Buttel, F. and Newby, H. (eds) *The Rural Sociology of the Advanced Societies: Critical Perspectives*. Montclair, New Jersey, Allanheld, Osmun, 201–214.

Friedland, W. J., Barton, A. E. and Thomas, R. J. (1981) *Manufacturing Green Gold: Capital Labor and Technology in the Lettuce Industry*. Cambridge, Cambridge University Press.

Friedmann, H. (1978a) Simple commodity production and wage labor in the American Plains, *Journal of Peasant Studies*, VI (1), 71–101.

Friedmann, H. (1978b) World market, state and family farm: Social bases of household production in the era of wage labor, *Comparative Studies in Society and History*, XX (4), 545–586.

Friedmann, H. (1986) Patriarchy and property: A reply to Goodman and Redclift, *Sociologia Ruralis*, XXVI (2), 186–193.

Garrison, W. L. and Marble, D. F. (1957) The spatial structure of agricultural activities, *Annals of the Association of American Geographers*, XLVII, 137–144.

Gilbert, A. (1988) The new regional geography in English and French-speaking countries, *Progress in Human Geography*, 208–228.

Gilbert, J. and Akor, R. (1988) Increasing structural divergence in US dairying: California and Wisconsin since 1950, *Rural Sociology*, LIII (1), 56–72.

Goldburg, R., Rissler, J., Shand, H. and Hassebrook, C. (1990) *Biotechnology's Bitter Harvest: Herbicide-Tolerant Crops and the Threat to Sustainable Agriculture*. Biotechnology Working Group.

Goodman, D., Sorj, B. and Wilkinson, J. (1987) *From Farming to Biotechnology: A Theory of Agro-Industrial Development*. Oxford, Basil Blackwell.

Gottlieb, R. and FitzSimmons, M. (forthcoming) *Thirst for Growth: Water Agencies as Hidden Government*. Tucson, AZ, University of Arizona Press.

Gregor, H. F. (1982) Large-scale farming as a cultural dilemma in U.S. rural development – the role of capital, *GeoForum*, XIII (1), 1–10.

Grigg, D. B. (1974) *The Agricultural Systems of the World*. London, Cambridge University Press.

Hayenga, M., Rhodes, V. J., Brandt, J. A. and Deiter, R. E. (1985) *The U.S. Pork Sector: Changing Structure and Organization*. Ames, Iowa State University Press.

Harvey, D. W. (1983) *The Limits to Capital*. Oxford, Basil Blackwell.

Hightower, J. (1973) *Hard Tomatoes, Hard Times*. Cambridge, Mass, Schenkman.

Kaufman, H. M. (1983) *Financial Institutions, Financial Markets, and Money*. New York, Harcourt, Brace & Jovanovitch.

Klohn, W. (1988) The role of farmer-cooperatives in U.S. agriculture. Paper presented at the annual meeting of the Association of American Geographers, Phoenix, Arizona, April 1988.

Liebenluft, R. F. (1981) Competition in farm inputs: an examination of four industries. Policy Planning Issues Paper, Federal Trade Commission, Washington, DC.

Mann, S. A. and Dickinson, J. M. (1978) Obstacles to the development of a capitalist agriculture, *Journal of Peasant Studies*, V (4), 466–481.

Mann, S. A. and Dickinson, J. M. (1980) State and agriculture in two eras of American Capitalism, in Buttel, F. and Newby, H. (eds) *The Rural Sociology of the Advanced Societies: Critical Perspectives*. Montclair, New Jersey, Allanheld, Osman, 283–326.

Marion, B. (1986) *The Organization and Performance of the U.S. Food system*. Lexington, MA, Lexington Books.

Marion, B. *et al.*, (1986) Monopsony Power in Fed Cattle Markets. Paper presented at the Annual Meetings of the American Agricultural Economics Association, Reno, Nevada, July 1986.

Marsden, T. K. (1984) Capitalist farming and the farm family: A case study, *Sociology*, XVIII (2), 205–224.

Marsden, T. K., Whatmore, S. J. and Munton, R. J. C. (1987) Uneven development and the restructuring process in British agriculture: A preliminary exploration, *Journal of Rural Studies*, III (4), 297-308.

Marsden, T. K., Whatmore, S. J., Munton, R. J. C. and Little, J. K. (1986a) The restructuring process and economic centrality in capitalist agriculture, *Journal of Rural Studies*, II (1), 271-280.

Marsden, T. K., Whatmore, S. J., Munton, R. J. C. and Little, J. K. (1986b) Towards a political economy of capitalist agriculture: A British perspective, *International Journal of Urban and Regional Research*, X (4), 498-521.

McConnell, G. (1969) *The Decline of Agrarian Democracy*. New York, Atheneum.

Mooney, P. H. (1983) Labor time, production time, and capitalist development in agriculture: A reconsideration of the Mann-Dickinson thesis, *Sociologia Ruralis*, XX (3/4), 279-292.

Morgan, D. (1977) *Merchants of Grain*. New York, Viking.

Munton, R. J. C. (1988) Agricultural change: A re-examination of the dualist thesis. Paper presented at the annual meetings of the Association of American Geographers, Phoenix, Arizona, April 1988.

Murray, R. (1977) Value and theory of rent, Part I, *Capital & Class*, III, 100-122; Part II, *Capital & Class*, IV, 11-33.

National Research Council (1989) *Alternative Agriculture*. Washington, DC, National Academy of Sciences.

Newby, H. and Buttel, F. H. (1980) Toward a critical rural sociology, in Buttel, F. and Newby, H. (eds) *The Rural Sociology of the Advanced Societies: Critical Perspectives*. Montclair, New Jersey, Allanheld, Osmun, 1-35.

Pfeffer, M. J. (n.d.), The social relations of subcontracting: The case of contract vegetable production in Wisconsin. Working Paper No. 2, Center for Comparative Studies in the Sociology of Agriculture, University of Wisconsin, Madison, Wisconsin.

Roberts, R. S. and Lighthall, D. S. (1988) Groundwater Quality: The Role of Agricultural Politics and Policy, in Vladimir Novotny (ed) *Non-point pollution: 1988 - Policy, Economy, Management and Appropriate Technology*. Bethesda, American Water Resources Association, 9-21.

Scott, A. J. (1988) *Metropolis: From the Division of Labour to Urban Form*. Berkeley, University of California.

Scott, A. J. and Storper, M. (eds) (1986) *Production, Work, Territory: The Geographical Anatomy of Industrial Capitalism*. London, Allen & Unwin.

Soja, E. W. (1989) *Postmodern Geographies: The Reassertion of Space in Critical Social Theory*. London, Verso.

Spencer, J. E. and Horvath, R. J. (1963) How does an agricultural region originate? *Annals of the Association of American Geographers*, LIII, 74-92.

Storper, M. and Walker, R. (1989) *The Capitalist Imperative: Territory, Technology and Industrial Growth*. Oxford, Basil Blackwell.

Vogeler, I. (1981) *The Myth of the Family Farm: Agribusiness Dominance of US Agriculture*. Boulder, Colorado, Westview.

Walker, R. A. (1985) Class, division of labour and employment in space, in Gregory, D. and Urry, J. (eds) *Social Relations and Spatial Structures*. London, Macmillan, 164-189.

32

Whatmore, S. J., Munton, R. J. C., Marsden, T. K. and Little, J. K. (1987a) Towards a typology of farm businesses in contemporary British agriculture, *Sociologia Ruralis*, XXVI (1), 21–37.

Whatmore, S. J., Munton, R. J. C., Marsden, T. K. and Little, J. K. (1987b) Interpreting a relational typology of farm businesses in Southern England, *Sociologia Ruralis*, XXVI (2–3), 103–122.

CHAPTER 2

The Rural Environment in a Post-Socialist Economy: The Case of Hungary

Miklós Persányi

The Socialist experiment in the rural areas of Eastern Europe

Lenin set as one of the aims of the socialist cultural revolution the abolition of differences between the city and the village. During the past 70 years in the Soviet Union and 40 years in Eastern Europe, immense effort has been devoted to this cause, involving violent upheaval and massive experimentation. There were still feudal remnants in the rural areas of Eastern Europe some 40–60 years ago. Not only have these been swept away but the vast poverty of the rural masses has been eliminated by great social and techno-economic changes. But many of the interventions, such as the centralised system of harvesting and storage, have proved unsuccessful and have been abandoned. For a long time, though, through ideological or political imperatives, the authorities in some countries, including Romania, Czechoslovakia and the German Democratic Republic, continued relentlessly pursuing grandiose but unworkable measures. In some instances, indeed, it was only the overthrow of the Communist regimes in 1989 that brought such projects and schemes to a halt.

Because, until recently, development policy did not stress the environment, a structure of settlements and production has been established which was and is wasteful of land, material and energy, with deleterious consequences for both the natural and the built environment. Systems of central planning pursued their prescribed economic and industrial goals with an inflexibility devoid of holism or local sensitivity: they were thus incapable of handling the complexity of the environment and, when trying to solve a specific problem, often created many others.

The historical changes brought about in rural areas by the socialist experiment along Stalinist and post-Stalinist lines coincided with the enormous technological shift of the post-war period. Technical change in the Eastern European countryside has thus taken place in quite different social and political circumstances from those in the West. Indeed, East-West developmental differences are much greater between rural areas than urban ones because of intrinsic differences between the two. The countryside of Eastern Europe, compared with the cities, retains advantages in terms of human contacts and physical conditions but suffers many material and cultural disadvantages, such as lack of employment and poor services. The urbanisation of the countryside is far from complete.

Across Eastern Europe, the settlement network is planned centrally. Radical and forceful efforts to reshape it have further increased the problems by multiplying them or generating new difficulties. In most countries, including Hungary (Gyenei, 1989), a dominant feature of post-war settlement policy was a virulently anti-village mentality. The need to redress some of the awful harm thereby done in the name of misguided modernisation policies has begun to be addressed, particularly with the process of democratisation. In some countries, though, the deliberate destruction of cultural and natural values has continued. In Romania, the systematisation programme which involved the levelling of villages and the forced removal of the villagers to consolidated agro-industrial complexes was only halted after the overthrow of the Ceausescu regime in 1989. In the past, there were similar experiments in Hungary too: including a project for the liquidation of individual farms in the fifties, first by the creation of 'farm-centres', and later the unsuccessful introduction of soviet-type 'kolkhoz-cities' (huge farming co-operatives). In the sixties there was also the so-called 'settlement development concept' which resulted in the planned reduction of smaller villages. Through the agglomeration of agricultural enterprises and the amalgamation of local councils, the majority of Hungarian villages were subordinated and deprived of their rights (Gyenei, 1989). Recently, counter pressures have emerged and some local communities have regained control over their own villages by referendum.

Eastern Europe has yet to experience the counterurbanisation which Western countries are going through and which started in Britain and the USA in the fifties or sixties (Enyedi, 1988). So-called 'socialist practice' has supported every kind of centralisation – caricatured by Gyenei (1989) as 'the bigger, the more socialist'. This practice considered urbanisation as valuable in itself, and vigorously pursued the concentration of population. Authoritarian systems generally prefer having fewer units to direct, but the primary goal was based on the idea that higher living standards could be achieved for the people through concentrated services, supplies, and the like. But society, particularly rural society, does not always concur with such theories.

Urban-industrial development emerged in Eastern Europe historically much later than in the highly developed regions of the world. This process reached the Western margins of the region, but it advanced haltingly, and the industrial boom in Central and Eastern Europe was very different from the 'classic' Western pattern of development of the same period (Enyedi 1988). Industrialisation started in Hungary, for example, in the 1860s, and reached the Balkans in the 1920s. The structure of industry became indigenous, adapting to a region which was overwhelmingly rural. There was, therefore, no need for an intense urban concentration and industry drained less labour from agriculture which had surplus manpower. This industrial revolution was very slow and interrupted. The industrial areas emerged – for example, in Hungary, at the turn of the century – as enclaves in a society which remained substantially rural and feudal for a long time. The cities did not generate industrialisation, but industry stimulated urbanisation which proceeded very often in a rather imperfect way.

By the middle of this century, in almost every socialist country (except the German Democratic Republic and Czechoslovakia), between a half and two-thirds of the population was rural. Most of these people lived from agriculture, but after 1950 rural depopulation gathered pace. The main goal of the centrally planned economy was 'laying the material foundations of socialism' which stressed development in keeping with the interests of the industrial-military complex and justified on ideological grounds (Glatz, 1987).

One of the typical features of Central and Eastern European urbanisation is that, from this period, industrial and urban development were completely interwoven, with the capital for industrialisation being drained from agriculture (Enyedi, 1988). The growing industrial cities were developed at the expense of the villages and non-industrial towns. The period of industrial take-off, which coincided with the urban boom, eventually slowed down in most of Central and Eastern Europe and recently has practically finished (see Figure 2.1). Meanwhile, the rural sector has remained substantial. The urban population of the region is only 55–60 per cent, and, though much lower than in Western Europe, is a characteristic feature and not a mark of underdevelopment. There is no need for further urbanisation. Nowadays the inequality between settlements is one of the most serious social inequalities in the region, and this is the outcome of urbanisation. In many respects, living conditions in rural and urban areas show wider and wider disparities. The only solution must be to focus on the modernisation of rural areas and to tackle the problems caused by the long neglect of, and discrimination against, the villages and their inhabitants (Enyedi 1989).

Social processes

The state of the environment is not necessarily better in the Eastern European countryside, because of its lower level of development, than in the West. On the contrary, there are many environmental problems, even though people live in these areas closer to nature and further from 'urban' technologies, which does confer certain environmental advantages. But in the last three or four decades many new and aggressive technologies, with substantial consumption of energy and materials and with major pollution

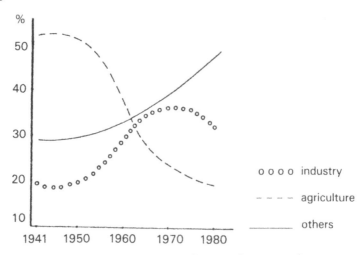

Figure 2.1   Hungary: rate of employment by economic sectors

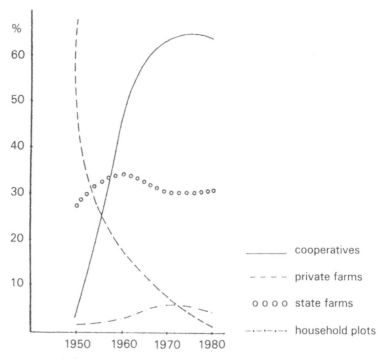

Figure 2.2   Hungary: land area by social sectors

problems, have displaced the traditional methods of production which are more harmonious with nature.

Rapid social changes have also radically altered traditional village life. There have been successive changes in land-ownership (Figure 2.2). In Hungary, in 1945, for example, most of the large estates were distributed to the peasants and the rest were transformed into state farm enterprises. In the late forties the collectivisation of small-holdings began. It was interrupted in 1953, but after the forced reversal of the early process of democratisation in 1956, it was recommenced, and by 1962 the 'socialist transformation of Hungarian agriculture' was complete. As a result, large scale co-operative and state farms came to occupy 93 per cent of the agricultural land. Later, and especially after the 1986 economic reforms, small-scale production on household plots was encouraged. Substantial private production capacities now exist, but real opportunities for private enterprise arose only in the late eighties. Most recently of all, with the reappearance of market-economy ideas, the possibilities for the reprivatisation of agricultural enterprises and co-operatives are being considered.

Meanwhile, the rural population itself has been considerably transformed. Many moved into the cities; others live an ambivalent commuting life holding jobs in urban factories, but residing in villages and working with the family on household plots in their spare time. Sweeping change also typifies purely agricultural employment and the working conditions of agricultural workers: no longer are they farmers with a broad general knowledge of husbandry but rather specialised, skilled operators of agricultural assembly-lines.

Simultaneously, the traditional social relationships of rural societies have been broken up. Systems of norms, human networks, and the hierarchies of local communities were systematically rearranged. The staggering economic changes were joined to other violent measures, especially in the fifties, such as the widespread harassment and internment of members of the middle peasantry and restraints on the churches and religious customs. In addition, rapid technological and infrastructural changes transformed traditional lifestyles, e.g. in housing (with new, more comfortable homes, equipped with electricity, running water, and bathrooms), or in transport (with a massive growth in car ownership), not to mention the revolution in the mass media.

All of these changes have had big impacts on the rural environment, including some profound indirect consequences. Changes in people's mentalities, for example, can be detected in the careless, untidy appearance of public places; and the loss of traditional values and constraints has resulted in the sprawling, unregulated development of settlements without regard to their historic from of appearance.

It is no longer possible to establish a strict dichotomy between urbanised and rural areas. The division between cities and villages is based on administrative distinctions. Several new towns developed in the last few decades, however, are little more than housing estates: many characteristics of urban infrastructure are missing, the sewage system, telephone lines, pavements, metalled roads, and even sometimes running water. In such respects, there is often little difference too between the outer suburbs of the bigger cities and 'real' villages apart from their distance form the urbanised zones. Suburbs and the surrounding villages, on the other hand, share many of the advantages and disadvantages of cities.

Because of the vague boundaries of rural areas in Hungary, it is difficult to find absolutely definitive rural data. Nevertheless, one can delineate some significant features of rural environments by classifying them according to settlement types. Some 40 per cent of the 10.6 million population of Hungary live in villages in purely rural areas. The others live in and around cities and towns, including many who live in rural settings. There are 125 cities or towns, of which Budapest, the capital, is by far the biggest, with a population of more than 2 million. There are, in addition, 2,933 villages, with a third of them having fewer than 500 residents, and a quarter having between 500 and 1,000. The settlements differ not only in their scale but also in housing conditions, infrastructure, employment and the quality of the environment.

Changes in production

Rural conditions are predominantly determined by the means and organisation of food production. Hungarian agriculture has good natural and historical advantages, and has achieved substantial increases in production in the last two decades. Large-scale farms have developed a relatively effective symbiosis with the joint household plots. Small-scale family farming rarely deals with some types of crop (e.g. corn, sunflower or sugar beet), but has a greater share of other products (e.g. meat, fruit, vegetables). They produce 22 per cent of total agricultural output, and 45 per cent of net production (KSH, 1989). The performance of Hungarian agriculture is outstanding amongst the countries of Eastern Europe. Beyond satisfying domestic needs, one-third of its output is exported, accounting for 20 per cent of the nation's total exports. However, because of the current oversupply on world markets, the need to subsidise agricultural exports now produces the greatest deficits for the Hungarian economy (Csorba, 1987).

The rapid expansion of agriculture has been brought about by the intensification of agricultural methods and through the application of science to the techniques and procedures employed. Production and consumption have increased continuously since the sixties (Figure 2.3). Industrial systems have emerged in horticulture and livestock breeding. Pressures to intensify arise not only from the imperative to expand output but also from the loss of agricultural land to other uses as well as the increased use of land within agriculture for storage, transport and waste disposal and the abandonment of marginal land ill-suited to intensive farming methods.

The rapid growth of intensive state agriculture brought about greatly increased environmental pressures and hazards. In 1935 the mechanical hauling capacity was only six per cent, by 1950 40 per cent, and in 1980 99 per

Figure 2.3 Growth of Hungarian agriculture 1950 = 100%

Year	Total agric. production	Production per hectare
1938	113	111
1950	100	100
1960	120	121
1970	146	149
1980	206	213
1987	214	223

cent, when it amounted to about 7.5 million kw. The mechanical hauling capacity per unit area increased 31 times, and the number of tractors 12-fold between 1950 and 1980. Large-scale farms which frequently work the land of several villages have large monocultural areas often far removed from each other. Moving big machines, harvesting and transporting the harvest results in higher fuel and energy consumption and costs (Prugberger, 1989). Chemicalisation of agriculture is another key factor. Overuse and careless use of chemicals have polluted soils and watercourses and have harmed natural ecosystems. In 1975, 41,250 tonnes of pesticides were produced; by 1987 this was 77,581 (Figure 2.4). About 65,000 tonnes of this were sprayed, amounting to about 10 kilograms per hectare. During the same 12 years the production of artificial fertilisers increased from 700,000 tonnes of active agents to 1.06 million (KSH, 1989) (Figure 2.5). The average use of artificial fertilisers is about 230 kilograms per hectare, which, like pesticide use, is quite high by international standards (Csorba, 1987). All of these developments result in the increased technological dependence of agriculture, and demand more energy and more raw and artificial materials and, in consequence, cause more serious and long term environmental damage.

In addition, many large-scale state and co-operative farms have diversified into non-agricultural activities. The rate of growth of such activities has far outstripped that of agricultural production, increasing sevenfold between 1970 and 1985, compared with an increase of just a half in agricultural and forestry output. As a result, some villages have become very industrialised but this rarely involves advanced technologies. Typical activities include metal working, packaging and clothes making. In consequence, though employment opportunities may be improved, at the same time sources of industrial pollution and hazardous practices are dispersed into rural areas where local people and administration are poorly prepared for handling them. Some activities, such as waste disposal, scrapyards and incinerators, have been moved out to rural areas specifically because of the pollution and nuisance they cause.

The agricultural industries have no real interest in environmental protection. Economic control-systems support improved output but not conservation and farms have become exploiters, not users, of natural resources. Some of the state subsidies (such as hectarage payments, price

40

Figure 2.4 Supply of pesticides, 1968–1984

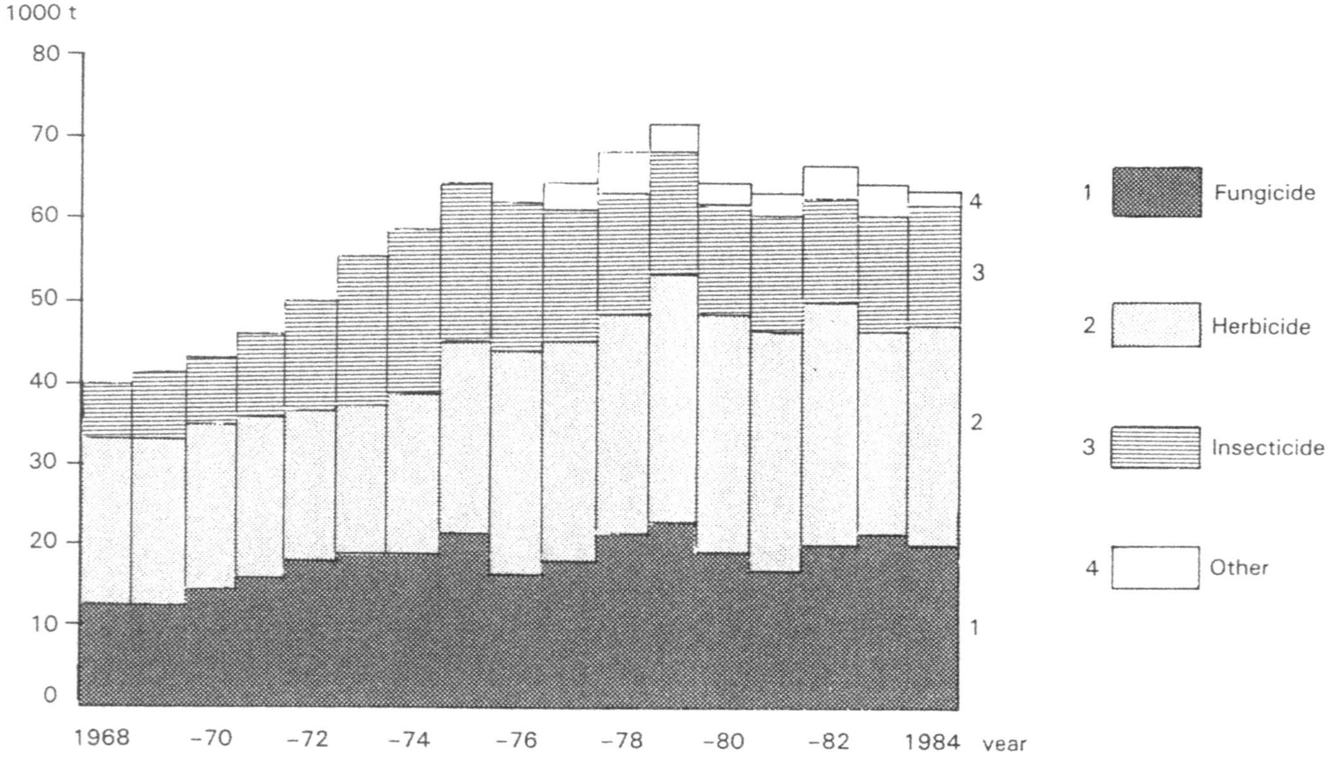

Figure 2.5 Supply of artificial fertilisers (active agents), 1951–1984.

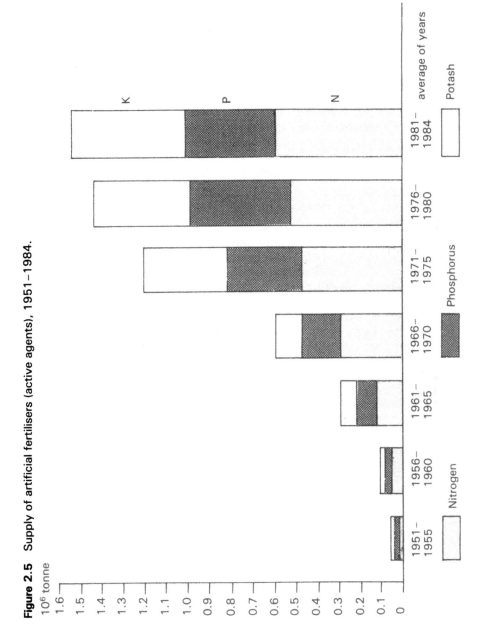

supports and grants for land reclamation and improvement) distort the real costs of production and militate against the preservation of natural habitats. The management of agro-business, moreover, has changed in favour of experts in engineering and chemistry, and the traditional agronomists have been forced into a subordinate role.

In most villages, the large-scale farms are the only employers. They thus have economic and political power, sometimes a monopoly. Most local people are at the mercy of these farms even if it is in their ownership as in the case of cooperatives. This defencelessness is experienced not only by individuals but also by the representative bodies – the local councils – even though they are organs of state power. Large-scale farms, at their own discretion, subsidise poor local councils in the development of the villages. They have better contacts with higher levels of power which stress the continued growth of production. They employ the people with technical expertise and knowledge in the locality. Therefore it has been exceptional for local councils to seek to limit the activities of large scale farms and their associated industries, even if they are environmentally hazardous.

The contradictions between agricultural development and the environment

The successes of the 'Hungarian green revolution' have been regarded as something of a miracle all over Eastern Europe. However, they have been less the consequence of centralised planning and state redistribution than of the greater autonomy of the co-operatives and large-scale state farms in Hungary and of the greater commitment and personal interest of the producers. These features, however, have not enabled Hungarian agriculture to avoid the environmental problems of intensification. Indeed, harmful consequences have accompanied the mechanisation and chemicalisation of agricultural production throughout the world, and the socialist countries have certainly been no exception. On the contrary, for the latter, such problems have been compounded by the mistakes of their centrally planned economies. Lax standards, a lack of accountability and over-centralisation have caused as much damage as the technology itself, and there has been a single-minded commitment to the industrialisation of production as the key to the broader social transformation of the countryside.

The rigid central planning and control of Hungarian agriculture of the fifties and the subsequent post-Stalinist state management of the sector through economic regulations and subsidies have created an irrational land-use system and product-structure. These state influences, for example, have been the cause of the high energy and material costs in agriculture and hence its poor competitiveness in the world market. Currently, experts criticise the narrowly quantitative attitude towards production and call for greater attention to what is produced, its quality and at what cost. The following examples illustrate the contradictions (Madas, 1989).

Large-scale programmes to improve soil fertility through the application of artificial fertilisers were promulgated during the sixties and seventies and boosted yields considerably. These programmes were curtailed at the end of the seventies, however, when the disproportionate financial costs were disclosed. Environmental disadvantages also came to light, such as nitrification of underground waters, acidification of soils, and degradation of soil structure. The use of farmyard manure had practically been abandoned, and once useful side-products had thus come to be regarded as wastes, creating their own pollution problems. Although these technocentric attitudes are changing and manuring is on the increase, the area dressed with organic manure is still only about five per cent of the total farmland.

The distortive effects of ill-considered subsidies are particularly remarkable in the case of the structural ratio of animal husbandry. Ruminants, notably cattle, have lost ground to other livestock which, though needing greater bought-in feed, are more susceptible to intensive production methods. The ratio of cattle to pigs, for example, was 1:5 in 1984, whereas the average for both the European Community and Comecom was 1:1, and for the USA it was 1:0.5. This is the reason why about one million hectares of meadow and pasture are practically redundant in Hungary, why the import of proteins is so very high, why more artificial fertilisers are needed, why intensive breeding complexes are such sources of severe pollution, and why most animal manure goes to waste. The construction of large, intensive livestock units with slurry systems was very much the fashion in the 1960s and 1970s, but the issue of what to do with all the liquid manure remained unsolved, and it has become a major pollutant of soil and water (Várallyai *et al.*, 1989).

Likewise, land improvement has been encouraged by central programmes, but less attention has been given to the prevention of soil deterioration, through the misuse of land, which now affects half of the total arable area (Dargai, 1988). Even the measures taken under the rubric of land reclamation, drainage or irrigation have in some areas caused more damage than benefits, but have been driven forward by the availability of central funds. The rational planning and evaluation of such programmes have been undermined by the influence of patronage in the disbursement of funds, and lax accounting procedures. Not infrequently the execution of individual projects has been careless and needlessly destructive from an environmental point of view, involving, for example, the disruption of underground, water-resistant clay layers, or the removal of lines of trees and hedges to create vast fields (Éri, 1989; Madas, 1989).

Real values and relationships have also been deformed by state support for the development of the means and methods of 'modern industrial' agriculture. The production and sale of agricultural machinery, fertilisers, and pesticides, and the establishment of large animal breeding complexes have received various direct and indirect subsidies. Therefore such technology became artifically cheap and could easily out-compete traditional agriculture based on more harmonious methods, even though in reality agro-production incurred considerable, but largely hidden, costs.

Perhaps the greatest structural problem of Hungarian agriculture is that production is irrational in terms of its regional distribution. Large quantities of agro-products have been produced on land ecologically unsuitable for the specific crop or livestock. The fault lies not with the command and control system of the 1950s but with subsequent agricultural programmes which have subsidised, either on a hectarage or an output basis, the production of certain commodities, such as maize and wheat. These programmes have encouraged the establishment of large monocultures with their attendant environmental disadvantages. Farms have also been stimulated to cultivate unsuitable land, because they are assured of a return even though yields may be poor.

The final example of distorted and damaging development arises from a set of measures whose formal intention at least is environmental protection. The so-called 'quantitative land-protection' aims to minimise the loss of agricultural land to urban or industrial development. Strict land controls were set up in the early eighties, and there are high charges for the development of farmland differentiated according to the quality of land. Most of the funds thus raised are channelled into land improvement. But problems arise in the misallocation of this money. Large-scale agro-industries, for example, have been subsidised in carrying out schemes not concerned with land protection, and even directly harmful to the environment (Éri, 1989). Forests have been felled and grasslands ploughed up, thus increasing the risks of water and wind erosion. Important habitats such as small woods, old pasture, steppes, wetlands, hedges, copses and thickets have been reclaimed even though the land is of marginal productive value. The problem arises here from the lack of accountability in the expenditure of public funds.

In the words of a progressive agricultural economist,

> The general judgement of the performance of agriculture in Hungary depends on the volume of its output and its export earnings especially in hard currencies, and these parameters therefore substantially determine the place of environmental protection among agricultural goals and the limits of environmental investment by the agro-sector.... Moreover, present agricultural policy leads to the deterioration of the environment, and neither the country nor the agro-sector possesses sufficient income or capital to mitigate the consequences. (Éri, 1989)

The first steps to a solution would be the removal of all economic regulations and incentives which run contrary to environmental interests (e.g. preference for ploughed land, or price subsidies for fertilisers, currently 22 per cent for nitrogen and 37 per cent for phosphorus), the decentralisation of the direction of agriculture and the introduction of special environmental levies. There are no clear forecasts about what might arise in the near future, although radical changes are possible, including the reprivatisation of land and the break-up of large farms, which will undoubtedly pose new challenges and opportunities in the relationship between agriculture and the environment.

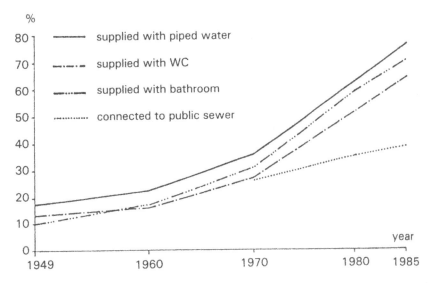

%

—————— supplied with piped water

—.—.— supplied with WC

—..…… supplied with bathroom

………… connected to public sewer

Figure 2.6 Proportion of dwellings with piped water supply and connections to the public sewers

The state of the environment in rural areas

All rural settlements have, to some degree, absorbed the great social changes of the post-war period. Technological change has rapidly spread throughout the Hungarian countryside through the agency of state farms and large co-operatives. The long tentacles of cities and industry have reached everywhere, shattering traditional values and leaving their lasting marks on the rural environment. Here are some examples of the environmental consequences.

One of the biggest environmental problems facing Hungary is the pollution of underground water. The ideological commitment to urbanise rural amenities and to raise living standards across the country led to a single-minded commitment to introduce piped water to all settlements. The necessary sewerage systems, though, have not been constructed at the same rate (Figure 2.6). In 1945, 25 per cent of the population had piped water and by 1987 it was 88 per cent. Over the same period, the proportion of the population linked to a sewer went from 18 per cent to 49 per cent. During the last 15 years the number of dwellings with running water but without sewerage has increased almost four-fold, yielding 146 million cubic meters of sewage per annum. Some 26 million cubic meters of it are collected by tank-trucks, but the rest – the sewage from more than 3 million people – simply seeps into the soil, or into ditches and streams. In some cases, sewage outlets have simply been directed into old wells. As a consequence, whereas in 1971 30 per cent of underground water needed purification for drinking, the figure is now 80–85 per cent. Because of pollution, there are 726 villages –

a quarter of the total number – whose water supply does not meet established health standards, and drinking water has to be transported in tanks, bottles and plastic bags to these villages. The problem is specifically rural. There are only 400 settlements in Hungary with sewerage systems and these include all the cities and major towns (Csáky, 1989). Not only is bacterial contamination of water sources a problem in rural areas but also the run-off of agricultural chemicals. Methaemoglobinaemia (blue-baby syndrome), for example, has been a significant problem caused by high nitrate concentrations (World Health Organisation, 1985).

The situation with solid wastes is no better. Some 16.5 million cubic metres of solid wastes are produced in the Hungarian settlements. Organised, permanent garbage-collection services are established in 800 settlements, including the larger and more urbanised villages. The service is absent from deeper rural areas. Thus, whereas garbage is collected from practically all homes in Budapest, it is done so from only half of the rural dwellings. A major problem is the handling and dumping of collected waste. Recycling and selective collection are only in their infancy. There are 2,600 dumping sites in Hungary, but only 58 per cent of them meet environmental and health standards. There are often no handling facilities and many are near capacity. They are a significant cause of local environmental nuisance. The problem is even worse at settlements without organised garbage collection. In these villages local people try to get rid of their garbage wherever they can, and thus, throughout the countryside, the margins of villages and the edges of roads and watercourses are strewn with rubbish (Jambor et al., 1989).

The built environment of villages has also changed greatly. Much traditional rural architecture has been lost during the last 20–30 years. The ancient village form, linear and gap-toothed, has been infilled with characterless box-like family houses and overwhelmed by uniform blocks of flats.

Macro technological, social and economic changes have also left their mark. The traditional Hungarian landscape had evolved over the centuries and was in harmony with the physical environment. This harmony has been disrupted by developments which take no account of natural features. It is most striking in the case of dense housing and leisure complexes, incongruously sited in rural settings. At the same time, small villages in underdeveloped regions are becoming derelict as they lose their population. A distinctive feature of the traditional Hungarian countryside was the water margins but these have been extensively altered by the removal of trees and bushes from the edges of rivers and lakes and the construction of artificial watercourses with narrow steep banks or lined with concrete. The upper reaches of the Danube are becoming more and more industrialised. Here there are industrial towns, factory zones, and waste dumping sites. The water barrage system under construction at Gabcikovo-Nagymaros will result in further changes to the natural state of the river (Möcsényi et al., 1989).

Formerly, agriculture existed in reciprocal relationship with the rural landscape, shaping it and in turn being shaped by it. But large-scale farming

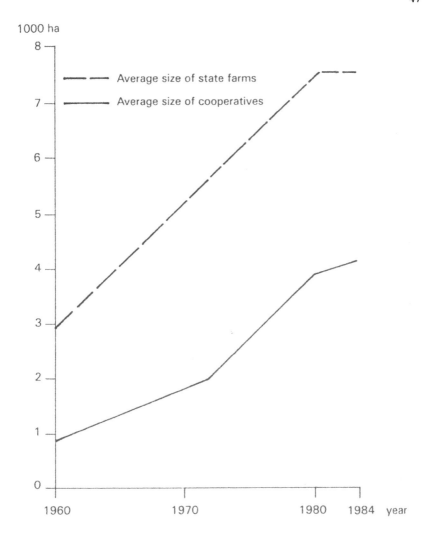

Figure 2.7 Average size of farms

has displaced traditional farming to the marginal lands. Large-scale farms have achieved higher yields on the majority of land, but this result has been attained at high costs. Overcentralised development and neglect of the environment have brought about both production and ecological problems. The trend of development has been technocentric with a preference for bigness (see Figure 2.7). Fields have been enlarged and their natural forms have given way to harsh geometric patterns. Areas recalcitrant to machinery have been neglected or abandoned, including such traditionally important zones of cultivation as hillside orchards and vineyards. Extensive monocultures have been established according to the dictates of mechanisation, e.g. the use of big tractors with the same chassis as military vehicles, or aerial crop protection using planes and helicopters. Hedges, spinneys, groves, and farmsteads have been removed. These features had tended to control wind and water erosion, and surface water flow, and had been important habitats. Landscapes have been impoverished and the natural enemies of pests have diminished. Most of the buildings of large-scale agriculture – e.g. animal breeding complexes, barns, dryers, refrigeration plants – are stark and brutal in their appearance, their siting, materials and design making little, if any, concession to the landscape. Because of mass recreation demands, in many areas traditional smallholdings have been extensively subdivided into small weekend plots. These mini 'shanty towns' are not only unsightly but lack any infrastructure and thus suffer problems of sewage and rubbish disposal. The plots are also intensively cultivated with often very heavy use of agricultural chemicals.

Technical change has influenced the state of Hungarian woodlands too. The woodland area has increased to 18 per cent, but the age and species structure of forests have been subordinated to short-term economic demands rather than to natural circumstances. The rate of plantation with fast-growing and high-yielding species (such as pines, poplars, acacia) has increased at the expense of natural forests (e.g. oaks, beeches). The health status of forests has declined – 10 per cent of the woodlands (primarily under oak) are diseased and dying. One of the major causes is pollution, particularly acid rain.

The remnants of natural habitats have shrunk into smaller and smaller areas, even while, in the last two decades, organised nature conservation has built-up a substantial structure in Hungary. About six per cent of the total territory is under protection, and more than one thousand (1,034) plant and animal species are protected by law. However, there are many conflicts in practice, particularly in rural areas. Weak state administration of conservation and the diffuse social support it enjoys are no match for the powerful, vested interests and bureaucracies of state utilities, industry, mining, and agriculture. There are frequent conflicts between conservationists and large scale agro-industries particularly over nature protection areas. This is provoked by such factors as over-fertilising, over-spraying, clearing of woods, and intensive breeding of game, because, although many nature protection areas are owned by the state, most are cultivated by agro-industries.

Some 40 plant and 53 animal species have become extinct in Hungary historically, and 1,130 species – two and half per cent of the total — are endangered. The direct causes are the increased pressures, largely brought about by technological change, including, for example, mechanical damage (through trampling, waste-dumping, over-grazing); the shift from extensive to intensive farming (on meadows and tillages); the use of pesticides; the transformation of natural habitats, through the alteration of water levels, eutrophication and pollution; and the direct destruction of natural habitats (e.g. through the ploughing up of old grasslands, the cutting down of ancient forests, the canalising of brooks and rivers, the construction of artificial embankments, land drainage, surface mining, the dumping of wastes, and the removal of topsoil) (Kovacs *et al.*, 1989).

Last but not least let us focus on the most important element of the rural environment: the soil. The extent of agricultural land has decreased in Hungary year by year. In 1950 92.2 per cent of the land surface was given over to agriculture and forestry; and by 1986 it was down to 88.7 per cent. The decrease has slowed down to an average of 9,000 hectares per year, but there are several developmental demands which will ensure that it is not curtailed for the forseeable future. Technological change and the consequent increase in arable and livestock yields have been the main factors in the altered balance of cultivation. The area under tillage, pastures, and vineyards has decreased but orchards and woodlands have increased (from 1.6 per cent to 4.7 per cent and from 12.5 per cent to 17.8 per cent respectively in the last four decades).

Soil degradation has occurred at a faster rate than improvements in soil fertility. Deleterious effects (acidification, salinisation, deterioration of soil-structure) are primarily a consequence of inappropriate agro-technology (the misuse of fertilisers, the poor planning or implementation of irrigation, inept ploughing). Annually, 800–1100 million cubic metres of topsoil with humus is washed off from hilly fields resulting in the loss of 1.5 million tonnes of organic material. Secondary salinisation and water logging affected 125 thousand hectares following the construction of the first water-barrage on the river Tisza (planning was much more cautious for the second barrage, and in the main these problems were avoided). Average yields on arable land doubled between the mid-60s and the late 70s through mechanisation, new plant varieties and increased application of artificial fertilisers. But the use of heavy machinery has led to problems of soil compaction and fertilisation has had various environmental side-effects: soils across the country are becoming more acid, by about 1 pH on average; surface waters are eutrophying; underground waters are becoming polluted by nitrates and toxic materials; and heavy metals are accumulating in the soil.

Public reactions

With the mounting tide of environmental problems, the environmental awareness of Hungarians has also grown markedly. Representative polls in 1988 disclosed that very few people were entirely satisfied with the state of the environment in the country, and while a third of those questioned considered it 'acceptable', the same proportion regarded it as 'completely bad'. Some 36 per cent of people had a strong interest in environmental issues, 47 per cent a moderate interest and 16 per cent little or none. The majority of the population (54 per cent) perceived environmental problems in their own neighbourhood (OPI, 1988; Kulcsár, 1988).

There is much direct evidence that environmental concern is higher in urban areas than in the countryside and this is confirmed by opinion survey data. It is easy to understand, because the urban population experiences a greater incidence of environmental problems. The relative lack of concern amongst rural people should not necessarily be interpreted as stemming from indifference. Indeed, environmentally friendly behaviour has a stronger tradition in rural areas, where responsibility for the future has been deeply rooted in the norms and values of local communities. Individual behaviour damaging to the environment is much rarer and more deviant in rural than in urban areas. Despoilation of the rural environment is more a consequence of new means of large-scale production which leave little scope for personal responsibility. Exogenous technological changes impose on rural inhabitants new and environmentally unsustainable patterns of life and consumption, yielding, for example, much more undegradable garbage, throw-away packaging, increased dependence on private cars, and higher consumption of energy and water.

In the past, the rural population has welcomed the consequent improvement in its material comfort and has been unaware of the long-term environmental side-effects. Because of the tangible benefits and the accompanying, modernising propaganda, rural people with their lower educational levels have often been slow to realise the environmental disadvantages, and their opportunities for action even then have been limited, particularly where overriding economic interests have been involved. Rural people, therefore, have not usually provided a warm welcome for urban-based environmental groups campaigning in favour of endangered natural values. Only since the mid-80s has nature conservation become sufficiently popular to restrict economic interests in some cases. In these years there have been several environmental conflicts that conservationists have actually won: such as the local defenders of the thermal lake at Héviz against bauxite mining; biologists at Budapest University defending Szársomlyó Hill nature protection area against limestone mining; and scientists objecting to the impact of the plans for the Danube dam system on the Szigetköz nature protection area. Tension was nevertheless detectable between the concerns of the 'urban greens' and the immediate interests of the rural population in almost all of these conflicts.

In recent years, the environmental awareness of rural people has been increasing significantly and has been expressed in a number of protests, mostly against waste dumping or processing sites. Initially, these protests were about the protection of residential land values and other local economic interests and did not stem from the ecological concern of the participants. Such protests reflect the great social changes sweeping the country in which local autonomy has increased and the relationship between power and the citizenry has moved towards greater democracy. Thus the people of the village are not simply spectators or passive recipients of these wider changes but increasingly have the possibility and the courage to act on their own behalf.

The first rural environmental protest burst out against the establishment of a hazardous waste dumping site at Zsámbék, 20 miles from Budapest, in 1981 (Tamás, 1986). More recently, such rural protests have become quite common – almost a permanent feature of life. Taking just one year, 1988, the following local environmental protests in rural areas had national reverberations: against the location of a dumping site for intermediate radioactive wastes from the Paks nuclear power plant at Ófalu; against enlargement of an isotope dump at Püspökszilágy; against illegal dumping of hazardous wastes at Monorierdó and Apajpuszta; against the establishment of hazardous waste dumping sites at Kuncsorba, Kápolnásnyék and Aszód; against the construction of a lead-battery reprocessing plant at Gyöngyösoroszi; and against bauxite mining which threatened the thermal lake at Héviz. A typical example was the opposition of six villages to the siting of a temporary dumping site for hazardous wastes in Bács county leading eventually to the authorities abandoning the plan.

At the same time depots for toxics, pesticides and other chemicals have operated for decades without any reaction from rural people, even though they pose a greater hazard than many of the establishments currently being opposed. The level of chemicalisation in private gardens and smallholdings is uncontrollably high. The serious problems of agricultural pollution remain unchallenged. Expansion of piped water in rural settlements is proceeding without the necessary development of collective sewage disposal. Villages are becoming more motorised, demanding new roads, and covering fields with concrete. Initiatives on organic farming remain insignificant against the backcloth of intensive, industrialised agriculture.

It must be stressed that the main reason for the environmental protests that do occur in rural areas is not deep-seated ecological concern. Rather these manifestations reflect the grievous economic, political, and cultural injustices that rural society has suffered and which have made it distrustful of centralised power and its technocrats. This is the main reason why, during the current period of democratisation, Hungary is witnessing a widespread mushrooming of local amenity protests, in some respects akin to the NIMBY-syndrome found in the advanced capitalist societies. People, for example, want waste disposal problems to be solved, but not close by.

Rural people are at the end of their tether, their patience and self-denial exhausted. Too often in the past demands have been placed upon them and only rarely have their own needs been recognised. Now, therefore, they are unwilling to tolerate environmental damage or risks on behalf of others, only on their own.

References

Csáky, Ferenc, (1989) Felszin alatti vizek (kézirat) in Hazánk környezeti állapota, KVM Budapest.

Csorba, Zoltánné, (1987) Struktúra, átalakítás és környezetvédelem a mezőgaz-dasági termelésben (kézirat) Országos Tervhivatal TTFCS, Budapest.

52

Dargai, László, (1988) A mezőgazdálkodás regionális kérdései, in Az agrárpolitika megújításának főbb kérdései. Agrárgazdasági Kut. Int. Budapest, 227–312.

Enyedi, György, (1988) A városnövekedés szakaszai. Akadémiai Kiadó, Budapest.

Enyedi, György, (1989) (Interjú az MTA RKK fóigazgatójával) Magyar Mezőgazdaság.

Éri, Vilma, (1989) Az alkalmazkodó mezőgazdaság környezetvédelmi kérdései. MTA Közg. Int., Budapest.

Gerlach, György (Szerk), (1989) Környezetminőség és környezetvédelem Magyar-országon, Műszaki Könyvkiadó, Budapest.

Glatz Ferenc, (1987) Ember, természet és az új történetelmélet, História, 2.

Gyenei, Mária (1989) A lélekharang értünk is szól, Élet és irodalom, 19.

Horváth Eszter (Szerk.), (1986) A környezet állapota és védelme, Központi Statisztikai Hivatal Budapest.

Jámbor, Imre, et al., (1989) Települési környezet (kézirat), in Hazánk környezeti állapota, KVM, Budapest.

Kovács, Margit, et al., (1989) Az élővilág (kézirat), in Hazánk környezeti állapota, KVM, Budapest.

Központi Statisztikai Hivatal, (1989) Statisztikai Évkönyv 1987. KSH, Budapest.

Kulcsár, László, (1988) Környezetgazdálkodás és lakossági tudat (kut. beszámoló gyorsjelentés, kézirat), GATE, Gödöllő.

Madas, András, et al., (1989) Környezetvédelmi követelmények a mezőgazdaságban. Környezeti Rendszerfejlesztő és Tanácsadó Kft., Budapest.

Möcsényi, Mihály, et al., (1989) A táj (kézirat), in Hazánk környezeti állapota, KVM, Budapest.

Országos Piackutató Intézet (1988) A lakosság véleménye néhány környezetvédelmi kérdésről (kézirat), OPI, Budapest.

Prugberger, Tamás (1989) A földek védelmében, Élet és Tudomány, 22, 692–693.

Tamás, Pál, (1986) Érdek és kockázatfelismerés, OMFB Rendszerelemzési Iroda, Budapest.

Várallyai, György, et al., (1989) A föld (kézirat), in Hazánk környezeti állapota, KVM Budapest.

World Health Organisation (1985) Health hazards from nitrate in drinking water, Environmental Health, 1. Copenhagen: WHO.

CHAPTER 3

Technological Change, Farm Management and Pollution Regulation: The Example of Britain

Philip Lowe, Graham Cox, David Goodman, Richard Munton and Michael Winter

Introduction

There is gathering public concern over the impact on the natural and global environment of expanding production and consumption activities. Increasingly, governments are being pressed to adopt a more strategic approach in tackling environmental problems, particularly so that ecological considerations might be effectively integrated into the choices that producers and consumers make. The design of suitable measures, though, presumes an understanding of the responses they would provoke and, in this regard, there is no greater challenge than that presented by agriculture.

It must be said, however, that there is comparatively little experience of the environmental regulation of agriculture and that, perhaps in implicit recognition of the difficulties that might be involved, farmers have tended to escape many of the controls that have been applied to other industries (OECD, 1989). Agriculture is, nevertheless, one of the most regulated fields from the point of view of production. A complicating factor in contemplating appropriate environmental protection measures, therefore, is the changing direction of agricultural policy as policy makers, partly in response to environmental pressures, reassess the overwhelmingly 'productivist' orientation of the post-war period. Aspects of a revised policy package are contained in recent statements of the European Commission (1988) and the British Government (ALURE 1987). Such policy shifts may ultimately offer the prospect of fully combining the environmental and production regulation of agriculture, but Britain is not alone at present in falling well short of such integrated management of the agricultural sector (OECD, 1989).

The farming industry itself now shows signs of adjustment to a post-productivist era, for example in land abandonment in parts of Europe (Conrad, 1987) and a decline in the real level of fixed capital stock in British agriculture (Harrison, 1989). Nevertheless, in the absence of new forms of regulation, industrial farming methods will continue to affect the environment adversely. Inevitably, current efforts to redirect agricultural policy into a more environmentally benign direction carry with them a sense of closing the stable door after the horse has bolted. A leading agrarian historian, for example, has judged that of all the agricultural revolutions claimed for different historical periods only one merits the name, by virtue of its speed, scale and ubiquity, and that is the post-war agricultural revolution (Mingay, 1990). Clearly, the associated changes cannot be undone nor the practices and technologies unlearnt: and certainly with respect to pollution, it would seem that the consequences and the problems are starting to mount. There are also many yield-boosting innovations still in the pipeline, of which the somatotrophins are but the latest, which will encourage the further concentration of production and increase pollution risks.

In addition we could be on the threshold of a major new phase of technological change in agriculture induced by developments in biotechnology, though it is yet to be seen whether these effect the scale of transformation brought about in the post-war period by advances in chemical, mechanical and breeding techniques. Nevertheless, new plant and animal biotechnologies promise significant increases in productivity and productive capacity. They are also likely to lead to new linkages between agriculture, food processing and the chemical and energy industries. In helping open up industrial outlets for farm produce, modern biotechnologies may ease the crisis of overproduction and, by incorporating pest or disease resistance into crop plants, they may also solve certain environmental problems such as excessive pesticide use. In the shape of genetically engineered organisms, however, biotechnologies also pose quite novel environmental hazards, quite apart from the environmental consequences following from any intensification of production they stimulate.

Although policy adjustments may eventually lead to less intensive farming technologies (and here biotechnology may also play a leading part), their adoption is likely to be uneven between sectors, localities and farm businesses. It is for these reasons that strong demands for improved methods of regulation will continue to be articulated.

Our purpose in this chapter is to raise some of the key issues such developments pose for social science. Initially, therefore, the chapter illustrates some of the major trends and looming problems with specific reference to water pollution in Britain. There then follow sections reviewing conceptual and analytical themes relating to technological change, farm management and pollution regulation. These are the central components in the 'pollution production process' (Figure 3.3), a full understanding of which is a necessary condition for the establishment of a coherent policy and institutional framework to deal with agricultural pollution.

Agriculture and water pollution in Britain: trends and prospects

In the past, agricultural pollution has attracted much less attention in Britain than the more readily observable impact of agricultural development on wildlife habitats and rural landscapes. One consequence is that there is much less information and data concerning agricultural pollution than on these other environmental changes. Since the early 1980s, however, the issue has assumed much greater prominence and this in turn has stimulated increased monitoring and investigation.

The broad trends over the past 10–15 years can be summarised as follows:

(1)   a growth in the public recognition and political salience of an expanding array of agricultural pollution problems;
(2)   a significant broadening in the geography of such problems with many of the traditional sources of farm pollution, such as pesticides, fertiliser run-off, straw burning and animal wastes, formerly associated mainly with the intensive arable, vegetable and livestock production systems of Eastern England; but the emergent problems of the 1980s, particularly slurry and silage effluent, associated more with the pastoral (particularly dairy and beef) farming of the West;
(3)   a shift of attention from discrete, local and specific issues to a general appreciation of agricultural pollution as a generic and structural problem of modern, intensive farming systems;
(4)   a shift from a concern mainly with wildlife and 'nuisance' effects to ecological and public health implications.

Despite broadening concerns in recent years, however, the major pre-occupations remain with water pollution and with pesticides: other types of farm-based pollution, such as noise, air pollution and soil contamination and erosion, have received much less attention. The main types of water pollution arising from contemporary agriculture are as follows.

Nitrates

Nitrate concentrations in both ground and surface waters are rising in many areas. The main source is arable agriculture where intensification in the last few decades has increased nitrate leaching from soils. In 1987 British farmers spread 1.6 million tonnes of fertiliser nitrogen at a cost of around £600 million and the Agricultural and Food Research Council estimated in its 1988 annual report that between 10 and 30 per cent was lost, either to the water supply or the atmosphere. A Royal Society study of the nitrogen cycle had earlier warned that, owing to slow transit times, the nitrate concentration in many supply wells will rise over the next 20 to 30 years to well above the maximum acceptable level specified by either the European Community or the World Health Organisation (WHO).

The highest nitrate levels occur in the intensive arable areas in the south and east of England, and the problem is most pressing in those areas of eastern and central England which, with their low rainfall and chalk, limestone and sandstone aquifers, are most dependent on ground water sources. Concentrations in underground waters are expected to reach 150 to 200 mg/litre in the future, if agricultural losses remain stable (Croll and Hayes, 1988). Already, several borehole stations in the worst affected areas have had to be taken out of public supply.

Although there has been only one recorded death from infant methaemoglobinaemia (blue-baby syndrome) in Britain in the last 40 years, this is regarded as the main health hazard associated with nitrate consumption. With regard to cancer risks, there has been little challenge to the Royal Commission on Environmental Pollution's 1979 pronouncement that 'there is no evidence that unambiguously associates nitrates and N-nitroso compounds in human tissues or body fluids with carcinoma of any organ in man'. For many years British water authorities worked to the WHO European standard for nitrates in drinking water (100 mg/l). It was the need to comply with the European Community's Directive on Drinking Water which served to sharpen conflict over the issue, particularly when the government's implementation strategy, encouraged by agro-chemical interests, included seeking derogations for about 50 supply sources which failed to meet the directive's maximum admissible concentration for nitrate of 50 mg/l. A threat of legal action by the European Commission led the government to drop these derogations in 1988. The Commission also forced an alteration in the method of testing compliance with the law from an average level over three months to a single result, with the effect that the number of people receiving supplies over the limit rose from one to four million. The crucial issues remain the timetable for improving these supplies to bring them into line with the limit and how this should be achieved.

As the UK's strategy of a liberal interpretation of the EC standard has run into political and legal obstacles, so greater consideration has been given to technical and operational solutions (Nitrate Co-ordination Group, 1986). The main short-term options are blending and source modification or replacement. Removal by treatment is likely to be costly – adding about a third to the total costs of water treatment and distribution – and might generate its own water quality problems. It has been estimated that the cost of achieving the 50 mg/l standard would be £200 million over the next 20 years (Nitrate Co-ordination Group, 1986). This has encouraged the exploration of more fundamental solutions, including the curtailment of nitrate use and of farming practices which increase leaching in sensitive catchments (Department of the Environment, 1988b; Consultants in Environmental Sciences, 1988). Bound up with these choices is who should bear the cost of prevention or treatment – the farmers, the fertiliser companies, the water consumers or the exchequer.

In 1990 a pilot scheme was begun in which farmers in 10 designated Nitrate Sensitive Areas (NSAs) were to be compensated by the Ministry of Agriculture for adapting their farming practices to reduce nitrate leaching.

Figure 3.1 Farm pollution incidents in England and Wales, 1979 to 1988

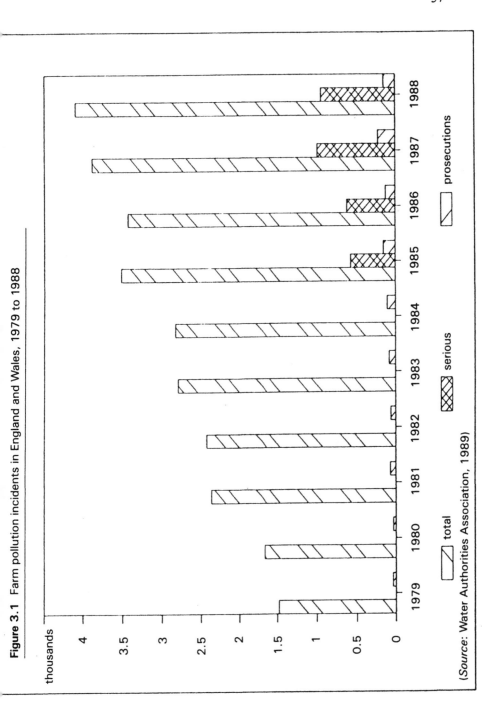

(*Source:* Water Authorities Association, 1989)

In an additional nine areas intensive advisory campaigns were conducted towards the same goal. The only agricultural systems with sufficiently low leaching rates, though, are likely to be low to medium productivity permanent grassland and forestry. In any case, the very limited experiment in borehole protection zones represented by the NSAs is likely to be overtaken by the EC's Nitrate Directive. A draft of this issued in 1989 would require the establishment of water protection zones in areas where nitrate levels exceed 50 mg/l involving extensive and severe restrictions on farming practices, in order to protect inland, coastal and marine waters, as well as drinking water.

Farm wastes

Figure 3.1 shows the growth of farm pollution incidents over the past decade. About a fifth of all recorded water pollution incidents are due to farming, with the other major sources being industrial effluent and sewage. However, whereas the effluent from large industrial concerns and sewage works is regularly, if not continuously, monitored, that from farms is not. A pollution incident caused by farming is recorded only when someone reports it, arising, for example, from a major fish kill or from the need to shut down a public abstraction point. Undoubtedly, many cases of farm pollution go

Figure 3.2 Farm pollution incidents in England and Wales, 1988.

Type of waste/pollution or cause of pollution	1988		1987 to '88	1988
	no.	%	% change	no. of prosecutions
cows slurry stores	801	19	14	41
solid stores	194	5	31	1
yard/parlour washings	836	20	2	11
land runoff/treatment system failure	441	11	49	9
silage liquor	815	20	− 19	55
pigs slurry stores	231	6	6	16
yard washings	59	1	9	0
land runoff/treatment system failure	109	3	15	5
poultry	64	2	10	0
sheep dip	18	0	6	2
pesticide	52	1	4	1
mineral fertiliser	19	0	6	0
vegetable washings	16	0	− 52	0
oil spillages	93	2	− 27	0
fish farms	10	0		2
others	383	9	54	5
total	4141	100	6	148

(*Source*: Water Authorities Association, 1989)

unreported. The ones that are recorded, therefore, tend to be more serious than those from other sources; and very great damage can be done because of the large amount of organic matter often discharged in such incidents and its high Biological Oxygen Demand (BOD). Thus, farming accounts for two-thirds of the pollution incidents which result in prosecutions.

Figure 3.2 presents a breakdown of the water pollution incidents caused by farm wastes and highlights the significance of pig and cow slurry and silage effluent. All the other categories, such as oil spillages, poultry waste, mineral fertilisers and vegetable washings, are comparatively minor. Growing pollution problems from livestock wastes have been associated with the development of intensive husbandry and particularly with the trend, since the 1960s, towards the indoor housing of animals in large numbers in intensive livestock units.

This trend has been most marked for chickens and pigs. Whilst poultry litter is usually handled in solid form, pig manure is usually handled mainly as slurry and therefore creates greater disposal problems and risk of water pollution. The largest concentrations of piggeries are found in Norfolk, Suffolk and Humberside and the main problems relate to the inadequate storage and treatment of slurry, and land run off due to excessive application. In 1977 it was estimated that one quarter of the pigs were on holdings with insufficient arable land to make profitable use of the manure produced, and in 1979 the Royal Commission on Environment Pollution remarked that slurry treatment systems had been 'adopted to only a negligible extent' (RCEP, 1979 paras 5.10 and 5.31). The problem has to some extent been contained in the eastern, traditional pig rearing areas, but has grown elsewhere, particularly in the North and South West, as ill-equipped farmers have sought to diversify into pig production, including some dairy farmers in the aftermath of milk quotas.

The major source of farm pollution of water involves dairy and beef farming, which have accounted for 75–80 per cent of farm water pollution incidents in England and Wales during the past four years – though between a third and a quarter of these incidents arise not from livestock wastes but from silage liquor (see below). The problem is consequent upon the growth in herd sizes (the average dairy herd expanded from 46 to 61 cows between 1978 and 1988) and the trend towards greater housing, particularly of dairy cattle. There has also been a marked shift from the bedding of dairy herds on straw to their housing in cubicles, with the result that there is a liquid slurry to be disposed of. To a lesser extent, similar trends are apparent in the beef cattle industry. The geography of the problem reflects the geography of beef and dairy farming, and is thus concentrated in the western half of the country. Surveys in a number of dairy catchments have found that about half the farms are either polluting water courses or at risk of doing so (Water Authorities Association, 1988, 1989). Improved storage and treatment of effluent would require substantial investment in plant and structures, beyond the means of many of the smaller dairy farmers.

Another trend with considerable pollution implications is the growth in the production of silage for the winter feeding of livestock. This partly reflects a shift from hay making, because silage making is less vulnerable to unpredictable weather conditions and earlier cutting is possible which allows quicker regrowth of the grass. It also reflects the efforts of farmers to reduce their reliance on bought-in feedstuffs, particularly following the imposition of milk quotas. In consequence, the amount of grass silage made in England and Wales increased from about five to 35 million tonnes between 1970 and 1988. Silage effluent can cause very serious pollution not least because of its very potent BOD value (which can be as high as 80,000 mg/litre, compared with the usual maximum of 20 mg/litre for treated sewage effluent). It may also be very acidic. The amount of effluent produced depends on the moisture content of the ensiled crop. Farmers are advised to wilt the cut crop – that is, to leave it in the field to dry for 24 hours before storing it – to minimise the effluent produced. However, weather conditions, particularly in the wetter western areas, may prevent adequate wilting, and additives are available which permit good silage to be made from wet material. The appropriate siting and adequate construction of silos and the provision of sufficient storage for the effluent are therefore important considerations to prevent pollution, but these are often overlooked.

In the past, farm pollution has been treated with a great deal of leniency. Even in recent years, only about four per cent of farm pollution incidents on average have led to prosecutions, and fines have often been derisory. In addition, farmers have enjoyed exemptions from many controls applied to other industries; including, for example, the Control of Pollution Act 1974, which exempted farmers if pursuing 'good agricultural practice'. There are signs, however, that official attitudes are hardening in response to the growing volume of farm pollution. In 1990, for example, regulations were introduced setting minimum standards for the construction and maintenance of silage and slurry stores. At the same time, the farming lobby has successfully pressed for greater financial assistance for farmers to bring their facilities up to scratch.

Pesticides

Traditionally, the limited concern that has arisen concerning pesticide contamination of waters has focused on gross pollution incidents: that is, on the careless disposal of surplus pesticides, including sheep dip (containing chemicals used to combat sheep scab and the only significant source of pollution associated with the upland sheep-farming areas of Wales and the North of England). Each year, such incidents make up a small proportion (1–2%) of the total number of recorded cases of water pollution by agriculture.

Recently, there has also been concern over the 'background' contamination of ground and surface waters with pesticides run-off, though there is little reliable information of the extent of the problem. This issue was raised by publicity of the failure of some water sources to achieve the standard specified by the EC Drinking Water Directive. The Directive sets two maximum admissible concentrations for pesticides; no more than

$0.1\,\mu g$/litre of any one pesticide, and no more than $0.5\,\mu g$/litre of 'total' pesticides, may be present. A survey of pesticides in drinking water in England and Wales between July 1985 and June 1987 showed that the levels for individual pesticides were exceeded on 298 occasions, while breaches of the $0.5\,\mu g$/litre standard were recorded on 76 occasions. A total of 16 pesticides featured in these incidents, the most common being a number of water soluble herbicides which persist in the soil (Friends of the Earth, 1988).

Presently, treatment is by filtration through activated carbon. As yet there has been no specific policy response although the issue seems set to take a somewhat similar course to the nitrate controversy. The prospect of restrictions on the use of specific pesticides in sensitive catchments is a possibility (European Institute for Water, 1988).

The broader framework for the registration of pesticides and the regulation of their use derives from the Food and Environment Protection Act 1985. This placed on a mandatory basis the previously voluntary clearance agreement for new products between the government and the relevant industry associations. The pressure for change had come from a variety of sources including industry, the Royal Commission on Environmental Pollution and environmental groups as well as the European Commission. The legislation was introduced against the background of a considerable growth in pesticide consumption. The number of approved products had grown from 540 in 1974 to almost a thousand in 1985. By the early 1980s, 97–99 per cent of all main crops, cereals and vegetables were sprayed at least once, and annual industry sales had reached about £330 million by 1983 (British Agrochemical Association, 1984). The 1985 legislation established a new structure governing statutory codes of conduct in the development, marketing and use of pesticides. Users are required to have been trained in the safe and efficient application of pesticides and are obliged to comply with the conditions of approval relating to use. The Act also included powers to set mandatory standards for residues in food in line with adopted European Community directives.

Since the early 1980s the number of issues connected with pesticide use has increased and the debates over the acceptability of different substances and application methods have intensified. It is generally agreed that fatalities arising from pesticide use in the UK are extremely rare and less common, for example, than tractor accidents. However, there is fairly widespread public suspicion of the health effects of pesticides in general, and demand for organically grown vegetables and other pesticide-free foods has grown rapidly. The hazards to farm and forestry workers of applying pesticides have also received some attention and the farm workers' trade union has as a result played an active part in the pesticide debate. The impact of pesticides on wildlife, though, has received much less attention in recent years especially compared with the late 1960s when the use (now greatly curtailed) of the organochlorides was indicted in the marked decline of several raptor species. Declining populations of a number of plant and invertebrate species, however, are partly attributable to pesticide use. Controversy over application methods has been confined mainly to aerial spraying which accounts for only about two per cent of total pesticide use. There is, however, an active campaign by environmental bodies to ban it altogether because of its prevalent association with spray drift problems.

From this brief view it should be evident that the development of a coherent policy and institutional framework to deal with agricultural pollution is still a distant prospect. The approach typically has been piecemeal and reactive though it is also clear that the European Community has injected into British practice a more systematic and formal approach to the setting and enforcement of standards (Haigh, 1987). The achievement of more rational arrangements would, in addition, require a greater appreciation of what might be termed the pollution production process (see Figure 3.3). We now turn to examine some of the key component systems in this process, relating to technological change, farm management adjustment and pollution regulation.

Technological change

The standard analysis of industrial innovation is not appropriate when explaining technological development in the agro-food system – a system which does not constitute merely another branch of manufacturing and thus is not reducible to industry (Goodman and Wilkinson: Chapter 6). This is because the dual biological constraints represented by agricultural production and the physiological requirements of human consumption have created unique problems for industrial organisation and innovation. The

Figure 3.3 Agriculture as a pollution production process

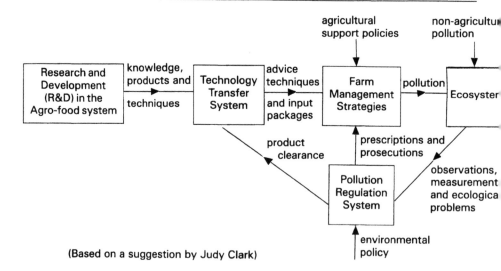

(Based on a suggestion by Judy Clark)

centrality of biological processes has imparted singular characteristics both to the industrialisation of agriculture and food production and to rural social structures, which have resisted direct and *unified* transformation by industrial capitals (Goodman, Sorj and Wilkinson, 1987). The result has been partial and historically discontinuous appropriations of rural production activities, and these separate appropriations define the origins of distinct agro-industrial capitals.

Biological constraints therefore have led to innovations by capitals located outside the immediate production process, with major consequences for the overall development of agriculture. As discrete rural activities are appropriated, the individual sectors so established become autonomous sources of innovation. Critical biological constraints, including photosynthesis, gestation, species diversity, and land as space, have led to the fragmentation of the innovation process. This fragmentation helps to explain the mainly atomistic structure of agriculture, centred on family labour forms of production, characteristic forms of state intervention, and the degradation of the rural environment. Industrial capitals pursue independent R&D strategies to promote sales of their inputs, disregarding the separate and cumulative impact of innovation on agriculture's 'factory floor' – the environment. This disregard is manifest in soil mining, habitat destruction, agro-chemical pollution, monocultural crop specialisation, genetic erosion, and other prevalent problems.

This analysis suggests that technological tendencies (internal combustion, inorganic chemicals, genetics, molecular biology) and associated corporate R&D strategies have a major role in restructuring the rural production process and defining the economic context of farm business behaviour. In this respect, the institutional apparatus of government support established since the 1930s has provided the vital foundation for rapid technological change. Indeed, it is arguable that the social transformation of agriculture is due less to the revolutionary character of innovation *per se* than the institutional incentives to early adoption and technological competition introduced by the state. Insofar as modern farming technologies are implicated in damaging the environment, then explanations as well as solutions must be sought by extending the analysis beyond farmers' behaviour to the political economy of the agro-food system as a whole.

Thus whilst technological change is important in its own right in understanding farming change, it also represents a key link *between* farm management strategies, environmental consequences and regulation. In particular, the continuing speed of technological change, reinforced by plant and animal biotechnologies, raises the questions of how appropriate are present regulatory structures and whether they are sufficiently resourced to meet, for example, growing public concern over agricultural pollution and the prospect of the deliberate release of genetically modified organisms into the environment. Important related issues are whether the point of regulation should be moved upstream (to embrace the R&D system, for example, in relation to biotechnology – Tait: chapter 8); and whether upstream regulation should seek to anticipate possible farm-level environmental consequences of technological innovation. Such a move might imply strengthening the institutional mechanisms of technology assessment and the wider application of Best Practical Environmental Option (BPEO) methodologies. An emerging principle of environmental regulation is that it should increasingly become precautionary and anticipatory rather than mainly reactive (DoE, 1988a), and this reinforces the need for investigations of farm business adjustment processes and their environmental impacts to be set within an agro-food system perspective

The analysis of post-war trends in agricultural technology emphasises the convergence of mechanical and chemical technologies on genetic innovations to establish integrated technological 'packages' which can be readily applied to differing farm systems. By attenuating the intrinsic risks and uncertainties of agricultural production, public intervention in agricultural markets to support farm incomes has accelerated the diffusion of these advanced 'packages'. This technology-policy model was, however, thrown into question by the international farm crisis of the mid–1980s. The crisis assumed many guises – over-production, the fiscal strains of farm support, proposals for agricultural trade reform, severe farm indebtedness, declining farm incomes and the continuing rural exodus – and its legacy is an extremely complex agenda for farm policy change (Goodman and Redclift, 1989). For the moment, policy directions are confused, hesitating between free market solutions and greater reliance on administrative regulation and *dirigiste* structural programmes. This hesitancy also reflects the greater political significance of farm policy, which increasingly is pervaded by 'green issues', ranging from pollution to the kind of rural society which should be maintained (EC, 1988).

This questioning of the inherited productivist model, which has greatly widened the constituency of interests involved in farm policy, occurs on the eve of a new technological revolution in agriculture associated with modern biotechnologies, and adds its own uncertainties. By conferring a generic capacity to modify the biological cycles underlying food production and human nutrition, these innovations will create a new technological base for the agro-food system. The potentially revolutionary impacts of biotechnologies in agriculture, primary processing and food manufacturing have rightly been emphasised (US Office of Technology Assessment, 1981). New plant and animal biotechnologies promise to bring faster rates of growth in productivity and aggregate productive capacity, adding to the complexity of structural adjustment in agriculture. It is worth stressing, though, that biotechnologies are 'enabling technologies', with a wide variety of possible applications. In plant breeding, for example, biotechnologies can be used to confer biological resistance to disease and pests or, alternatively, to proprietary agro-chemicals. But not everything which is technologically feasible will be realised. Much will depend, of course, on how rural production and social development policies are re-defined, including the public regulatory framework and the locus of control over biotechnology R&D.

In practice, the deployment of agri-biotechnologies is increasingly in private hands, with wider university-industry contract research relations

(Kenney, 1986), increasing concentration in the seed and agro-chemical industries (Goodman, 1987), and a changing division of labour in plant breeding research (Buttel, 1986; Kloppenburg, 1988). Corollaries include increasing recourse to trade secrecy in research and mounting pressures to extend intellectual property rights to genetically modified organisms and new life forms. In the UK, the new technical division of labour was signalled by decisions taken in 1987–8 to concentrate public sector resources on basic research, leaving applied or 'near-market' R&D to industry. A similar re-orientation occurred earlier in the United States following publication of the Winrock Report in 1982 (Rockefeller Foundation, 1982). These changes are defended using the rhetoric of world technological rivalry and 'national competitiveness' (Byman: chapter 7). However, the result is to cede increasing control over the research agenda and deployment of agri-bio-technologies to the corporate sector (Munton, Marsden and Whatmore: chapter 5). Analyses of technological innovation need to take account of these changing institutional relationships in the research base of the agro-food system.

In the primary processing and food manufacturing sectors, modern biotechnologies are likely to lead to significant advances in fermentation techniques and separation methods. Such innovations will increase inter-changeability between the agricultural feedstocks used in food production, and also create new non-food outlets for agricultural crops (Wilkinson, 1987). These avenues of adjustment to the 'crisis of over-production' are already being vigorously pursued by 'downstream' agri-business firms (Goodman, 1989).

On the other hand, farm policy reform leading to greater emphasis on social objectives and more rigorous conservation standards will also have important implications for farm management practice. As yet, however, little is known about how agri-business firms might adapt their R&D strategies in response to stricter environmental regulation.

A typical dilemma facing the agri-chemical industry relates to which of the following paths agricultural policy and regulation might take in response to problems of nitrate and pesticide pollution:

Regulatory/ policy choice	Problems for farm adjustment	Issues for technological change/R&D
Treatment vs	Increased regulation and enforcemernt of procedures for the use of agro-chemicals	Development of active ingredients which are highly specific in action and rapidly biodegradable
Prevention	Technical, financial and support problems of moving to a low input – low output system	Considerable demand for products and techniques related to biological agriculture (organic farming, integrated pest control, developments in nitrogen fixing, etc) but limited profitability.

Changing food consumption patterns arising from greater public awareness of health and nutrition introduce further uncertainty, and the market power of large retailers emphasises these trends. The retail multiples have the means to exert considerable control over agricultural production technologies, particularly the use of agro-chemicals and veterinary products, in response to consumer concerns

Nonetheless, although low-input farming systems are now receiving some official encouragement, the main thrust of EC adjustment strategy is still focused on product diversification through the development of alternative uses for major crops and the reduction of farm support. Proposals to produce ethanol from cereals appear to be gaining ground and in December 1989 the EC announced a proposed change in its set-aside arrangements which would support cereal production for non-food, industrial uses. This follows an earlier 1986 EC regulation to stimulate the use of sugar and starch inputs as feedstocks for the chemical industry. Primary processing industries, at times assisted by joint research programmes coordinated by the EC Biotechnology Concertation Unit, are successfully developing new speciality, high value non-food products, particularly for starch and oilseed crops (Wilkinson, 1987).

These emerging patterns of innovation are forging new modes of integration between agriculture and industry which transcend traditional agro-food chains, creating the longer-term prospect of a 'bio-industrial processing complex' formed by the integration of the agro-food system and the chemical and pharmaceutical industries (Goodman and Wilkinson: chapter 6). Little social science research has been conducted in Britain into these emerging technological tendencies and industrial scenarios, nor have their transmission to farmers and their environmental consequences been examined.

Farm adjustment and environmental consequences

The relationship beween social and economic processes and their environmental consequences are rarely simple or direct, and they generate important feed-back effects. The farm adjustment process is uneven, and especially difficult to predict at the local level and for individual businesses. Yet an ability to comprehend change at these scales is being increasingly demanded by shifts in public policy which cast farmers as managers of countryside change and require regulation and support to be precisely targeted. There are, for example, growing calls for income support for small producers rather than generalised price support, and the need to target environmental regulatory measures towards vulnerable localities (e.g. Environmentally Sensitive Areas) and sources of pollution (e.g. Nitrate Sensitive Areas). Such pressures culminated in the Countryside Policy Review Panel's (1987) demand for farm-based, multi-purpose planning designed to integrate farm and environmental management practice (see also Lowe et al., 1986).

At present these developments sit somewhat uneasily within a policy context for the rural environment still largely oriented towards voluntarism and minimal controls over producers (see Cox *et al.*, 1989; 1990). Even so, they do argue for the importance of farm-based enquiry and analysis, although this cannot be conducted in isolation from the broader economic conditions and policy adjustments facing the food system as a whole, and the agricultural industry specifically. These changes affect the goals of families engaged in farming, which in turn structure their responses to policy measures, attitudes to risk (e.g. level of borrowing, the intensity with which the land may be farmed), and the deployment of family labour. Such considerations will determine household intentions towards the expansion or abandonment of particular farm enterprises and other sources of income (only some of which will be concerned with food protution) and the technologies to be used in the management of land.

Among the more important policy changes currently confronting British farms are those designed to encourage 'rural enterprise' and to de-regulate the land-use planning system, as much as changes to agricultural policy itself. Together, these create a new and more *uncertain* policy context, encouraging farmers, *inter alia*, to entertain a wider range of novel enterprises (diversification) and a less intensive use of land (extensification). The *potential* significance of these sources for the consumption of new and existing agricultural technologies is made clear by Buckwell (1989, p. 157) when he argues that

> ... all the while farmers expect that the general system of product price support will continue, the fact that the level of support does not guarantee rising, or even stable, long-run terms of trade, will not necessarily discourage investment. Only when ... there are real fears that the market props might be taken away is it reasonable to anticipate significant disinvestment in agriculture.

In the meantime, though there may be a shift in the rationale for new technology from 'high-output' to 'efficiency of inputs', a general retreat from high technology farming is unlikely. The investment in R&D in the food system is simply too great; the esoteric nature of many agricultural techniques and practices has created its own forms of technological dependence at the farm level; and the funds so far made available to compensate farmers for reduced income (as under land diversion, or 'set-aside'), or to encourage them to diversify into non-agricultural enterprises, are perceived as too limited compared with established sources of commodity price support (Gasson, 1988; Gasson and Potter, 1988). Off-farm employment opportunities have improved in recent years and there is growing demand for a wider range of goods and services from farms, including various leisure, sporting and retailing activities. Yet a recent study of farm household income changes, while showing a wide range of expectations regarding the future, found more farmers anticipating greater reliance on agricultural income than those envisaging growing dependence on non-agricultural income sources (Shucksmith *et al.*, 1989).

Thus, although the changing policy context has created new options for farming families, with several farming sectors experiencing a cash-flow crisis during the later 1980s, it has placed an even higher premium on adaptability and responsiveness in the allocation of capital and labour resources, and challenged established modes of thought and husbandry practices. The cash-flow crisis, which has arisen from a combination of depressed incomes and high debt burdens, exacerbated by rising real interest rates (Harrison and Tranter, 1989; Cox *et al.*, 1989, Hill, 1989), has not only tied a significant proportion of farms more closely to the dictates of finance capital but also to other more powerful interests in the food system, including the purveyors of industrial technologies (see Marsden *et al.*, 1990). These kinds of change are likely further to polarise experience at the farm level, stretching further the credibility of treating agriculture as a single industry and demanding the greater targeting of policy.

Despite some classic studies of the farm operator (e.g. Gasson, 1973), amidst these changing circumstances we remain ill-informed about the goals of farming households and their members. The literature on farming as a family business is still dominated by enquiries conducted under quite different farming circumstances. In their exhaustive review of this literature Gasson *et al.* (1988, p. 34) note that

> ... the successful financial performance and continuity of the farm as a family business depend not only on the satisfactory functioning of the business enterprise but also on the continuity of family structure and processes.

Yet evidence is accumulating that these conditions are increasingly not being met, especially on smaller and more economically marginal family units (Marsden *et al.*, 1989; Symes and Appleton, 1986; Hutson, 1987). The commitment among offspring to farming as a full-time (or even part-time) occupation (as opposed to retention of land occupancy rights) is weakening, revealing a shift in one of the traditional values underpinning farming, that of family continuity. The significance of this reduced commitment is further emphasised by larger social changes which are progressively impacting upon the farm household, including, for example, much higher participation in the paid workforce among women, rising material aspirations among the young (including greater personal mobility), and altered divorce laws granting the spouse greater say in the division of family assets (Whatmore *et al.* 1990). The implications for farming enterprises and the consumption of technology remain matters for conjecture.

Some evidence is, however, becoming available on the shifting pattern of advice which farmers seek and receive, which itself is underpinned by differing and potentially conflicting ideologies. On the one hand, the increasing technological and financial complexity of modern farming has accentuated many farmers' dependence on private sector sources where economic considerations are paramount (Tait, 1978 & 1985; Munton *et al.*, 1987b; Eldon, 1988; Carr, 1988) while, on the other, voluntary and state sectors are emerging as among the most significant sources of conservation advice (Cox, Lowe and Winter, 1990).

The extent of contact between farmers and sources of conservation advice remains very patchy and farmers' views of its relevance to the management of their businesses are variable and selective (Carr, 1988). A recent evaluation of farm conservation advice demonstrated the tendency even of receptive farmers to select such advice and modify it according to their own perceptions of appropriate conservation practice (Centre for Rural Studies, 1990). For many farmers this is taken to imply habitat creation, classically through tree planting and digging ponds; and farm conservation advisers report difficulties in persuading farmers of the importance of managing or retaining existing, semi-natural features or of the need to integrate conservation into general farming practices and plans.

Such findings are in keeping with other survey work which suggests that the most important source of influence on farmers' practices are those within the farming community itself (including the family, neighbouring farmers and the landlord) or closely assoicated with it, like the Agricultural Development and Advisory Service (ADAS). Even with regard to environmentally sensitive practices such as straw burning, hedgerow removal, tree planting and pesticide use, these sources remain the most salient; and conservation organisations even then are typically ranked below other sources of advice such as the farming media, the National Farmers' Union and commercial reps (Carr, 1988). The limited and selective impact of conservation advice is compounded by biases within: with its preoccupation with nature and landscape conservation, it has typically neglected pollution and wider health and ecological concerns.

Farmers' growing dependence, in contrast, on private sector sources of advice is particularly apparent in relation to pesticide use. In one survey of fruit and vegetable growers in East Anglia, 62 per cent favoured a commercial source of advice, generally the pesticide salesman (Tait, 1978). Subsequent surveys of cereal, sugar beet and oilseed rape growers indicated an even greater reliance on commercial advisers, with a majority having their fields frequently monitored in spring and early summer by a pesticide salesman (Tait 1985; Lawson 1982). Under these circumstances, 'the monitoring and forecasting information generated in the non-commercial sector was reaching the farmer almost exclusively through the commercial sector' (Tait 1985, p. 232).

Detailed evidence on the responsiveness of farmers to environmental regulation or incentives remains limited, especially in relation to how such concerns enter the farm adjustment process. Potter (1986a & b), though, has noted how farmers tend to become interested in voluntary conservation schemes only after major programmes of farm improvement have been undertaken. There is also a marked tendency for farmers to regard conservation practices as merely an adjunct to farm management, to be implemented on economically marginal parts of their farms, and as a source of income loss for which they need to be compensated. The needs of business security and family income have to be met first, and this has major implications for the operation of environmental policies. Typically, those most prepared to engage in environmental projects

> ... have already modernised their businesses, and altered landscapes, (and do so) to use grants *after the event* to replace individual features [with the effect that] conservation grants appear to be less useful in protecting *existing* vulnerable landscapes, with policy generally being unable to direct attention to damaging farm practices at the time of their occurrence. (Marsden and Munton, 1990).

In terms of this experience, the designation of spatial policies, such as Environmentally Sensitive Areas (in which farmers receive payments for farming in a traditional and sympathetic manner) makes sense but leaves much of the countryside vulnerable to further environmental damage.

Other research indicates that it is the initiation of conservation practices, however modest, which are crucial to longer-term adjustments in farm management. Those farmers who have significant areas of semi-natural habitat or woodland on their farms are most willing to entertain the diversion of further land from intensive agricultural production. This is not to suggest, however, that such operators are persuaded more generally of the merits of less intensive systems of production. Conservation simply has its place within a carefully zoned property. Multiple use may be exhibited at the level of the farm but be strikingly absent at the field scale. In their study of the potential responsiveness of farmers to land diversion, Gasson and Potter (1988) also demonstrate quite clearly the financial filter through which conservation practices have to pass. Not only do levels of compensation need to be competitive with the returns from existing farming enterprises, but they suggest that

> ... those who are most sympathetic to the idea of diverting land to conservation uses, and who are willing to offer most acres, would in fact be offering a smaller share of productive capacity than less willing and able participants ... such schemes are likely to meet with considerable resistance from small-scale, financially constrained farms. Far from redistributing income, any payments are likely to be channelled mainly to the better off. (pp. 349–50)

Such conclusions are in keeping with the absence of convincing evidence to support the notion that the occupiers of either small or part-time farms are more likely to be better conservators of the farmed landscape than those operating large units (Munton *et al.*, 1989). The one exception is 'hobby farming households', through their independence of income from the farm, although Sinclair (1983) found more generally that farmers who held, or had held, non-farming jobs were more sympathetic to conservation than others. Large farmers may have attracted more criticism from environmentalists because they achieved the means to alter the landscape earlier and with more extensive impact than smaller operators. But it was only large private landowners that Newby and his colleagues (1977) found could afford to retain a traditional landscape if they so chose. Otherwise once farmers become engaged with the technological treadmill most, if not all, will begin initiating significant alterations to the landscape.

The timing and comprehensiveness of such alterations in individual cases is difficult to pin down, although Potter (1986a & b) has drawn attention to the differing 'investment styles' of farm operators. He contrasts those with a 'systematic' style aimed at regular and comprehensive attempts to expand the business, often resulting in highly visible and controversial changes to the landscape, with those with an 'incremental' style who make many, small-scale changes, dictated by a risk-averse approach to the investment of limited and fluctuating funds. Both categories of operator are, however, generally committed to further land improvement, with occupancy change often the crucial catalyst. Rates of landscape change are faster on land that changes hands than on land which remains in the same business, with land acquisition itself being an irregular and often opportunistic event except for the very wealthy (Sinclair, 1983; Marsden and Munton, 1990).

By and large, the response of farmers to environmental issues and concerns is much less significant than the environmental effects of their responses to agricultural production policy. Indeed, a number of studies have shown that whatever the attitudes of farmers are towards nature or landscape conservation their behaviour tends to be dominated by economic and farming considreations (Newby et al., 1977; Carr, 1988). Even some of the responses to reduced levels of production may have adverse environmental consequences. For example, as we have seen, the adaptations to husbandry induced by milk quotas, particularly a reduction in the purchase of bought-in feed, have led to an increase in the intensity of grass-land management and silage making (Halliday, 1988). This, alongside the continuing concentration of milk production in the hands of a smaller number of large-scale producers, a process much eased by the UK's slack quota trading procedures, has contributed to an increasing incidence of water-course pollution in dairy areas from silage effluent and slurry (Water Authorities Association, 1989). Elsewhere, in eastern England, cereal producers, concerned that similar kinds of quota might be introduced to control cereal output, expanded their acreage in the mid–1980s on to more marginal land, and the fact that this form of supply control now seems most unlikely to be introduced cannot repair the environmental damage done thereby (Munton et al., 1987b).

The possible impacts of diversification on the environment are much more complex and will, clearly, vary according to the type of diversification and the strategy adopted by the farmer and/or household members. Some forms of farm diversification have tended to be the preserve of members of the farm household not directly responsible for farm management decisions. Classically, farm tourism has been under the direction of farmers' wives and has not directly affected farm management practices. Bouquet (1987) has shown how such income is treated as distinct from farm income and allocated for distinctive purposes, often to do with improving household facilities. Winter (1984) has shown how this separation serves to insulate the farmer and his terrain from the impact of tourism and recreation. Thus there is, in the majority of cases, neither environmental enhancement through attuning the management of the farm to the likely demands of tourists for a pleasant environment nor, conversely, environmental destruction prompted by an injection of capital from tourist income. Diversification into game management might be expected to be more beneficial, and a number of surveys of farmers have found positive attitudes towards wildlife and habitat conservation amongst those with an interest in shooting and other field sports, whether as a hobby or a commercial activity (Westmacott and Worthington, 1974; ADAS, 1976; MAFF, 1985). However, Macdonald (1984) also found that such an interest, while heightening farmers, appreciation of wildlife, also increased the number of bird and animal species they regarded as pests.

One of the problems of investigating the impact of farm adjustment specifically on pollution is that the biological and chemical processes are very complex, may take many years to show, and are often consequent upon quite subtle changes in land management and farming technology. Thus, whereas the loss of some landscape features and habitats is relatively easy to measure (if not evaluate) and often clearly attributable to major changes in management, some deterioration of habitats is more incremental due, for example, to recurrent fertiliser or pesticide run-off, in contrast to major accidents. Analysis of such changes, and linking them in to the rather broad-brush views of farm adjustment hitherto employed, represents a serious challenge. This is especially so if, compared with landscape conservation where there has been a long history of public controversy, it is the case that farmers regard pollution control 'as a technical and statutory function, not of itself an act of good farm management' (Clark and O'Riordan, 1989, p. 32).

What are the factors, for example, which persuade farmers to use particular kinds of pesticide and what determines the way they apply them? What factors influence a farmer's judgement on the suitability of weather or soil conditions for particular agricultural operations? Are these really questions of technical or economic competence, as they have traditionally been viewed, or, as now seems more likely, are they in essence questions of sociology and psychology (Tait, 1978, 1985; Carr, 1988)? And under these circumstances, to what kinds of regulation (or incentive) will the farmer be sensitive?

Clearly, as already indicated, an important issue here is the farmers' assessment of different kinds of risk within a farm management strategy, and how they may be traded off. Tait (1978, 1982, 1983), for example, has examined farmers' use of pesticides in relation to their attitudes to the risks involved. Though many farmers expressed strong concern over the environmental and personal health hazards, this was not often correlated with pesticide usage. The attitude to financial risk, though, was significantly correlated with behaviour, with farmers who were more risk averse using more pesticides than others. Clearly, such trade-offs depend upon the information available to farmers, their changing financial circumstances, and other pressures (including with regard to pollution incidents, the chances of detection). The assessment of risk is not an identical technical exercise for every farmer: there is no optimum or generalisable solution when such a broad range of factors interplay. One farmer's high risk strategy, such as investment in high-cost pollution technology with no guarantee of correspondingly increased returns, is for another farmer a matter of low risk. A farmer's attitude to investment and borrowing is crucial here and on this hinges much of the variation in farm adjustment strategies over the medium term.

The regulation of farm-based pollution

Farming practices pose some of the more acute practical and conceptual challenges for social scientists and policy makers concerned with environmental regulation. This is in part because of the progressively more intrusive impact which highly intensive methods of production make upon the environment. (As the most extensive user of land, agriculture is, after all, the prime social force creating and recreating the physical environment.) But, additionally, the extensive and fragmented nature of the industry means that prevailing regulatory models formulated to tackle problems of a different nature in other sectors can often have only a limited application. Indeed, we argue in this section that although its structure, of a great many small producers catering for myriads more consumers, would appear to make it an ideal candidate for market-oriented regulatory initiatives, proper appreciation of the distinctive character of agricultural activity entails the recognition that other approaches are almost bound to be necessary.

The comparative absence of effective controls over agriculture has become more readily apparent as regulatory mechanisms have developed in response to urban and industrial pressures on the environment. The anomaly stems in part, of course, from fundamentalist perceptions of farming as a naturally conserving land use. But it is also a function of the way in which environmental controls have conventionally been formulated and promulgated: for the most part through the setting of specific standards and their administration by regulatory agencies and inspectorates. Such systems are designed to deal with large industrial concerns, concentrated and acute forms of pollution and point sources. Diffuse sources, by contrast, pose intractable problems of regulatory strategy and only recently have governments and officials given serious consideration to how these problems might be overcome (Lowe, 1988).

Any assessment of the case of agriculture must surely emphasise the extent to which its character calls into question one of the key principles embodied in prevailing models of regulation. Its present treatment, moreover, effectively subverts another. The first embodies a presumption in favour of treating pollution and damage to the environment as unwanted externalities of the production system. The second, meanwhile, asserts that the regulatory effort should internalise the true social costs of production: an injunction typically characterised as the 'polluter pays' principle.

The distinction between the internalities and externalities of production which is, in any case, often only a convenient fiction, ceases to be in any way appropriate in relation to agriculture as soon as environmental concerns are accorded a serious status. As an extensive land use the activities associated with it produce not only marketable goods but also, at one and the same time, distinct rural environments. Indeed, rural environments as aspects of processes of production are in a perpetual state of creation and re-creation. Agricultural goods and the rural environment must be seen, to use the term favoured by economists, as in a relationship of 'joint supply'. But even that term, with its implied notion of separateness, is redolent of the language of internalities and externalities whose appropriateness we wish to question.

Such thinking is, of course, central to the approach adopted in *Blueprint for a Green Economy* (Pearce *et al.*, 1989) which has been so dramatically propelled to the forefront of government thinking on environmental matters in Britain. The view is advanced that policy should be based on a process of identifying what consumers would be prepared to pay to enjoy environmental 'goods', and accept by way of compensation for environmental 'bads'.

The argument, then, is that environmentally sensitive policies - both present and across generations - are best pursued by generating appropriate market signals based on the price so ascribed. The case is, at first sight, a persuasive one; not the least because the ambition to assess and monetise degrees of concern is accompanied by the presumption that the effort - and it must, inevitably, be a very considerable one - can deliver the sort of precision that policy makers value.

Arguably, however, the formalisations of cost-benefit analysis promise an exactitude which, in one vital sense, can only be spurious. Certainly, an implication of the argument presented is that by comparison with processes of contingent valuation, the determination of standards, for instance, on a political basis is bound to be somewhat arbitrary. But as has long been recognised in standard critiques of neo-classical economics the sorts of valuations which society may wish to make cannot be determined by aggregating the utilities of individuals. Processes which are essentially social are involved in treating questions which are irreducibly ethical; and to suppose that such necessarily political decisions can be resolved through translation into some species of economic calculus is bound to be something of a pretence. It is to confuse preference with ethical judgement since the soundness of ethical argument is not equivalent to willingness to pay, however relevant economic information might be to the making of a good argument.

As Sagoff (1988) has argued, environmental goals do not necessarily stem from self interest - from our willingness as consumers to pay in markets - but are related, rather, to our sense of who we are and our preparedness to act on our beliefs so that they may find their way, as public values, into legislation. Environmental goals presuppose shared values which have to be argued on their merits: and that necessarily political process is very different from the exercise of hypothetically pricing our interests at the margin.

The intractability of quantifying benefits and costs of an ethical or aesthetic nature is notorious (Mishan, 1967). But more fundamental than what might be considered a purely technical difficulty is the recognition that cost-benefit approaches can entail a category mistake which, in some respects, is mirrored by the inappropriateness of speaking of internalities and externalities in relation to agricultural production. The category mistake occurs when the attempt is made to shadow-price public values as externalities or private transactions. At first sight the idea of 'pricing' ethical and ideological beliefs as if they were externalities looks an attractive one for the reasons that Pearce finds so persuasive. But it has its dangers and they too have long been recognised (Collard, 1972, p. 68).

The ability, as Sagoff (1988, p. 92) puts it, to 'find "free rider" problems, unpriced values, and transaction costs in every doorway and under every stone' crucially undermines the credibility of market analysis. It can be used, ultimately, to justify almost any policy. Private and public preferences must be seen rather as conceptually distinct. Public 'preferences' express what people believe is best for the community as a whole rather than their own wants or desires. Thus, in arguing for or against a public policy they seek creatively to develop and change the views of others rather than merely register already existing views. That process is necessarily public whereas:

> The genius of cost benefit analysis is to localize conflict among affected individuals and thereby to prevent it from breaking out into the public realm. (Sagoff, 1988, p. 97).

There are good reasons of a very general conceptual nature, therefore, for recognising the irreducibly political nature of many issues relating to environmental regulation. But there are, in the case of agriculture, additional and particular reasons for expecting political processes to dominate. To appreciate why that is so we need only briefly consider the way in which policy processes in agriculture have typically overturned the 'polluter pays' principle. Government has begun to recognise that the production of marketable goods simultaneously recreates the rural environment. Accordingly, measures have been introduced which combine efforts both to constrain production and generate certain conservation benefits.

Nevertheless, we are some way from achieving an integrated approach to production and environmental regulation in agriculture and the progress that has been made has involved paying farmers not to pollute or otherwise harm the environment. The character of these policies has stemmed in large part from the particular view that has been taken of property rights (Bowers, 1988, p. 166) and there are strong reasons for supposing that such considerations will continue to prevail (Cox, Lowe and Winter, 1988).

The extent to which they prevail will, of course, be limited by broad trends in regulatory strategies. Under diverse pressures, including those from the environmental lobby and the European community, and under the impact of privatisation, a profound shift in the style of British regulation is occurring (Haigh, 1987; Lowe & Flynn, 1989). This involves a move from a largely informal and decentralised approach to an increasingly formal, legalistic and centralised one. The transition will have a profound effect in the agricultural sector, because here the style of regulation has traditionally been informal and decentralised and, in many respects, largely voluntary. In 1987, the

House of Commons Select Committee on the Environment called for a 'far more interventionist and regulatory approach to farm pollution'. What little evidence there is, however, suggests that formal regulation of increasing farm pollution raises a range of particularly intractable administrative, compliance and enforcement difficulties (Hawkins, 1984; Royal Commission on Environmental Pollution, 1979, 1983, 1986; House of Commons Select Committee on the Environment, 1987; Agricultural Training Board, 1988; Water Authorities Association, 1988).

Unfortunately, though we know more about the economic behaviour of farms than any other types of business, we know less, as social scientists, about the interaction of farmers with regulatory agencies and the law than for industrial concerns (for the latter see, for example, the various monographs of the Oxford Centre for Socio-Legal Studies, e.g. Richardson, 1982 and Hawkins, 1984). This limited understanding is ironical because, arguably, one of the most significant sources of business uncertainty now facing farmers is the rapidly shifting prospects of environmental and planning controls. Moreover, the pressures on farmers as well as on regulatory officials, to curtail pollution and achieve higher environmental standards will come not only from changes in national and European policy but also from shifts in an increasingly sensitive public opinion. There is, therefore, an important deficiency to be overcome, not only in understanding the effectiveness of present and future regulatory measures but also in anticipating how farm business strategies might respond to an increasing volume of environmental controls.

We expect that farmers will face increasing controls because market mechanisms alone are unlikely to be adequate for attaining the policy objectives that have already been articulated. For all the advantages of price signals so clearly identified by Pearce *et al.* there are uncertainties associated with their use which militate against too exclusive a reliance on such a strategy. Despite their comparative crudeness, controls do provide a direct and more predictable handle on what is going on provided, of course, there is adequate monitoring and inspection.

References

ADAS (1976) *Wildlife Conservation in Semi-Natural Habitats on Farms: a Survey of Farmers Attitudes and Intentions in England and Wales.* London, HMSO.

Agricultural Training Board (1988) *The Food and Environment Protection Act 1985: Its implications for Training in Pesticide Use in Agriculture.* Beckenham, ATB.

Agriculture and Food Research Council (1988) *Annual Report.* London, AFRC.

Bouquet, M. (1987) Bed, breakfast and an evening meal, in Bouquet, M. and Winter, M. (eds) *Who From Their Labours Rest? Conflict and Practice in Rural Tourism.* Aldershot, Avebury.

Bowers, J. (1988) Farm incomes and the benefits of environmental protection, in Collard, D., Pearce, D. and Ullph, D. (eds) *Economic Growth and Sustainable Environments*. Basingstoke, Macmillan.

Buckwell, A. (1989) Economic signals, farmers' response and environmental change, *Journal of Rural Studies* 5, 149-60.

Busch, L., Bonnano, A. and Lacy, W. B. (1989) Science, technology and the restructuring of agriculture, *Sociologia Ruralis*, Vol 29 (2).

Buttel, F. H. (1986) Biotechnology and public agricultural research policy, in Rhodes, V. J. (ed) *Agricultural Science Policy in Transition*. Bethesda, MD, Agricultural Research Institute.

Buttel, F., Larson, O. F. and Gillespie, G. W. (1990) *The Sociology of Agriculture*. New York, Greenwood Press.

Carr, S. (1988) *Conservation on Farms, Conflicting Attitudes, Social Pressures and Behaviour*. Unpublished PhD thesis, Open University.

Centre for Rural Studies (1990) *Farmers and Conservation Advice* Occasional Paper, no. 9. Cirencester, Centre for Rural Studies.

Clark, A. and O'Riordan, T. (1989) A case for a farm conservation support unit, *ECOS* 10 (2), 30-5.

Collard, D. (1972) *Prices Markets and Welfare*. London, Faber.

Conrad, J. (1987) *Alternative Uses for Land and the New Farm Workers*. Berlin, International Institute for Environment and Society.

Consultants in Environmental Sciences (1988) *Effects of Nitrate Removal on Water Quality in Distribution*. London, CES.

Countryside Policy Review Panel (1987) *New Opportunities for the Countryside*, CCP 224. Cheltenham, The Countryside Commission.

Cox, G., Flynn, A., Lowe, P. and Winter, M. (1988) *Alternative Land Uses for Britain*. Berlin, The Science Centre.

Cox, G., Lowe, P., and Winter, M. (1988) Private rights and public responsibilites; the prospects for agricultural and environmental controls, *Journal of Rural Studies*, 4, No. 4. 323-47.

Cox, G., Lowe, P. and Winter, M. (1989) The farm crisis in Britain, in Goodman, D. and Redclift, M. (eds) *op cit*.

Cox, G., Lowe, P. and Winter, M. (1990) *The Voluntary Principle in Conservation: A Study of the Farming and Wildlife Advisory Group*. Chichester, Packard.

Croll, B. T. and Hayes, C. R. (1988) Nitrate and water supplies in the United Kingdom, *Environmental Pollution*, 50, 163-87.

Department of the Environment (1988a) *Protecting Your Environment - A Guide*. London, DoE.

Department of the Environment (1988b) *The Nitrate Issue*. London, HMSO.

Eldon, J. (1988) Agricultural change, conservation and the role of advisers, *ECOS* 9 (4), 14-20.

European Commission (1988) *Environment and Agriculture*, EEC Comm. (88), Final. Brussels, The Commission.

European Commission (1988) *The Future of Rural Society*. Bulletin of the European Communities, Supplement 4/88.

European Institute for Water (1988) Proceedings of the Conference on *Pesticides in Drinking Water*, Como (unpublished).

Friends of the Earth (1988) *An Investigation of Pesticide Pollution in Drinking Water in England and Wales*. London, FoE.

Gasson, R. (1973) Goals and values of farmers, *Journal of Agricultural Economics*, 24, 521–42.

Gasson, R. (1988) Farm diversification and rural development, *Journal of Agricultural Economics* 39, 175–82.

Gasson, R. *et al.* (1988) The farm as a family business: A review, *Journal of Agricultural Economics* 39, 1–41.

Gasson, R. and Potter, C. (1988) Conservation through land diversion: a survey of farmers' attitudes, *Journal of Agricultural Economics* 39, 340–51.

Goodman, D. E. (1987) *Some Tendencies in the Industrial Reorganization of the Agro-food System*. University College London, Department of Economics, Discussion Paper No. 87–25.

Goodman, D. E. (1989) Some recent tendencies in the industrial reorganization of the agro-food system, in Busch, L., Buttel, F. H. and Friedland, W. H. (eds) *The New Political Economy of Agriculture*. Charlotte, NC, University of North Carolina.

Goodman, D. E. and Redclift, M. (eds.) (1989) *The International Farm Crisis*. London, Macmillan.

Goodman, D. E., Sorj, B. and Wilkinson, J. (1987) *From Farming to Biotechnology; a Theory of Agro-Industrial Development*. Oxford, Basil Blackwell.

Haigh, N. (1987) *EEC Environmental Policy and Britain*. Harlow, Longman.

Halliday, J. (1988) Dairy farmers take stock, a study of milk producers' reaction to quota in Devon, *Journal of Rural Studies*, 4, 193–202.

Harrison, A. (1989) *The Financial Structure of Farming*. Reading, Centre for Agricultural Strategy.

Harrison, A. and Tranter, R. (1989) *The Changing Financial Structure of Farming*, Report 13, Centre for Agricultural Strategy, University of Reading.

Hawkins, K. (1984) *Environment and Enforcement: Regulation and the Social Definition of Pollution*. Oxford, Clarendon Press.

Hill, B. (1989) *Farm Incomes, Wealth and Agricultural Policy*. Aldershot, Avebury.

House of Commons Select Committee on the Environment (1987) *River Pollution*. London, HMSO.

Hutson, J. (1987) Fathers and sons: family farms, family businesses and the farming industry, *Sociology*, 21, 215–29.

Kenney, M. (1986) *Biotechnology: The University-Industrial Complex*. New Haven, Conn, Yale University Press.

Kloppenburg, Jr., J. (1988) *First the Seed*. Cambridge, Cambridge University Press.

Lawson, T. J. (1982) Information flow and crop protection decision, in Austin, R. B. (ed) *Decision Making in the Practice of Crop Protection*. British Crop Protection Council Publications, Monograph, no. 25.

Lowe, P. (1988) Environmental politics and agriculture in Western Europe, *Agriculture et Environnement*. Arlon, Belgium, Fondation Universitaire Luxembourgeoise.

Lowe, P. and Flynn, A. (1989) Environmental politics and policy in the 1980s, in Mohan, J. (ed) *The Political Geography of Contemporary Britain*. London, Macmillan.

Lowe, P., Cox, G., MacEwen, M., O'Riordan, T., and Winter, M. (1986). *Countryside Conflicts*. Aldershot, Gower.

Macdonald, D. W. (1984) A questionnaire survey of farmers' opinions and actions towards wildlife on farmlands, in Jenkins, D. (ed.) *Agriculture and the Environment*. Cambridge, Natural Environment Research Council.

MAFF (1985) Survey of Environmental Topics on Farms in England and Wales. MAFF Statistical Notice No. 244/85. Guildford, Government Statistical Service.

MAFF, (1989) *Report of the Working Party on Pesticide Residues*. London, MAFF.

Marsden, T. K., Munton, R. J. C., Whatmore, S. J. and Little, J. K. (1989) Strategies for coping in capitalist agriculture; an examination of the responses of farm families in British agriculture, *Geoforum*, 20, 1–14.

Marsden, T. K. and Munton, R. J. C. (1990) Farmed landscape change and the occupancy change process, *Environment and Planning A* 22 (forthcoming).

Mingay, G. (1990) British rural history, in Lowe, P. and Bodiguel, M. (eds) *Rural Studies in Britain and France*. London, Pinter.

Mishan, E. J. (1967) A survey of welfare economics 1389–59, in American Economic Association and the Royal Economic Society *Surveys of Economic Theory*. London, Macmillan.

Munton, R. J. C. and Marsden, T. K., (1990) Occupancy change and the farmed landscape: an analysis of farm-level trends, 1970–1985, *Environment and Planning A*, 22 (forthcoming).

Munton, R. J. C., Marsden, T. K. and Eldon, J. (1987a) *Occupancy Change and the Farmed Landscape*. Unpublished report to the Countryside Commission, Cheltenham.

Munton, R. J. C., Marsden, T. K. and Eldon, J. (1987b) Farmers' responses to an uncertain policy future, in Baldock, D. and Conder, D. (eds) *Removing Land from Agriculture: The Implications for Farming and the Environment*. London, IEEP/CPRE.

Munton, R. J. C., Whatmore, S. J., and Marsden, T. K. (1989) Part-time farming and its implications for the rural landscape: a preliminary analysis. *Environment and Planning A*, 21, 523–36.

Newby, H. *et al.* (1977) Farmers' attitudes to conservation, *Countryside Recreation Review* 2, 23–30.

Nitrate Co-ordination Group (1986) *Nitrate in Water* Pollution Paper no. 26. London, HMSO.

OECD (1989) *Agriculture and the Environment*. Paris, OECD.

Pearce, D., Markandya, A. and Barbier, E. (1989) *Blueprint for a Green Economy*. London, Earthscan.

Potter, C. (1986a) Processes of countryside change in lowland England, *Journal of Rural Studies* 2, 187–95.

Potter, C. (1986b) Investment styles and countryside change in lowland England, in Cox, G., Lowe, P. and Winter, M. (eds) *Agriculture, People and Policies*. London, Allen & Unwin.

Richardson, G. *et al.* (1982) *Policing Pollution*. Oxford, Clarendon Press.

Rockefeller Foundation (1982) *Science for Agriculture*, New York, Rockefeller Foundation.

Royal Commission on Environmental Pollution: Reports for 1979, 1983 and 1986. London, HMSO.

Royal Society (1983) *The Nitrogen Cycle in the United Kingdom*. London, Royal Society.

Sagoff, M. (1988) *The Economy of the Earth*. Cambridge, Cambridge University Press.

Shucksmith, D. M. *et al.* (1989) Pluriactivity, farm structures, and rural change, *Journal of Agricultural Economics*, 40, 345–60.

Sinclair, G. (ed) (1983) *Uplands Landscape Study*. Martletwy, Environmental Information Services.

Sir William Halcrow and Partners (1988) *Assessment of Groundwater Quality in England and Wales*. London, HMSO.

Symes, D. and Appleton, J. (1986) Family goals and survival strategies: The role of kinship in an English upland farming community. *Sociologia Ruralis* 26, 346–63.

Tait, E. J. (1978) Factors affecting the usage of insecticides and fungicides on fruit and vegetable crops in Great Britain. II. Farmer specific factors, *Journal of Environmental Management* 6, 143–51.

Tait, E. J. (1982) Farmers' attitudes and crop protection decision-making, in Austen, R. B. (ed) *Decision Making in the Practice of Crop Protection*. British Crop Protection Council Publications, no. 25.

Tait, E. J. (1983) Pest control in brassica crops, *Advances in Applied Biology* 8, 121–88.

Tait, E. J. (1985) Rationality in pesticide use and the role of forecasting, in Brent, K. J. and Atkin, R. K. (eds) *Rational Pesticide Use*. Cambridge, Cambridge University Press.

US Office of Technology Assessment (1981) *Impacts of Applied Genetics: Micro-Organisms, Plants and Animals*. Washington, DC, US Congress.

Water Authorities Association (1988 & 1989) *Water Pollution from Farm Waste*. London, WAA.

Westmacott, R. and Worthington, T. R. (1974) *New Agricultural Landscapes*. Cheltenham, Countryside Commission.

Whatmore, S. J., Munton, R. J. C. and Marsden, T. K. (1990) The rural restructuring process: emerging divisions of agricultural property rights, *Regional Studies* 24 (forthcoming).

Wilkinson, J. (1987) *Europe within the World Food System: Biotechnologies and New Strategic Options*. FAST Programme Exploratory Dossier 11. Brussels, Commission of the European Communities.

Winter, M. (1984) Farm-based tourism and conservation in the uplands, *ECOS* 5, no. 3, 10–15.

CHAPTER 4

The Role of Agricultural Technology in Sustainable Development

Michael Redclift

The environmental consequences of uneven and combined development

It is important to begin by exploring the context in which agricultural technology programmes are developed and implemented. In this regard, the concepts of 'uneven' and 'combined' development are helpful, referring, as they do, to two related but analytically distinct processes, with characteristic environmental consequences (Smith, 1984).

Uneven development can be defined as the historically rooted process which differentiates 'developed' areas of capital concentration from 'underdeveloped' areas whose main assets are natural resources and cheap labour. At the global level, uneven development distinguishes between 'First', 'Second' and 'Third' Worlds.

Combined development refers to another dimension of the development process which is of increasing importance today: many regions of the world, notably but not exclusively in developing countries, have characteristics of both 'development' and 'underdevelopment'. Indeed, as the development process leaves nowhere untouched, capital, advanced technology and industrial organisation penetrate areas of developing countries which only decades ago would have been left at the periphery of the international division of labour. In these areas, state-of-the-art technology and highly anachronistic labour processes are often juxtaposed. What we see, in effect, is a combination of 'First World' development and 'Third World' underdevelopment in spatial proximity rather than across a continental divide. In O'Connor's (1989) words

... combined development puts together the most profitable features of development and underdevelopment in a new unity which maximises profit(s).

In practice, we need to consider uneven and combined development together, but appreciating the analytical distinction enables us to understand their separate environmental consequences. It also enables us to identify the potential contribution of the national state to improved resource management, and the constraints on its ability to act.

The global food system

The decades following the Second World War witnessed enormous advances in the security and efficiency of farmers in the developed countries. Scientific research establishments developed hybrid cereals that were high yielding, and the result of these and other advances were rapidly passed on to farmers. At the same time the economic policy context became increasingly favourable to farmers, initially in North America, but also in the European Economic Community and Japan. Farmers were able to capitalise their holdings, improve their access to subsidised credit and acquire machinery and the necessary chemical technologies without running a serious risk of default. The rationalisation and modernisation of agriculture were accomplished through shedding labour on a huge scale – only half the numbers engaged in agriculture in the 1950s were still there in the 1980s (Goodman and Redclift, 1988) but this transition was relatively painless while the industrial economies were growing rapidly.

One important consequence was that the developed countries produced agricultural surplus at a time when most developing countries were experiencing rapid population growth and insufficient agricultural growth. The problem for developing countries was perceived as one of production and, during the 1960s and 1970s, the International Agricultural Research Centres were established in an attempt to move the technological initiative towards basic food provisions in the South. While the United States was still exporting part of its grain surplus under Public Law 480, the International Centres were gearing up to the challenge of developing 'advanced' high yielding technologies for poor countries. The partial success of these programmes is demonstrated by the fact that high yielding cereal varieties helped produce a 27 per cent increase in food production per capita in Asia between the mid-1960s and late-1980s.

The medium to long term consequences of the 'Green Revolution' have been widely debated (Bowonder, 1981; Pearse, 1980). Among the most important effects worth considering in the present context was a shift in the diet of many people in developing countries towards foods which benefit most from technology and policy interventions. In the South a division became apparent between land on which high yielding varieties could be utilised, which was mainly irrigated, and areas of rain-fed agriculture where the environment appeared to represent a 'brake' on development potential.

In the first case, new technologies could modify or remove constraints on productivity growth; in the case of poorer areas, technology could not be easily developed and transferred without a complex process of local selection and adaptation. The interest in 'farming systems research' in the 1970s and the 1980s reflected the need to give more attention to poorly-endowed or environmentally-vulnerable areas.

These shifts in both the production and consumption of food in the developing countries did nothing to arrest the progress in producing more food in the North. By the 1980s, as Tubiana (1989) has observed, the global food trade had effectively been reversed: the industrialised countries were now supplying a significant proportion of the developing countries with food. In 1967 the developing countries had accounted for 16 per cent of world demand for agricultural products: by 1980 the same countries accounted for 26 per cent of world demand. A major re-organisation in the structure of trade for primary products had occurred, partly as a result of the developed countries' abilities to exploit the opportunities represented by new agricultural technologies, some of which had been devised with the needs of poor countries in mind. At the same time, in the developing countries the selective agricultural modernisation that occured in some areas – notably parts of Latin America and Asia – did not resolve food problems, it merely changed them. On the one hand, the introduction of high yielding varieties, under controlled conditions, carried implications for the environment in relatively 'rich' agricultural areas. On the other hand, marginal farmers were forced back on their physical environment in a way which was ultimately damaging to their own chances of survival, and served to reduce long-term sustainability. In Latin America and Africa, countries experienced a reduction in food security, and their burden of debt since the early 1980s has made it more difficult for them to advance strategies of their own. Interest rates rose and the international terms of trade moved against the products of most developing countries at a time when they were being exhorted to export more.

The developed countries, experiencing a rise in living standards, promoted increasingly intensive forms of cattle production domestically, partly as a way of absorbing their own grain surpluses. In some cases, such as the European Community, they also began to import more forage crops from the developing world, such as soya from Brazil and cassava from Thailand. Within the developing countries these new demands served to divert land away from food crops for direct human consumption, encouraged by governments offering inducements to export producers. The shift towards forage crops is only one example of the wider process through which monocultivation and increased agricultural specialisation in the South have tended to deplete land resources and displace peasant farmers, favouring a high degree of commoditisation. In the 'receiving' industrialised countries the environmental impacts were equally important: animals were increasingly part of a 'production line' and the disposal of animal waste became a major problem, contaminating water courses in most of the countries of northern Europe (Lowe et al.: Chapter 3).

As we have seen this problem of uneven development is matched by the effects of combined development when changes in technology and capital investment, originating in the developed world, are combined with small-scale 'peasant' agriculture. The effect is often to add pollution problems to those of resource erosion. Pesticide problems in developing countries are usually worse than in developed countries, precisely because of the conditions under which they occur. Effective controls on pesticide misuse are impossible to enforce and much of the human cost is paid by agricultural labourers unable to resist or contain the process. The effects in local ecosystems is often equally damaging (Thrupp, 1988). In many cases combined development exploits loopholes in the law, or systems of legal protection, enabling natural resources to be utilised in ways clearly at odds with the interests of local people. One illustration is the use that is made of developing countries for dumping highly dangerous toxic wastes. The essence of these activities is that specific areas become the focus of attention for capital, although often located at a considerable distance. As O'Connor expresses it, within capitalist development 'nature' is the point of departure for production but typically not a point of return' (1989:3).

In some cases a country's economic policy towards rural areas, and the environmental consequences of this policy, can be viewed as a composite of uneven and combined development. Since 1960, for example, Mexican rural policy has had two separate objectives: in the irrigated areas of North and North-West Mexico the main objective has been to 'modernise' agriculture, utilising available technology and supporting packages of credit and insurance. The social and environmental effects in these more favoured regions have not always been beneficial (Hewitt, 1976; Sanderson, 1986). The emphasis in rain-fed regions has been different, and principally directed towards resisting or occasionally conceding peasant demands for land. Most small producers have, as a consequence, been marginalised from technological change and have seen the economic benefits go elsewhere. Their own environments have suffered from the demands placed upon them by an increasingly impoverished population.

It is not difficult to identify other examples of the damaging environmental effects of uneven and combined development: cattle ranching in Latin America is often cited (Rich, 1985) and the depletion associated with tropical hardwoods. The principal distinction that needs to be pursued here, however, is linked to the way the rural environment is 'managed' in areas of very different resource potential in the South. The discussion of uneven and combined development enables us to identify the dynamic processes which determine the direction of change in different ecological zones and the real meaning of increasing 'sustainability' in these different areas. Before examining the application of technology to different environmental areas, we need to scrutinise the concept of 'sustainable development'.

Sustainable development

The problem with referring to sustainable development is that, like so many terms in the development lexicon, its very strength is its vagueness: sustainable development means different things to different people.

One point of departure is to define what Barbier (1989) terms **sustainable economic development**. This refers to the optimal level of interaction between three systems – the biological, the economic and the social – a level which is achieved 'through a dynamic and adaptive process of trade-offs' (p. 185). Economists, notably David Pearce, continue to emphasise the *trade-off* between systems or between present and future needs, as the key issue (Pearce, 1986). In similar terms it is argued (Pearce *et al.*, 1987) that:

> sustainable economic development involves maximising the *net benefits* of economic development, subject to maintaining the services and quality of natural resources over time.

For economists interested in the environment, then, issues like *environmental accounting*, which aim to give a numerical value to environmental losses and costs, are essential instruments in seeking to achieve greater sustainability.

Of immediate contrast is what Barbier sees as the much less narrowly defined concept of **sustainable development**. This is expressed in the Brundtland Commission's phrase of 'development which meets the needs of the present without compromising the ability of future generations to meet their own needs' (Brundtland, 1987, p. 43). The Commission's report, *Our Common Future*, placed the emphasis in sustainable development on *human needs* rather than the trade-offs between economic and biological systems, an approach which a lot of economists would have difficulty in endorsing. Brundtland (p. 46) mapped-out a very political agenda, arguing that:

> ... sustainable development is a process in which the exploitation of resources, the direction of investments, the orientation of technological development and institutional change *are all in harmony*, and enhance both current and future potential to meet human needs and aspirations.

The important thing to notice about this approach is that it regards sustainable development as a policy objective, rather than a methodology. It is an over-arching concept, a highly desirable end-point of development aspirations. Such an approach is unapologetically normative, and places both the responsibility for problems, and the political will to overcome them, in the hands of human actors.

An even more 'human-focused' approach is provided by Robert Chambers, in his concept of **sustainable livelihoods**. Chambers served on the Advisory Panel on Food Security, which fed into the Brundtland Commission's final report. He argues (Chambers, 1988) that:

> *Sustainable livelihood security* is an integrating concept ... livelihood is defined as adequate stocks and flows of food and cash to meet basic needs. Security refers to secure ownership of, and access to, resources and income-earning activities, including reserves and assets to offset

risk, ease shocks and meet contingencies. Sustainable refers to the maintenance or enhancement of resource productivity on a long-term basis.

Part of the interest in the discussion of sustainable development is the way the concept has borrowed from both the natural and social sciences. Chambers's definition, which places the emphasis on poor people coping with stress, is a case in point. Gordon Conway, in a series of very influential papers, argued that 'sustainability (is) the ability *to maintain productivity*, whether of a field, farm or nation, in the face of stress or shock' (Conway and Barbier, 1988, p. 653). Originally, Conway had been thinking primarily in ecological terms, about the ability of natural systems to cope with system disturbance, but this led him (through a broader commitment to people rather than things) to seek to define a concept which retained the idea of system disturbance, but added that of human beings as self-conscious actors in the development process. Other writers, such as Bartelmus (1986, p. 12), an environmental planner, have defined sustainable development more in terms of conserving stocks of what we might term 'natural capital', in contrast to the traditional economic view that resources and the environment were chiefly important as ways of generating income, or income flows:

> [Sustainable development] is development that maintains *a particular level of income* by conserving the sources of that income: the stock of produced and national capital.

This does not exhaust the possibilities for defining sustainable development, but it does point to a number of significant areas of both convergence and divergence:

(1) There is little agreement about what needs to be sustained, present or future populations.
(2) Does this population need to be sustained in terms of its minimum (perceived?) needs at a particular level of consumption? Or does this level of needs/consumption require changing?
(3) There are different 'levels' at which sustainability is important, e.g. the farm level, the field level and the village level in Conway's agro-ecological analysis. Or the level of the village, region and nation, according to other accounts. These distinctions are important because what is sustainable at one level may not be sustainable at another (and vice versa). An example is that of the Santa Cruz area in Eastern Bolivia, where farming systems are 'sustainable' in agro-ecological terms, but are being undermined by contraband trafficking of, and the resultant high prices for, coca leaves, the raw material for cocaine (Redclift, 1986).
(4) Some writers refer to sustaining levels of production, and others to levels of consumption. Again, this is important since it can be argued that what makes development unsustainable at the global level are the patterns of consumption in the rich countries, while most efforts to tackle development problems are essentially production-orientated.

Sustainable development, then, is either about meeting human needs, or maintaining economic growth or conserving natural capital, or about all three.

One aspect of sustainability deserves attention when we consider the role of agricultural technologies, in particular. Some areas of the globe obviously have greater potential for resource exploitation than others, but 'development' still has an impact even on areas where the resource base is relatively poor. It is logical, then, to think of 'sustainable development' as a concept with different implications for natural resource utilisation in different areas. Five environmental zones can be delineated (see Figure 4.1), each with its own 'sustainable potential'.

- Vulnerable 'low resource' areas, suffering from chronic land degradation;
- 'Enhancement' areas with continued potential for sustainable intensive cropping;
- Forestry areas;
- Fisheries;
- Genetic reserve areas (which might be located in any of the above, but particularly forestry areas).

'Low resource' areas

In vulnerable 'low resource' areas, such as the Sahelian countries, conditions are unfavourable to accelerated agricultural development. Even to support the existing population it is necessary to do much more to conserve soil and water resources. In some cases it may be possible to restore degraded land, but in many cases the battle has already been lost. Reversing the process of land degradation will prove costly and often unsuccessful. In semi-arid areas, in particular, 'sustainable development' can be translated as resource conservation and income supplementation. People will continue to migrate to find employment and to supplement their livelihoods. Under these circumstances agricultural development must be conservation based but aim also to meet the short term necessities of farming families. A balance will have to be struck between ensuring that resources are not depleted to exhaustion, while delivering benefits to the population in the form of current utility. Agricultural technology in these zones will continue to be designed not to maximise yields of single crops but to accommodate to precarious environmental conditions. If poor people are to be persuaded to act more sustainably under these conditions it will require fundamental shifts in the systems of incentives and market signals.

'Desertification' can be defined as a process of continued decline in productivity due to the impoverishment and depletion of vegetable cover, exposure of the soil to wind and water erosion, the reduction of the soil's organic and nutrient content and the deterioration of soil structure and water retention capacity. When desertification is advanced the land can neither be brought back into productive use nor reclaimed profitably, in the short term.

Drought is only part of the problem, although it does highlight the inadequacy of existing resource management systems. Extensive areas of the developing world are at risk of desertification; some have already succumbed. 'Moderate' desertification generally involves a loss of productivity of up to a quarter, while 'severe' desertification means a loss of up to half the land's previous productivity. Current estimates suggest that over 80 per cent of rangelands in Africa and the Near East are moderately to severely desertified. In Asia the comparable figure is 35 per cent (IFAD, 1988, p. 6). Serious degradation of land due to soil erosion has been reported throughout Asia, in Nepal, Bhutan, Thailand and India. In Latin America, the Andean countries have been affected by desertification as well as Mexico and Central America.

In the past the approach to problems of land degradation in general, and soil erosion in particular, was to treat these as physical problems requiring technical solutions. Soil science concentrated on understanding physical processes albeit, as Hudson (1988) has argued, against a background of developed country experience and institutions. The knowledge gained about soils enabled advances to be made in technical prescriptions – terrace construction, contour cultivation – without improving our understanding of *why* land degradation occurs.

The most important proximate causes of accelerated soil erosion are incorrect land use and bad land management, through land being worked in a way that exceeds its capacity. The underlying causes are structural: development proceeds in an uneven way, impoverishing some locations just as it enriches others. Poor farmers in environmentally vulnerable areas do not act in ways which intentionally degrade the land.

Incorrect land use and poor land management are due to a combination of factors – economic, social and political – which constrain the farmer's behaviour. A first step towards developing a soil conservation programme for resource-poor areas is, therefore, an analysis of why undesirable land uses are practised. The analysis might determine that several factors are at work: the pressure of population on the land tenure system, agricultural pricing policy, inappropriate technology, etc. Solutions that meet the needs of local people may not be economically feasible, or might meet concerted political opposition, but unless the underlying problems are made explicit there will be even less chance of the required institutional and legal changes taking place.

At the same time, an analysis of the structural impediments to a more sustainable agricultural system in low resource areas is essential if governments are to be prevented from embarking on costly development programmes that do not work, and devoting soil conservation programmes to the symptoms, rather than the causes, of land degradation. Many 'conservation-based' projects have failed because they were imposed from the top in a cultural vacuum, without any serious attempt either to involve local people or to understand their needs. As a result local communities, which were not involved in the planning or maintenace of the projects, saw no tangible advantages and abandoned them. According to the report by the

UN Food and Agricultural Organisation 'African Agriculture: the Next 25 Years' (FAO, 1986, p. 36) over one billion US dollars was spent by donors on *group ranches and grazing schemes* in Africa during a fifteen-year period. Most of these funds were wasted.

On the other hand donor-resistance to small-scale projects has led to their neglect over the same period. Such projects are often overlooked because the preparations needed are thought to be excessive compared with large, and expensive, projects. Nevertheless the greatest low-cost potential for increased food production in low-resource areas is through water harvesting, soil erosion control, alley cropping, use of crop residues as fertiliser, community afforestation and small-scale irrigation. To be effective, projects which incorporate these approaches need to be managed by communities themselves, something which national governments often wish to avoid. In some instances this is because they do not want to devolve decision-making. In others, it is because they lack the necessary administrative and technical organisation and staff. Governments may not wish farmers to maintain and operate their own small-scale projects, but unless this is done the projects will be abandoned, on the grounds that they do not meet local needs and local farmers do not reap the benefit. Sustainable natural resource development rests on three essential pillars: community management of local projects, sound land-use planning and the development of improved farming systems which emphasise ways of reversing the loss in soil *productivity*, rather than seeing erosion – and hence 'soil loss' – as the problem. The following guidelines are elements in an alternative approach to development, oriented to conservation at the farm and community level. They form part of a prescriptive strategy aimed at building environmental considerations into development planning.

(1) A positive view of the environment needs to be developed, on the basis of present and future livelihood creation: jobs, income and cost savings. This means a shift towards emphasising the *advantages* of better environmental practices, including a system of incentives.

(2) There is a need to develop labour and time-saving technology for fuelwood, water, food preparation and post-harvest storage, activities principally undertaken by women.

(3) Wherever possible farm grown inputs should be substituted for market purchases, which make additional calls on scarce finance. This will reduce the small farmer's external dependence.

(4) Non-farm sources of income need to be considered *together with* the measures needed to make farming systems more sustainable. In practice poor households will not employ more sustainable practices if they perceive them as at the cost of income-generation. In some cases efforts at income supplementation may prevent more sustainable practices from being adopted.

(5) Improved livelihood security is required, involving such essential features as land tenure rights and access to common property resources. If extended access to 'commons' is leading to increased

degradation, other means of bolstering the household's livelihood need to be given emphasis, to provide the essential income supplementation.

(6)   Government policies should be directed towards plugging gaps in the food system of *critical* importance to poor people in low resource areas: for example, post-harvest technology and storage, agroforestry, decentralised marketing, improved transport, better biomass utilisation and alternative sources of income generation. Plugging the 'agricultural technology' gap means sharing skills and knowledge in the implementation and adaptation of technology as well as developing appropriate technology.

(7)   Poor people's calculations, like our own, are based on what they know and what they can anticipate. Better environmental monitoring and forecasting are therefore necessary, and the resulting information and predictions should be much more widely disseminated.

'Enhancement' areas

'Enhancement' areas can be defined as those where there is a potential for intensive crop production, using existing technologies, but with more attention to the environmental costs of agricultural practices. Such areas are frequently irrigated or include reliable rainwater on rain-fed land. Soils are generally good. Agricultural technology has been developed in these areas to exploit the relatively favourable resource base and to raise the 'carrying capacity' of the land. The priority now is to ensure that the land's productive capacity is not seriously compromised, while reducing vulnerability to environmental hazards, many of which occur as a result of the technical transformation of agricultural production. Figure 4.1 indicates that 'enhancement' areas need to be considered within the context of other, geographically contiguous zones, such as watershed forests, which themselves need to be developed more sustainably.

The development 'success' story of the late 1960s and the 1970s was the so-called 'Green Revolution' which was devised for 'enhancement' areas and which served to transform the internal balance between irrigated and non-irrigated areas of developing countries. The Director General of the International Rice Research Institute has captured the rapidity of 'Green Revolution' advances in the following remark:

> India received nearly 10 million tonnes of food grains during 1966, largely from the PL480 Programme of the USA. It was in the same year that the Government of India initiated a High Yielding Varieties Programme in order to make food aid unnecessary as quickly as possible. Consequently, by 1971, a grain reserve of over 10 million tonnes was built up. (Swaminathan, 1986, p. 26)

The achievement of the selective-breeding programmes was to develop varieties of rice and wheat which, under controlled irrigated conditions, responded dramatically to chemical fertilisers. Problems of pests and disease also needed to be controlled technologically, given the greater

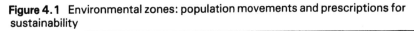

Figure 4.1 Environmental zones: population movements and prescriptions for sustainability

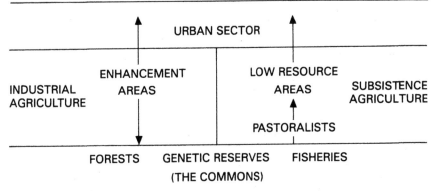

Arrows show migratory movement: population moving towards areas of employment or marginal sparsely populated zones.

- 'LOW RESOURCE' AREAS
  (low rainwater, poor soils, high risks, insecure tenure).
  Sustainable Development = resource conservation for basic livelihood maintenance *plus* income supplementation.
  Key – agricultural technology designed to accommodate to difficult environmental conditions – maintain 'carrying capacity'
- 'ENHANCEMENT' AREAS
  (irrigation, good soils, low risks, tenure varies)
  Sustainable Development = sustaining high yields but with minimum environmental costs
  Key – agricultural technology designed to exploit favourable environmental conditions – raise 'carrying capacity'.
- FORESTRY AREAS, FISHERIES, GENETIC RESERVE AREAS
  Sustainable Development = the prevention of genetic erosion, and the maintenance of livelihood opportunities within user management strategy.
  Key – the preservation of natural capital, rather than growth-based 'development'.

vulnerability of mono-crop cultivation practices to plant diseases. The management of this high input, high productivity system was a delicate one. Continued yield increases were dependent on a steady supply of relatively expensive inputs: the oil-based fertilisers, fuel and pesticides becoming steadily more expensive after the 1972/73 OPEC price rises. The problem in 'enhancement' areas today is not to extend the 'Green Revolution' benefits, but to minimise the costs of the new packages to the immediate natural environment. Conway has shown how 'sustainability' needs to be considered, together with productivity, stability and equity, in assessing the contribution an agricultural system makes to development.

In rich resource areas the only way to guarantee long-term productivity is to shift emphasis to the 'stability' and 'sustainability' dimension of the system. Methods of minimising environmental damage – of use in both vulnerable, resource-poor areas and in enhancement areas – place the emphasis on biological, rather than chemical, control, and seek to enhance productivity *after*, as well as before, the harvest. They can take one of the following forms, although combinations of each of these 'management interventions' will often prove essential:

● A biophysical subsidy, in the form of fertiliser application, can counter the stress of repeated harvesting, but carries risk for the environment, which can ultimately threaten sustainable utilisation.
● Another form of input, acting as a control agent, is a pesticide to counter pest or disease attack. To secure sustainability may necessitate repeated pesticide applications, and increase vulnerability at other points in the food chain and ecosystem responses.
● Alternatively, the strategy to withstand stress may involve the introduction of new genetic materials, which are disease resistant or can withstand conditions such as drought.
● Integrated pest management can also be used to ensure that sustainability is maintained. By introducing a biological control agent, such as a parasitic wasp, the intrinsic sustainability characteristics of the production system may be changed so much that there is no need for further intervention (Conway and Barbier, 1988).

For most developing countries, as Norse (1988, p. 7) argues, food security and the alleviation of rural poverty will depend overwhelmingly on the establishment of sustainable production systems in high potential areas, as well as the improved management of such systems in areas that are already heavily exploited. Figure 4.2 shows that, in Asia, cereal production – essential for the urban as well as the rural population – critically depends on

Figure 4.2 Contribution of cereal production in 'enhancement' areas to food production in developing countries (% of production in 1982/84)

Key: GR = good rainfed land (reliable precipitation); NF = naturally flooded land; IR = irrigated land; OL = other land.

	GR	NF	IR	OL
Sub-Saharan Africa	40	8	8	44
Near East/North Africa	22	9	34	33
Asia (excluding China)	5	27	57	11
Latin America	49	5	23	23
Developing countries overall	18	19	44	19

(*Source*: Agriculture: Toward 2000, Revised Version, 1987 [adapted from D. Norse, IFAD 1988])

Figure 4.3 Irrigation development in Asia 1966 to 1983

	Irrigated land as % of arable land		
	1966	1974/76	1983
Afghanistan	28.8	31.4	33.6
Bangladesh	7.0	20.7	20.7
Bhutan	—	3.9	4.2
Burma	7.8	16.3	16.5
India	16.8	20.5	24.0
Nepal	5.8	7.8	9.9
Pakistan	63.9	67.8	73.1
Sri Lanka	50.3	50.2	50.6
China	—	43.5	46.3
Indonesia	13.1	37.1	32.7
Malaysia	27.0	31.7	32.7
Philippines	10.4	15.6	17.8
Thailand	15.5	16.2	19.9

(*Source*: FAO Production Year Book, 1977 and 1984)

rich areas, of naturally-flooded or irrigated land, which must continue to produce food surpluses for the rising population as a whole. The problem can be put briefly and cogently. Over three-quarters of the world total of 750 million people living in absolute poverty, live in Asia. In that region 84 per cent of cereals are grown on flooded or irrigated land. Some three-quarters of Asian land under crops, though, is still rain-fed (Figure 4.3), and three-quarters of the rural population in Asia live in these areas. It can easily be appreciated, then, that maintaining and increasing staple food production on irrigated land is of vital importance for most of the world's rural poor (and many of the urban poor). It can also be appreciated why changes in natural resources and the environment in areas contiguous to irrigated river-basins and highly populated intensive farming systems are matters of the utmost concern. But with the possibility of global warming caused by the increasing concentration of 'greenhouse gases' in the atmosphere (emanating largely from the excessive use of fossil fuels by the industrialised countries), the threats now are no longer regionally confined. For resultant rises in sea level, or in the incidence or ferocity of monsoons, are likely to threaten large populations dependent on irrigated agriculture in countries such as Bangladesh.

In addressing the urgency of environmental problems in irrigated zones the following three issues need to be considered:

(1)   The salinisation, alkalinisation and waterlogging of existing and newly-irrigated land, as well as the widespread incidence of malaria, schistosomiasis and other waterborne diseases.

(2)   The dangers linked to mono-culture agriculture, under large-scale irrigation, which increase the susceptibility of crops to diseases and

pests. Environmental and health problems are associated with a possible doubling in the use of pesticides by the end of the century. This calls for preventative health measures, especially in areas where farmers have not been confronted with these diseases in the past. Mixed cropping and greater diversification of crop genetic materials can reduce these risks.

(3)   In areas where agriculture is only possible through wells there is a risk of over-exploitation of groundwater resources. Close monitoring of the groundwater tables is called for and stricter rules in allocating and exploiting water rights. There is not the same problem in countries like Bangladesh, India and Pakistan, where large-scale gravity irrigation is the rule (IFAD, 1988; Ahmad, 1988).

The underlying problems in irrigated areas are not simply those of technically advanced agriculture, they are those of fragile ecosystems. The key to the better management of their natural resources is the recognition that the future of highly productive agriculture rests on better integration between irrigation management and national resource planning, particularly the links between lowland and upland areas. Integrated water management needs to be extended outwards from areas with groundwater problems, to encompass watershed forests; and the conservation of forests and soils in nearby areas needs to take more account of the consequences for 'enhancement' areas. Such policies represent essential 'management intervention' but the only long-term solutions to poverty within both 'enhancement' and 'low resource' areas are radical approaches that ensure better management of assets through redistributing them.

As we saw in the discussion of uneven and combined development above, ecological vulnerability is often a consequence of the combination of 'high' technology and conditions of poverty. This leads us to consider another aspect of 'enhancement' areas that needs to be addressed: the richest agricultural areas, in terms of natural resource endowments, frequently have some of the poorest people. In recent years relatively rapid economic growth in areas that have benefited from high yielding varieties has widened income disparities within rural areas, and between rural and urban areas. Economic development within the agricultural sector has been associated with growing landlessness, especially in Asia and Latin America (ILO, 1977; de Janvry, 1981). According to a recent paper on rural Asia prepared for the International Fund for Agricultural Development (IFAD, 1988):

In addition to the acute population pressure in rural areas, which is increasing in spite of rural-urban migration, the existing pattern of land distribution is at the heart of rural poverty. The great majority of farms are uneconomically small. The smallholders along with about one-third of the rural householders who are virtually landless (as in Pakistan) constitute more than 40 per cent of the rural population. These people are deprived of basic needs, they are undernourished and dependent on subsistence agriculture, and they constitute the hard core of rural poverty. (Ahmad, 1988, p. 5)

The problem in most highly developed agricultural areas is that too many people occupy land that is in limited supply, and the situation is worsening. The cultivated area per rural inhabitant ranges from slightly over 0.3 ha in India, Pakistan and the Philippines, to 0.123 ha in Bangladesh. This increasing scarcity has had several negative consequences. There is an expanding number of farm holdings which are too small to provide an adequate family income. The corollary is an increasing fragmentation of farm holdings. There is also increasing landlessness, as the rural population becomes more dependent on agricultural and non-agricultural wage-labour.

In 1980 there were approximately 167 million landless or near landless families in developing countries, almost two-thirds of them in Asia. Most of the large flood plain and river basin systems, including the Ganges-Bramahputra, Irrawaddy, Indus, Mekong, Yellow and Nile, are heavily populated and there is every indication that landlessness will increase in these regions. In addition, in monsoon countries, problems are exacerbated by the concentration of 80 per cent of the rainfall within a five-month period. The rural population of monsoon Asia is exposed to 'natural' disasters, such as flooding, as well as chronic landlessness, and these disasters expose the poor to risks from which they have no retreat.

Many of the development projects undertaken in resource-rich areas can only be described as perverse from an environmental perspective. Some have been designed without any proper assessment of carrying capacity, othres have costs in terms of natural resources and ecological damage that exceed the short term economic benefits. Intensive irrigation programmes leading to salinity and alkalinity, agricultural projects which use water inefficiently, the indiscriminate use of fertilisers, pesticides and other harmful chemicals, all fall within this category. As the IFAD Report on Asia argues, large projects which attract publicity have their parallels in small projects which do not (Ahmad, 1988, p. 9). Unwise agricultural development has contributed to the felling of rain forests, the silting up of dams and the reduced productivity of the soil. It has used up scarce financial resources and depleted non-renewable resources. The answer, then, is to increase the security of the rural poor and, at the same time, to ensure that financial resources are dedicated to improving sustainable livelihood opportunities rather than prestigious, but unworkable, 'top-down' planning.

Despite the dramatic improvements in agricultural yields and grain production in the 1970s and early 1980s, the story since 1984 has been rather different. The momentum of the earlier years of the 'Green Revolution' has evaporated and production has reached a plateau. Since 1984 grain production in some of the most populous countries – China, India, and Indonesia – has not risen. Between 1986 and 1988 grain production actually fell by 14 per cent, most of the shortfall being made up from existing stocks (Worldwatch, 1989, p. 12). After impressive strides until 1983, in which the wheat harvest tripled, there has been no increase in grain production in India since 1983. In Indonesia, where rice output doubled between 1970 and 1984, it has remained stationary since that date. In Mexico, the original home of the 'Green Revolution', where improved varieties of both wheat and maize were successfully developed, and grain harvests quadrupled between 1950 and 1984, there has also been a decline in grain production of the order of 10 per cent since.

Perhaps most significantly of all, in China, economic reforms have helped that country to make up the backlog in agricultural technology development, increasing grain production between 1976 and 1984 by an impressive 50 per cent, but since 1984, there has been no further increase. And China is now endeavouring to follow its east Asian neighbours, Japan, Taiwan and Korea, in making a push towards rapid industrialisation. Each of these other countries, since their period of increased industrial growth between 1967 and 1978 which pulled workers and land out of agriculture, has experienced a decline in grain production, of one-quarter in Japan, one-fifth in Taiwan and one-sixth in South Korea. China, with its much bigger population, is relying on increased agricultural production during its own projected drive to industrialise in the 1990s. It can be appreciated that the success of this drive to develop rests heavily on a successful transition to industry, on a scale previously unheard of.

Forestry areas

Forests perform at least three essential sustainable development functions – environmental protection, livelihood support and fuel wood supplies – and these are considered in turn below.

The role of forests in environmental protection must be considered against the clear link between maintaining food production in 'low resource' and 'enhancement' areas and the rate of deforestation currently occurring (FAO, 1986, p. 2). In fact much of the world's agricultural land was formerly under forest vegetation, and currently an estimated 7.5 million hectares of closed forest and 3.8 million hectares of open woodland are cleared every year. Much of the land that is cleared is of poor quality and easily becomes eroded. Under forest cover it would serve a more useful productive function, maintaining the soil and water base. Furthermore, forests perform an essential resource conservation role in several critical ecological zones.

First, deforestation of mountainous and hilly land not only causes soil erosion on the land that is cleared, but also, through the effects on the water flow, a major threat to downstream areas. To protect agriculture in both areas from severe environmental degradation, measures need to be taken to manage watersheds in an integrated way. In addition to forest conservation and reforestation, the maintenance and rehabilitation of watersheds requires engineering works to control erosion and flooding.

Second, in arid and semi-arid lands wind rather than water is the main agent of erosion. Forests can contain soil erosion and stay green when grasslands dry up. Forest areas are therefore important reserves for feeding livestock during prolonged droughts. Similarly, tree planting can rehabilitate salt-affected land and sand dunes, by tapping moisture and nutrients in the deeper soil layers. Forests thus represent an important barrier against encroaching deserts and vulnerability to drought.

Third, forest cover is essential to protect soils in the humid tropics. Traditionally, shifting cultivation practices left tropical forests in ecological balance, and did not irreversibly degrade the soil. However, increasing population pressure has led to shorter fallows that do not enable fertility to be restored. One solution is to encourage permanent systems of cultivation, but many poor farmers in forested regions are already experiencing declining yields and cannot afford the improvements required to maintain fertility and prevent further degradation. One option is to develop agro-forestry, combining agricultural systems with tree planting, as an alternative to both shifting cultivation and intensive, permanent production systems.

Turning to forests as sources of livelihood, the scale of food sources gathered from forests is usually under-estimated: it includes wildlife, fruits, nuts, roots and fungi. In addition, in parts of Africa as much as 70 per cent of animal protein supplies are obtained in this way by the local population. Also forestry and the activities based on it are significant sources of rural employment and income. Forest management operations being labour intensive, are an important source of employment. Most of the employment is at the artisanal and household level: in carpentry, handicrafts, charcoal burning, and rubber tapping. The export of tropical woods and forest products is also an important source of foreign exchange for many countries. Forests are thus a key economic, as well as ecological, resource.

Finally, forests are a vital source of energy. Fuel wood comprises about 85 per cent of the wood used in the developing countries and accounts for more than three quarters of total energy consumption in the poorest of these countries. In general, the poorer the country the greater the dependence on fuel wood and the more vital it is that forests are conserved as a resource. Fuel wood is the principal means available to the rural poor to convert food supplies into an adequate diet. Many of the staple foods of the rural poor – such as cassava – require cooking to make them safe for human consumption. Other foods require cooking to make them palatable and free from pathogens. The scarcity of fuel wood is a major factor in the allocation of poor people's time, especially poor women's time. FAO estimated that in 1980 almost 100 million rural people in the developing countries were living in areas where existing levels of use could not be sustained. The problem is so complex and intractable that it is unlikely that we can do more than mitigate it, and an acute shortage of fuel seems bound to continue in the rural areas of developing countries, unless and until alternative sources of cheap energy can be made available on a massive scale.

Fisheries

Throughout history fishing communities have been practising what we now term 'sustainability'. In traditional societies rights to fish certain areas were carefully protected, and conserving fishing stocks was a matter of common concern. Fisheries are a classic example of common property resources, which belong to nobody and everybody. If traditional communal controls break down, unlimited access to these resources can easily lead to serious depletion of fish stocks, especially if technology is developed which enables the capture of fish to increase dramatically, while fishing areas are not re-stocked.

Because fishing normally provides no rights in a resource and no guaranteed return on its use, the livelihood of fishing families also represents a microcosm of the problem of marrying 'development' to 'sustainability'. Most fishermen and their families are poor; they possess virtually no collateral with which to negotiate and no rights in nature. In many respects they most resemble 'gatherer-hunters' or the poorest landless peasants. Without assets, most fishing communities are the 'sink-hole' through which the poorest people frequently drop. When the price for fish rises, as it did in the 1960s, this does not lead to re-investment or the protection of rights to fish. Instead, the number of poor people fishing increases rapidly, greater pressures are felt on fish stocks, and the most productive fishing grounds are over-fished.

In the 1970s the idea of 'maximum sustainable yield' gained currency among fishery experts, but in a situation where fishermen could not exercise restraint because of their poverty, it proved an impossible dream. When profits rose, more people came into the industry and this served to reduce the returns to poor fishing families. As with foresters, fishing is an activity, a way of life, that people will pursue at the margin and must continue to pursue even (or especially) when returns diminish. The concept of 'optimum sustainable yield' incorporates, to some extent, these social dimensions of the problem.

For all these reasons the best way to approach the livelihood choices of fishing households is through greater understanding of the pressures to which they are subjected, which inevitably lead to 'unsustainable practices'. Fishing communities need to have their rights to fish protected by institutional guarantees that work. They need to be encouraged and enabled to reinvest in the little capital they possess, and to have a clearly defined share in productive zones. The principle at work is not unlike that in forestry, but 'sustainable yield' implies a much shorter return: within three months not sixteen years. For small-scale fishing, barter and direct consumption remain

Figure 4.4 World fish production 1950–85 (million tons)

	Origin		Total	End-use	
	Marine	Freshwater		Food	Feed
1950	17.6	3.2	20.8	17.8	3.0
1960	32.8	6.6	39.4	30.8	8.6
1970	59.5	6.1	65.6	39.1	26.5
1975	59.2	7.2	66.4	46.0	20.4
1980	64.5	7.6	72.1	52.9	19.2
1985	74.8	10.1	84.9	59.6	25.3

(*Source*: FAO, 1987, World Fisheries, Situation and Outlook)

important, it is a 'petty commodity' activity that provides some protection from the ravages of unemployment.

The ability of fishing communities to act sustainably has been fundamentally altered by the pressures of technological expansion and growing urban demand. The explosive growth in world fish production since 1950 is shown in Figure 4.4. Underlying the early period of expansion in the 1950s was the growth in the world economy, but by the 1960s demand for fish had also risen dramatically in the developing countries. At the same time, a shift to intensive livestock rearing in North America and Western Europe led to a dramatic increase in the demand for fishmeal (see Figure 4.4).

Developments in fishing technology enabled these increased demands to be met. Two factors, in particular, assumed importance: the introduction of synthetic fibres in the manufacture of nets, and the freezing of catches at sea. These innovations, together with mechanical net hauling and stern trawling, as well as electronic aids, permitted widespread use of large nets and a dramatic increase in the size, versatility and operational range of fishing craft. Freezing at sea facilitated Japanese commercial fishing, and the spectacular expansion of the distant-water fisheries of Eastern European countries was a feature of the 1960s and 1970s.

Future demand for fish is expected to place serious pressures on the resource areas most affected. Total demand by the year 2000 is expected to exceed 100 million tons. An increase of that magnitude, on resource stocks which are already depleted, can only lead to disaster unless urgent attention is given to improved fisheries management. Social considerations require conscious allocation of limited fish resources to particular groups of fishermen, which might be achieved by legislation to protect delimited areas for the use of specified fishing gear or fishermen. It is especially important to protect and enhance small-scale or artisanal fisheries, which produce over 20 million tons of fish a year, most of it consumed by poor people. These are the populations at the vulnerable margins of fishery mismanagement and over-exploitation, drawn into a poor but inflated industry by necessity rather than choice. In coastal waters, where most fishing families operate, problems of environmental degradation – in mangrove areas, for example – already place a limit on 'sustainable yields'. Unless resource protection measures are combined with fishing rights legislation and government-assisted capitalisation, marine fisheries will continue to be overfished and the cost will be paid by the poorer groups for whom fish is their vital source of protein.

Genetic reserve areas

The principle that local people should participate more in the management and conservation of *genetically-important resources* represents a new and important departure, which must be encouraged. Important genetic reserves include tropical forest areas, but also some vital marine areas. Genetic resource conservation in these areas is a crucial part of global sustainability as proposed by the Brundtland Commission, since a high proportion of the world's naturally occurring species are found in relatively confined geographical areas, notably some tropical forested zones. Sustainable development in genetic reserve areas, wherever they are located, means preventing any genetic erosion, even to the extent of seeking to exclude growth-based development. The key objective is the preservation of natural capital, rather than the development or expansion of livelihood opportunities for people in the areas concerned. In practice, there is often a trade-off between seeking to achieve this conservation goal, as a priority, and seeking to protect the livelihood activities of communities of poor people dependent on agriculture, forestry and fishing.

The establishment of the International Fund on Plant Genetic Resources by FAO in 1987 is the latest stage in the process of assisting governments to conserve genetic variety. Individual countries' work on policies and strategies – including the evaluation of collections and improvements in plant breeding – will be supported. Field projects are being designed to help countries establish and utilise gene bank facilities. Regional training courses will be held in Latin America and Africa, and efforts are underway to establish an international network of base genetic collections in genebanks.

The destruction of natural ecosystems has shifted attention to gene-banking in LDCs. This kind of *ex situ* conservation, however, represents only part of the picture. Increased emphasis needs to be given to *in situ* conservation, through direct assistance to countries in the establishment of pilot areas where genetic conservation can be combined with sustainable utilisation.

Conclusions: towards a third track for agricultural technology

This chapter has explored the possibilites – and limitations– of developing agricultural technologies for specific ecological zones of the Third World. It was suggested that the concepts of uneven and combined development enabled us to undersand the context of environmental problems in developing countries which are a consequence of a development process centred in the developed countries. Conceptualising development in terms of both the 'successful' implementation of technologies from the North, and the progressive marginalisation of technologies from the South, enables us to appreciate the hidden dimensions of many of the projects designed to 'develop' agriculture in the poorer countries.

Two 'tracks' can be distinguished in the development of agricultural technology: one, a 'high tech' track, designed to encourage the adoption of genetically engineered technologies combined with purchased industrial inputs; and the other, a 'low tech' track, following a path much closer to the resources and practices available to the small farmer.

From what has been written it is clear that we have already reached the limits of the first track, of 'high tech' agricultural development, and evidence for this proposition is suggested by falling, or stationary, grain harvests in most countries of the South. At the same time, the limitations of relying on 'low-tech' agricultural technology are also clear: most poor farmers in 'low resource areas' face a series of almost insurmountable *structural* problems, from which technology, however appropriate, cannot save them. These problems include poor access to markets, deficient pricing, repressive tenurial systems, etc. Approaches like 'farming systems research' have a role to play in agrarian development, but they cannot transform the poverty of small farmers in developing countries. Indeed, the point about 'sustainable development' – as this chapter has also argued – is that unless the industrialised countries act more 'sustainably' the consquences not just for their environment but also for the environment of poor countries are very serious indeed. The recent concern about the effects of global warming, the reduction in the ozone layer and tropical deforestation (dictated by demand in the North) are all cases in point.

Part of the challenge to agricultural technology now is the development of a third track, which might be described as low-input/high tech. Ultimately, of course, integrating both tracks will depend upon much better research collaboration, and a measure of international agreement about implementation that is not easy to foresee. It will also depend on a much more far-sighted view of the environmental consequences of existing development models.

Some research institutions, like the International Centre for Tropical Agriculture in Colombia (CIAT), have already made strides in this direction. Programmes to improve the genetic make-up of basic tropical food crops, such as beans and cassava, have been geared to the needs of small farmers, who are unlikely to be able to acquire expensive industrial inputs. According to this approach, better environmental adaptability, better storage and, as far as possible, the preservation of genetic variety are the principal goals of agricultural technology. Other technological programmes, like those for integrated pest management and better storage and product utilisation, aim to link agricultural technology with the wider food system through a process of product integration (CIAT, 1988).

Much of the current research in biotechnology and genetic engineering also conforms in various ways to this model. Nevertheless it still has to be demonstrated that in practical terms these efforts are tailored to the needs of poor farmers and landless labourers, and that they can be used to strengthen the livelihoods of poor people, as well as generating increased production at low cost for the companies which have invested in their research and development.

Finally, it needs to be emphasised that the identification and management of more 'sustainable systems' of agricultural development should be linked to the international economy, in which 'sustainability' is rarely a goal, especially of the industrialised North. The discussion of uneven and combined development, together with the analysis of the differentiating effects of the introduction of agricultural technology in areas of variable resource endowment, suggests that the contribution of agricultural technologies (old and new; 'First', 'Second' and 'Third' track) depends entirely on the willingness of the developed countries' governments to seek global sustainability rather than national or regional self-interest. There is little evidence that anything short of global environmental disaster will serve to change the attitudes which already dictate so many of the policies of the industrialised countries.

References

Ahmad, Yusuf (1988) *Issues of Sustainability in Agricultural Development in Asia.* Rome, International Fund for Agricultural Development (IFAD), 11–13 October

Barbier, E. (1989) *Economics, Natural Resource Scarcity and Development.* London, Earthscan Publications.

Bartelmus, P. (1986) *Environment and Development.* London, Allen and Unwin.

Bowonder, B. (1981) The myth and reality of High Yielding Varieties in Indian agriculture, *Development and Change* 12 (2).

Brundtland Commission (World Commission on Environment and Development) (1987) *Our Common Future.* Oxford, OUP.

Chambers, R. (1988) Sustainable livelihood strategies, in C. Conway and M. Litvinoff. *The Greening of Aid.* London, Earthscan.

CIAT (1988) International Centre for Tropical Agriculture, *CIAT Report 1988.* Cali, Colombia.

Conway, G. and Barbier, E. (1988) After the Green Revolution, in *Futures* Special issue (eds D. Pearce and M. Redclift), 20 (6) 651–678.

de Janvry, A. (1981) *The Agrarian Question and Reformism in Latin America.* Baltimore, The John Hopkins University Press.

Food and Agriculture Organisation of the United Nations (1986) *African Agriculture: the Next Twenty Five Years.* Rome, FAO.

Food and Agriculture Organisation of the United Nations, (1987) *World Fisheries, Situation and Outlook.* Rome, FAO.

Goodman, D. E. and Redclift, M. R. (1988) Problems in analysing the agrarian transition in Europe, *Comparative Studies in Society and History*, 30 (4) 784–791.

Hewitt, C. (1976) *Modernizing Mexican Agriculture.* Geneva, United Nations Research Institute for Social Development.

Hudson, N. (1988) Soil conservation strategies for the future. Paper presented to the Vth International Soil Association Conference, Bangkok, Thailand, January 18–29.

International Fund for Agricultural Development (1988) Environment, sustainability, development and the role of small farmers: issues and options. A conference organised by IFAD, Rome, 11–13 October.

International Labour Office (1977) *Povertry and Landlessness in RuralAsia.* Geneva, ILO.

Norse, D. (1988) Policies for sustainable agriculture: getting the balance right. IFAD meeting, Rome, October.

O'Connor, J. (1989) Uneven and combined development and ecological crisis: a theoretical introduction, *Race and Class*, 30 (3).

Pearce, D. (1986) The Sustainable Use of Natural Resources in Developing Countries. Paper to the Economic and Social Research Council, University of East Anglia.

Pearce, D. *et al.* (1987) The meaning and implications of sustainable development. Paris, OECD.

Pearse, A. (1980) **Seeds of Plenty, Seeds of Change**. Oxford, Clarendon Press.

Redclift, M. R. (1986) Sustainability and the Market: survival strategies on the Bolivian Frontier, *The Journal of Development Studies*, 23 (1) 1.

Redclift, M. R. (1988) *Sustainable Development of Agriculture and Natural Resources*. Report for FAO, ms. draft.

Rich, B. (1985) Multilateral development banks: their role in destroying the global environment, *The Ecologist*, 15 (1/2).

Sanderson, S. (1986) *The Transformation of Mexican Agriculture*. Princeton, Princeton University Press.

Smith, N. (1984) *Uneven Development*. Oxford, Blackwells.

Swaminathan, M. S. (1986) Can Africa feed itself? An application of lessons learned in Asia to the challenge facing Africa, *Twelfth Ministerial Session of the World Food Council*. Rome, 17 June.

Thrupp, Lori-Ann (1988) Pesticides and policies: approaches to pest control dilemmas in Nicaragua and Costa Rica, *Latin American Perspectives*, 15 (4).

Tubiana, L. (1989) World Trade in Agricultural products: from global regulation to market penetration, in Goodman, D. E. and Redclift, M. R. (eds) *The International Farm Crisis*. London, Macmillan.

Worldwatch (1989) *The State of the World*. Washington, DC, Worldwatch Institute.

CHAPTER 5

Technological Change in a Period of Agricultural Adjustment

Richard Munton, Terry Marsden and Sarah Whatmore

Introduction

Between 1940 and 1980 governments and aid agencies unreservedly encouraged substantial investment in industrial technologies as a means of increasing agricultural productivity and reducing production costs. Rarely were the social and environmental impacts of these technologies a focus of attention. When treated at all, they were often regarded as short-term, external disbenefits to be absorbed as part of the price of 'modernisation' and the expansion of output, which in North America and the European Community, for example, has risen by about two per cent per annum since the mid-1960s.

The 1980s have seen a growing rejection of this orthodoxy. For many, the undoubted success achieved by agro-industrial technologies on the narrow front of productivity gains is no longer viewed as sufficient justification for their continued deployment. There is now overwhelming evidence that this 'technological strategy' is poorly related to the long-term prospects of the market, distorts public spending, and promotes substantial social and environmental costs. In the context of the EC, for example, budget expenditure under the Common Agricultural Policy has risen from 12.4 bn ECU in 1978 to almost 40 bn ECU in 1988, while the incomes of farming families from their agricultural operations have fallen, by as much as 50 per cent in real terms in the UK, and rural deprivation and social polarisation have increased (Lowe *et al.*, 1986). The numbers employed in agriculture in the EC have fallen by 60 per cent since 1960 with unwelcome knock-on effects on village life and the cost of providing services in peripheral rural regions; in the UK, the loss of wildlife habitat and valued landscape features has continued unabated (see Countryside Commission, 1986; Munton *et al.*, 1989); and water supplies have become increasingly polluted by agro-chemicals and animal wastes (Lowe *et al.*: chapter 3).

Increasing protest over these issues is not simply the result of new scientific evidence. It is also a consequence of a broader shift in policy and attitudes. At one level, for example, the British government has sought to restrain public spending as part of its macro-economic strategy while at another it has campaigned for environmental spending from the CAP budget (e.g. for Environmentally Sensitive Areas) in response to strong public pressure and a growing awareness of the political importance of 'green' issues. Among these are some of direct concern to agriculture, such as water pollution, food hygiene, animal welfare and a demand for 'natural' foods. Of wider significance is the changing view that different interests hold of the countryside. In particular, it is increasingly seen as a place of consumption for housing, recreation and amenity, and much less as the exclusive preserve for food production. Modern farming methods have lost much of the public confidence and political support they enjoyed when food security was regarded as a more immediate issue, and have done so just as the competitive position of farming is being increasingly challenged by new economic demands on rural areas.

These secular changes are contributing to a more critical attitude towards modern agricultural technologies. So far, most attention has centred upon the socio-economic and environmental impacts of farming methods. This concern has undermined the widespread acceptance of agro-industrial technologies as a necessary means of progress, an acceptance which has legitimated the role of industrial capital in agriculture. These technologies had led, in turn, to the assumption that farmers not only needed to, but *should*, embrace new cost-cutting techniques as the means of retaining their living. Much less analysis has been made of the production and transmission of these technologies and the economic interests they represent. Preliminary enquiries, especially in the United States, reveal quite clearly that technological change is tied directly to the development of the wider food system and its economic prospects. A revised research agenda is required which focuses upon the objectives of those promoting and funding research and development, the regulatory conditions under which they operate, and the control that the suppliers of new technologies can, or cannot, exert over the consumers of their products.

These issues assume particular significance today because of the changing balance in the sources of funding for agricultural R&D. Historically, the state took the lead in determining the research agenda and in funding most of the basic research. Consequently, current attempts in the UK and US to shift responsibility more towards the private sector are provoking considerable debate, especially on two related matters. First, the primary beneficiaries of agricultural R&D (and hence new technologies) were traditionally thought to be farmers. It was argued that, in order to retain national agricultural competitiveness, farmers needed a state-funded R&D programme because the small, individual size of their businesses meant they were incapable of sustaining one themselves. While the latter condition may still hold today, and to an even greater degree because of the 'scientification' of agricultural practice, the industrialisation of the food system has ensured that most of the benefits are not retained on the farm (see below). Off-farm industrial capitals gain most, and because many are major international companies with substantial resources, some governments now argue that these corporations should fund more of the research. Second, this position might seem eminently reasonable were it not for the fact that this attempt to 'privatise' R&D coincides with growing demands for a *greater* element of 'public good' in the production and application of modern farming technologies, especially in relation to the 'environment'.

An exploration of these questions and contradictions forms the basis of this chapter. In spite of their growing importance and recognition, they have attracted remarkably little detailed research by European scholars. There has, however, been a wider and more critical examination of similar trends in the United States and an attempt will be made to compare that experience with recent developments in the UK. But before addressing recent and nationally-specific changes in policy and practice, some more general observations about the nature of technological change in agriculture are required.

Technology and modern capitalist agriculture

During the past 150 years there have been several distinct phases of technological advance in agriculture, the most important being the mechanical, the chemical, the bio-chemical, and now the genetic. (For historical treatments which seek to examine simultaneously the sociology of technological innovation and the processes and consequences of technological change, see Goodman *et al.*, 1987; Kloppenburg, 1988.) From the perspective of agricultural production, these phases have been discontinuous and partial in their impact but persistent in transforming elements of the production process into 'industrial activities, and their reincorporation into agriculture as inputs' (Goodman *et al.*, *ibid.*, p. 2). The key point is that these technological developments have been designed specifically to 'reduce the importance of nature in rural production' (*ibid.*, p. 3). To this may be added the substantial reduction in the numbers working in agriculture, with technological change on the farm being dominated by process rather than product innovations, associated with increasing employment in the agricultural supply industries. Goodman *et al.* also discuss parallel advances in the food industry which sought first to reduce agricultural products to an industrial input and then to seek replacements for them altogether from among non-agricultural raw materials.

Together, these developments have reduced the economic importance of the farm production stage in the food chain. They have transferred large parts of the food production process to the urban economy, and farming families and their employees from the land to the factory. It is estimated that by 1973 64 per cent of the value-added in the US food chain could be attributed to the food industry (processing and marketing), 18 per cent to the agricultural supply industries, nine per cent to on-farm resources (e.g. family labour), and a mere nine per cent to the farming operation itself (Goss *et al.*, 1980, quoting Donald and Powell, 1975). More recent information supplied by Manchester (1985; quoted in Kloppenburg, 1988) suggests that the total contribution of the farm stage may now be as little as 13 per cent. Evidence for the UK (excluding net exports) provides a similar picture, with the food industry today accounting for 65 per cent of the value-added and the farming sector something in excess of 15 per cent (see Harvey, 1987). Put another way, in 1986 the total value of food products in the UK was in the order of £55 bn, while that of the farming sector was a mere £11 bn including industrial inputs worth £6.5 bn (Ward, forthcoming). The most noticeable feature of recent decades has been the steady growth in the economic power of the large retailing combines (Lang and Wiggins, 1985). In Britain, the five leading supermarket-chains now control 60 per cent of the domestic market. They have responded to, and moulded, consumer demand, sending strong signals over the consistency and quality of products down the food chain to processors and through them to farmers.

Current developments in biotechnology are potentially much more far-reaching in their effects than previous technological revolutions, although a crucial distinction needs to be made between their likely short-term effects on the *food system* as opposed to *agriculture*. On the farm, their initial applications (e.g. BST) are little more than an extension of existing techniques, evolutionary rather than revolutionary. Buttel (1989, p.11) even suggests that:

> ... current research goals [for biotechnology] tend to involve either patching up the problems – such as salinization, pest resistance, the expense of nitrogen fertilizer and biocides – that have been caused by previous agricultural technologies or obviating diminishing returns and productivity plateaus that have become manifest in current petrochemical technologies.

But this argument is potentially misleading if taken out of context as it underplays the integrated scientific nature of biotechnology and therefore the links between the individual techniques (solutions) being employed in different sectors of agricultural activity. Much more significantly, former technologies were concerned to improve the efficiency of 'natural' biological processes, leading to an *interdependent* food chain linking farming inputs, agriculture, food processing and retailing. Biotechnologies, however, have the ability to hasten the break-down of these established linkages, even if their implementation may face political barriers raised by agricultural, consumer and even some industrial interests disadvantaged by the change (Goodman and Wilkinson: chapter 6). The involvement of private capital at the 'cutting-edge' of this technology has been given a strong fillip by the agreement among many First World countries to allow the patenting of biological material and thus some ability by private capitals to retain the profits derived from marketing genetically-engineered products they have themselves produced (see Kloppenburg, 1988).

In Britain, the social impacts of technological change in the food system have been examined much less thoroughly than the environmental effects of modern farming methods. Even here, though, most research has tended to miss the main target. Too much attention has been directed towards the actions of farmers. While they are, of course, most immediately responsible for environmental change through their husbandry methods, this narrow perspective fails to acknowledge their growing dependence on other parts of a system which not only incorporates the suppliers of industrial inputs and technical support, and the processors and retailers of food products, but also the sources of credit and financial advice that facilitate the use of such inputs to meet the demands of the market. And beyond this immediate system, but bearing significantly upon it, lies the changing competitiveness of food interests within capital markets.

The inelasticity of demand for the major food products creates highly competitive markets, modest and unstable rates of return and a tendency for corporate restructuring. Securing brand loyalty to protect market share, and creating new, higher value-added versions of existing food products, dominate current attempts to extract additional profits from the 'upper end' of the consumer market. Of greater significance in the long run is the growing involvement of corporations whose major interests lie beyond the food system. This tendency is most evident in the context of industrial inputs (e.g. Ford, ICI) but is also to be observed elsewhere, as in the takeover in 1989 of Gateway (the UK's third largest food retailer) by the financial conglomerate Isosceles. These changes form part of the current evolution of multi-product, trans-national corporations and an associated international division of labour, making the system more vulnerable to change for reasons quite unrelated to food.

It is within these larger, off-farm, and even non-food, arenas that the trajectory of technological development is primarily determined. To date, these arenas have relied upon and been substantially influenced by public investment in agricultural R&D. The justification for a major public role has lain in the importance of agriculture to national economies, the strategic significance of food security, and the fragmented nature of the farming industry. As Cochrane (1979, p. 313) concludes:

> Technological advances can occur at the farm level only to the extent that new and improved technologies have been developed in public and private institutions, and have been made available to and extended to farmers.

These circumstances immediately lead to questions about the interests of those engaged in R&D and how their output is transmitted to farmers as well as other parts of the food chain. In general, less is known about the research endeavours of private organisations than publicly-funded programmes. Intense market competition leads to a reluctance to divulge information, but analyses of the corporate structure of the non-agricultural parts of the food system reveal a high level of concentration and the dominant position of a few companies. In the UK, for example, three corporations control 95 per cent of the fertiliser market; four, 75 per cent of agro-machinery; while three companies manufacture 90 per cent of all frozen food. But more important than this degree of concentration, in particular parts of the food chain is the extension of control by individual corporations into *several* areas of the food supply system.

One of the more radical examples of moves towards integrated control is provided by Unilever and its subsidiaries. They now have a major stake in animal feeds (BOCM Silcock) and seeds, as well as their traditional area of food processing. A more widely recognised example is provided by the petro-chemical and pharmaceutical companies, such as ICI, Monsanto and Ciba-Geigy. They have purchased seed companies in order to develop 'packages' of products such that the gains made from adopting a particular seed variety are then enhanced by using a range of agro-chemicals developed by the same company. This process is well-advanced in the United States where it has been extended to links with the new genetic engineering firms (e.g. Agrigenetics, DNA Plant Technology Corp.). These firms often begin as consultancy off-shoots of publicly-funded university research. Kloppenburg (1988, p.16) describes them as:

> ... born of the passionate marriage of academia and venture capital (and) devoted to the commodification of the research process itself ...

thus highlighting the changing relations between public and private investment, and public service and private profit, and the potential for a reduced flow of scientific information.

From their analyses of agricultural biotechnology in the United States, Kloppenburg (1988) and Buttel (1986) argue that industrial capital has proved adept at manipulating the publicly-funded research programme to under-write its own profits. A recent study by Curry and Kenney (1990) suggests that private corporations have not invested substantially in university biotechnology research programmes but, following major scientific breakthroughs, have been more inclined to invest in their own private consultancy spin-offs, effectively capturing the commerical benefits of the research once these were assured. Buttel (1989, p. 9) further suggests that:

> ... research information has been *indirectly privatized* – for example, when university scientists in the capacity of consultants to private firms transfer publicly-funded research information to private firms as part of these consultancy relationships. (our emphasis)

Less private capital has so far found its way into British universities, but the UK provides a different kind of example in the recent sale to Unilever of the Cambridge Plant Breeding Institute by the Department of Education and Science. The Institute was previously run by the Agriculture and Food Research Council (AFRC) and the National Seed Development Organisation, a commercial plant breeding operation managed by the Ministry of Agriculture. The sale conforms with Government policy to reduce public spending by selling public assets and to encourage private sector investment, particularly in 'near market' research (see below).

For most farmers, choice over technological strategy is constrained. With a long-term tendency for the real market price of farm products to fall, producers can only maintain or increase their margins by lowering unit costs faster than prices fall. This creates what Cochrane (1958) has termed the 'technological treadmill' (see also Dexter, 1977). In the EC, the most effective means of maintaining margins has been to apply ever-increasing quantities of industrial inputs. This management strategy has been strongly encouraged by falls in their real unit costs (Harvey, 1987), and the opportunity to sell into a guaranteed market. The EC has not been prepared to fund the cost in full because of its escalating amount, placing further downward pressure on support prices. Contrary to the objective of reducing the cost of public support, both the state and private capital employ an array of professional advisers to communicate new production techniques, in particular to 'innovative' and often large-scale producers who have then held a short-term economic advantage over their neighbours. Others are obliged to follow suit if they wish to remain in business, unless protected by special measures or able to farm independently of agricultural income.

As the competitive forces associated with this process unfold, the farming sector *as a whole* retains little economic benefit. Most of the economic gains accrue to off-farm industrial capitals and to a small elite of farmers capable of capturing some advantage from the process. Furthermore, under these conditions, the treadmill encourages the general adoption of capital-intensive technologies. These are often difficult to abandon quickly or without penalty because of their 'lumpiness', long investment horizons and a dependence that arises out of their growing sophistication. Farmers are increasingly removed from a detailed scientific understanding of the technologies they employ, in some instances their management function being reduced to 'reading the instructions on the packet'. They may be unsure of the implications of straying beyond the instructions, leading to a reliance on expensive off-farm technological expertise. This, in turn, binds them even closer to the products and advice of particular suppliers.

Such circumstances are most likely where farmers produce under contract (see Smith, 1984; and Heffernan, 1986, pp. 207–11) or do not have access to a cheap or free source of independent information. In the UK this process is being encouraged by the curtailment of what was previously a largely free state advisory service. Most non-environmental services now have to be paid for, and a recent survey reveals a growing preference for private sector sources of information (Eldon, 1988). One reason for this is falling farm incomes which have led industrial companies to employ a variety of inducements to maintain sales, including soft loans guaranteed by special deals made between them and the clearing banks (see Marsden *et al.*, 1990). In the short run these deals provide relief for hard-pressed farmers but, in the long run, only increase their dependence upon off-farm assistance and reduce their share of the value-added in the food chain. These links also reinforce the process of differentiation between farm businesses as those clients deemed worthy of such advantageous treatment are increasingly singled out from the remainder on the basis of strict cost-accounting and forward-budgeting criteria. It is hardly surprising that farmers retain an ambivalence towards agricultural research. On the basis of a recent empirical study conducted in New York State, Gillespie and Buttel (1989) suggest that farmers regard research as generally desirable but are cynical about the benefits it provides for them. They have reached the same conclusion as researchers about the distribution of the benefits from new technologies with the 'larger, more profit-orientated farmers with a high frequency of contact with extension...most likely to express favourable attitudes towards agricultural research' (p. 403).

The arguments outlined here suggest, first, that as the structure of the food system has altered, leading to a weakened economic role for agriculture, the financial gains from new technologies have increasingly accrued to off-farm interests. Second, because of the highly competitive nature of the food system, private corporations have found it increasingly necessary for their own survival to acquire the benefits of R&D, either through expanding their own efforts or by taking a proprietary interest in the products of publicly-funded research. As will be illustrated, these changes have had knock-on effects on the content and scale of public-sector research, as well as the relations between the public and private sectors. These are especially evident where, as a matter of policy, there has been a reduction in the real level of state funding for R&D. This has occurred in both the US and the UK, countries which have long-established and prestigious public-sector programmes.

The American experience

American scientists have been marking several recent anniversaries celebrating public initiative and financial support for agricultural R&D. Notable among these initiatives were the Morrill Act (1862), which established the state Land Grant Colleges, the Hatch Agricultural Experiment Station Act (1887) and the Co-operative Extension Act (1914). But from the start these initiatives were criticised for encouraging research of greater benefit to the larger farmers, for being too theoretical in approach and even for training farmers to leave the industry (Danbom, 1986; Marcus, 1987; Rasmussen, 1987; Cochrane, 1979). The crucial alliance became not that between farmers and scientists but between *professionals*, or those with a common interest in research, including a farming elite, senior agribusiness personnel, bureaucrats and some academics. The process of transferring economic power away from farmers was established early and put on an irrevocable course during the 1930s by Henry A. Wallace, then Secretary of State for Agriculture. His determination to promote science as the means of ensuring the long-term competitiveness of US agriculture in world markets was conveniently endorsed by the highly successful development of hybrid seed corn by American agronomists. The faith he extolled in science and technology remained broadly intact until the 1970s, largely on the back of major gains in productivity. Even the more severe critics of post-war technological change have been forced to acknowledge that higher productivity has led to consumer benefits in the form of greater food security, lower prices and a wider range of food products.

The new era of criticism has arisen from several separate sources (for discussions see Busch and Lacy, 1983; Dahlberg, 1986; Hadwiger and Browne, 1987). Ever since the publication of *Silent Spring* (Carson, 1962), environmentalists have regularly pointed to the adverse impacts of modern farming methods, while social scientists, building upon a long history of concern among extension officers, have drawn attention to the social consequences for farming communities of technological change and, in particular, the displacement of labour through mechanisation (e.g. Beradi and Geisler, 1984; Friedland, *et al.* 1981; Friedland, 1984). The case was argued most ferociously by Jim Hightower in his book *Hard Tomatoes, Hard Times* (1973) in which he sought to demonstrate that

> ...the tax-paid, land grant complex has come to serve an elite of private, corporate interests in rural America, while ignoring those who have the most urgent needs and the most legitimate claims for assistance. (p. xxvi).

This disparate coalition of critics may, individually, have had limited influence on the direction of agricultural R&D, although Hightower, for one, was elected Texan Commissioner of Agriculture in 1982; but collectively they helped to undermine the scientific and political credibility of the public research system (Browne, 1987). Committees of the land-grant scientific elite, set up to look into the state of agricultural research, accused the system of being pedestrian, duplicative and too concerned with problem solving rather than basic science (National Research Council, 1972; Rockefeller Foundation, 1982), and they advocated major changes to the organisation of publicly-funded work. These changes implied a greater degree of centralised direction and, most importantly, the need for better links between public research institutions and private organisations in order to encourage the rapid commercial exploitation of scientific advances (for further discussion see Buttel, 1986). But, as Buttel and Busch (1988) point out, these circumstances placed the public sector institutions at the centre of three conflicting forces – those representing agribusiness and federal interests which wanted an expansion in basic, generic science, the results of which could then be rapidly transferred to private capital for commercial exploitation; public interest groups which demanded a wider set of criteria upon which to determine research priorities than simply increasing productivity; and local interests (including farmers) which argued that their needs should have the highest priority as state funds for the Agricultural Experimental Stations are three times greater than those received from federal sources.

Meeting these conflicting demands has been made more difficult by the declining importance, in both cash and leadership, of the public sector. Between 1965 and 1980 the level of public funding did not change while that of private capital grew, increasing its share from 55 per cent to 65 per cent (Bonnen, 1983), in spite of claims made by Ruttan (1982) and others that the internal rate of return to public investment in agricultural R&D is substantially greater than for most other forms of public investment. This has led some agricultural economists to conclude that public agricultural R&D is under-funded. Three possible explanations of the tendency to under-funding have been put forward.

The first argues that the farming community, aware that it fails to capture most of the economic benefits of technological change, retains an antipathy towards public spending in this area, even to the point of not investing fully in new techniques. The latter assertion is not supported by the evidence with most farmers investing extensively if only in order to survive. What is true is that technological change has reduced the numbers engaged in farming and therefore their political influence over the scale and direction of R&D spending. It has also been suggested that technological advances have encouraged the specialisation and regionalisation of production, fragmenting at national level the farming interest where strategic decisions on R&D are increasingly being taken (Marcus, 1987). Whether this fragmentation can be said to reduce agricultural influence in Congress must be open to question, as it is the *highly-focused* interest groups, including commodity interests, which are seen as most effective in the lobbying process (Browne, 1989). Whether the same conclusion can be drawn for lobbying at state level, where most agricultural R&D funds are determined, is unknown. If it were, then another of Browne's conclusions would be distinctly unhelpful in the promotion of a generalised case for public R&D funds. He says:

> ... legislative people find little use for information about sector wide concerns, generalised farm or business problems, social conditions of underclasses, and public interest problems about the environment or nutrition. (p378)

A different position is taken by Kloppenburg and Buttel (1987). They treat public spending on R&D as part of a larger programme of state support for agriculture, including commodity pricing. These elements, they point out, hold contradictory consequences and lead to underfunding. Most new technologies are productivity raising, resulting in higher output in a broadly static market, driving *down* prices and *increasing* the public cost of commodity programmes. This can lead to fiscal crisis, especially where larger economic goals are directed towards reducing public spending, making the case for an increase in the R&D budget politically unsustainable. Again, there is a potential conflict between the different levels of public expenditure, the cost of support prices for farm products being borne by the Federal Government but the expected costs and benefits of R&D programmes being assessed largely at the state level.

The third explanation takes an even broader position. It starts by recognising that technological advance under capitalism is uneven and determined by the needs of capital accumulation. Public spending is viewed as a manipulable adjunct to private investment. It is then impossible to establish whether public research is underfunded in the absence of an analysis of its *modus operandi* with private capital, and possibly not even then because public and private initiative cannot be satisfactorily separated. During the 1980s the relations between the two have become increasingly complex, indefinite and variable between institutional settings.

These shifting and complex relations are well illustrated by recent experience in the United States where the R&D system has been responding, on occasion reluctantly, to encouragement from the federal government to privatise areas of research which are 'close to the market'. Such a policy has been actively promoted in some land grant universities where it has been thought to match particular institutional strengths. A specific illustration is provided by Charles Hess, Dean of the College of Agriculture and Environmental Sciences at the University of California-Davis. He argues that

> When the private sector has the ability to develop ideas and concepts into marketable products, then the private sector should take the responsibility to do it rather than the university. In this way the university will continue to fulfil its role of conducting basic research and training graduate students but not be in competition with the private sector. (Hess, 1986, pp.17–18; quoted in Kloppenburg, 1988, p.237)

Kloppenburg points out, however, that the ability of particular universities to take advantage of this strategy depends on their competitive strength in the search for funds for basic science. It also encourages differentiation between institutions, and as an approach to funding is regretted by those faculties who believe it distances them even further from their traditional clients, the farmers. But in today's R&D climate, the prestige to be derived from conducting basic science of interest to industrial capital is much greater than that from the more immediate problem-solving research and extension of concern to farmers.

Furthermore, this strategy makes the development of science itself increasingly linked to the interests of capital. This is most obvious in the United States in the area of biotechnology. Industrial capital, for example, has criticised the performance of public R&D, accusing it of focusing on 'old science' (such as organic chemistry) and being insufficiently in tune with 'new science' (molecular and cell biology). It has pursued this argument in government to the point of suggesting either that it should be accorded the lead in advancing 'new science' or it should be allowed and encouraged to develop new business arrangements with university departments and their consultancy spin-offs (Kloppenburg, 1988). All of these tendencies would suggest that public research is in some sense under-funded (or mis-directed) with the private sector believing it necessary (and profitable) to fill the gap. As we shall argue below, in spite of the institutional differences between the two countries, many of the same arguments permeate the present debates over the future of public funding of agricultural R&D in the UK.

The current debate in the UK

Until the 1980s, productivist goals dominated post-war agricultural policy in Britain (see, for example, MAFF, 1975). Their promotion relied upon a narrow interpretation of what lay within the 'public interest'. That 'public interest' was largely determined by a restricted policy community based, most visibly, on a close corporatist relationship between MAFF and the National Farmers' Union (see Cox *et al.*, 1986) and, less obviously, between MAFF and agribusiness interests (Cannon, 1987). Other arms of government have, in the words of Newby and Utting (1984, p. 267), been

> ...left to mop up the social consequences among those who were relatively disadvantaged by this policy – small farmers, farm workers, unemployed rural school-leavers, and so on.

To this list could be added environmental interests appalled at the consequences of modern farming methods.

A key means of implementing this policy has lain in the publicly-funded R&D programme and advisory service. A rudimentary advisory system for farmers was placed on a national basis just prior to 1914 when the Provincial Advisory Service (PAS) was established (see Holmes, 1988). In the inter-war period the PAS acted alongside a permissive rather than a statutory advisory service, offered by some counties but not others, providing farmers with limited and uneven access to the fruits of scientific advance. Spending increased several-fold, albeit from a very low base, but the system was subject to a familiar criticism from a farming community that often rejected it. Effectively, the system had little to offer the numerous small, under-capitalised farms, which made up the majority of farming businesses at the time, and which were managed on the basis of minimising expenditure of all kinds as the best means of surviving the farming recession. The long-term distributional implications of this message were not heeded by those responsible for promoting increased food production during and, especially, after the War. Once the objective of 'efficiency' was linked to productivity in the early 1950s, the numbers of farm workers and farmers began to decline, and have done so consistently ever since. Following the 1947 Agriculture Act, the research and advisory systems were substantially expanded. The real level of public spending on the Agriculture and Food Research Service rose by five per cent per annum until the early 1970s. It then levelled off before beginning to contract in recent years (see Harvey, 1988). This rise compares with an annual growth in the volume of the farming industry's net product of about 3.25 per cent, which has nevertheless fallen in value in real terms because of the decline in product prices and rise in input prices (Harvey, 1987). Wildly conflicting estimates have been made in recent years of the internal rate of return to public investment in agricultural R&D, ranging from the optimistic (e.g. Thirtle and Bottomley, 1988, who produce a figure of 70 per cent), to the cautious (e.g. Wise, 1986), to the pessimistic (Harvey, 1988). The debate between these authors reveals the extensive theoretical and practical difficulties of identifying and measuring the costs and benefits of R&D, and the limited practical value of trying to allocate public expenditure on the basis of internal rates of return alone (see Harvey, 1988, for a discussion of this issue). These difficulties have been exacerbated in recent years by the widening range of goals being set for agriculture, including variety and improved quality of food, economy of input and reduced impact on the environment. Success in meeting these goals is very difficult to assess quantitatively, and the inability to be precise has not worked to the advantage of those protesting at the declining level of government monies allocated to R&D programmes.

In nominal terms, the amount spent by government on agricultural research has fluctuated between £180 m and £200 m per annum during the 1980s. The Agriculture Departments (in England, Scotland and Northern Ireland) have been responsible for about three-quarters of the total. They have spent about £100 m in-house and £50 m in commissioned research through the Agricultural and Food Research Council (AFRC) on applied work. The remainder has been spent on basic science by the AFRC. The dependence of the Research Council on commissions obtained from MAFF arose out of the recommendations of the Rothschild Report (1972). This report suggested that civil research needed to be more directly related to the needs of society as formulated by government. In certain instances, the research councils and relevant government departments were to operate on a customer-contractor basis, and this led to half of AFRC's income being transferred to MAFF.

The spending out-turn for 1991–2 is expected to be 1 5–20 per cent lower in real terms than for the mid-1980s (House of Lords, 1988). This figure is based on the Government's own favourable view about future rates of inflation and comes on top of cuts made earlier in the decade. An overall decline between 1983 and 1992 of about 40 per cent in real terms is a reasonable expectation and is paralleled by similar reductions in spending on the advisory services. The Government is exhorting the private sector to pick-up the funding of 'near-market research' a concept with an elastic definition which the Government has chosen not to reveal in order to meet some of the shortfall. At present, farmers and horticulturalists contribute a further £20 m annually to R&D via levies, but claim that they cannot contribute more in the short term because of their diminished incomes. Elsewhere, the agricultural supply industries invest about £200 m per year, mostly on in-house product development, while in 1986 the food and drink industry allocated a mere £104 m, out of an estimated turnover of £56bn to R&D (House of Lords, 1988). In response to these changes in funding, research institutes have sought to diversify their sources of income to make them less reliant upon government monies. Rothamsted Agricultural Experimental Research Station, the largest station in Britain, has reduced its dependence on public funds from 86 per cent of its total income in 1984/5 to 74 per cent by 1988/9 but has still had to shed about a third of its permanent scientific posts over the period (RAERS, 1989).

The present Government is ideologically committed to encouraging the private sector to support research, and is using 'shock tactics', consisting of a very short adjustment period, to impel, if not compel, the private sector to respond. It is seeking to do so directly by refusing to fund projects which it views as commercially viable, and indirectly by reducing the level of funding for basic science. The latter is forcing institutions to adjust their research programmes towards more applied work capable of attracting private sponsorship. While certain gains may be obtained from this change in emphasis, such as ensuring the continuing relevance of applied research in a period of policy adjustment, the House of Lords Select Committee which investigated the future of agricultural research stated quite clearly what it regarded as the limits to this approach. It noted (1988, para 4.12, p. 29), for example, that:

> Public funding is necessary where research is needed to support public policy and particularly to secure optimum use of land, a major national resource. Animal health and welfare, nutrition for human health, food safety and quality standards, protection of the environment, and the provision of independent information and advice to the public are all areas which affect the public good and which cannot be left solely or even mainly to judgements based on profitability.

This conclusion addressed the other and related area of debate which concerns the priorities for R&D. As in the United States, these priorities are being influenced by the growth in environmental concern, the need for 'relevance' or commercial application, and the current pervasiveness of research in molecular biology and genetic engineering at all points in the food chain – the latter undermining the distinction traditionally drawn between research into 'agriculture' and 'food'. But change is slow. The 1985 report to MAFF of the Research Priorities Board still placed considerable emphasis on further improving farming efficiency and international competitiveness. Socio-economic and environmental issues were not ignored but neither did they have separate budgets. They were tacked on to larger, commodity-based programmes which in turn continued to reflect an 'agricultural' rather than a 'food' bias.

Such conservatism accounts in part for the critical stance adopted by another House of Lords Select Committee when it reported on the organisation of government-sponsored research in the area of agriculture and the environment (House of Lords, 1984). Not only was the Committee critical of the lack of coordination between government departments (MAFF and the Department of the Environment) but also the poor links between them and the relevant research councils. A lack of foresight and leadership was detected, the Committee noting (para 3.8, p.14) that:

> ... agricultural research has shifted its priorities towards lessening environmental impact and reducing inputs. The research trends have thus responded to public opinion. But agricultural research has not led public opinion.

This is a strong indictment given the powerful position accorded to MAFF following the Rothschild Report. But the Select Committee also paid scant attention to the contribution social science could make to our understanding of the relations between agriculture and the environment. At best, it seems, the assumed role of social science was a restricted one, relegated to assessing the impact of new agricultural technologies *once* they were in place. The Select Committee failed, for example, to suggest that a full socio-economic and environmental *ex ante* evaluation should be built into the *determination* of public research priorities. In general, it preferred the view (para 3.7, p.14) that the:

> ... existing research organisation has not served the country badly.... Most essential research on the interface between agriculture and the environment seems be carried out eventually. It may sometimes be considerably delayed but overall the fault is more one of timing than of neglect.

Even this lukewarm endorsement now seems to be wearing thin. The further expressions of intent, which appeared in the 1987 Report of the Research Priorities Board and placed greater emphasis on animal welfare, improving the conservation of the environment and socio-economic aspects of agricultural change, have only just resulted in measurable changes to the research programmes themselves. This is most visible in special initiatives, such as the Joint Agriculture and Environment Programme, organised by three research councils (AFRC, ESRC, NERC) which was begun in 1989 with a budget of £5.4m to be spent over three years. Within established research budgets, the changes in direction called for are being introduced patchily with, for example, proportionately more being spent on non-food crops (effectively farm forestry), but less on soils. In drawing attention to this, the same Select Committee pointed out in 1988 that, in response to its 1984 report, the Government had accepted that 'the Agriculture Departments should have responsibility for promoting research on the environmental effects of agricultural practices, whether or not such work appears likely to have benefit in terms of farming economics' (quoted in House of Lords, 1988, para 4.52, p.36). It then goes on to note that spending on core environmental work increased from 4.7 per cent of total MAFF R&D expenditure in 1982/3 to 7.2 per cent in 1987/8. During this same period, however, MAFF's total R&D expenditure declined sharply and, as the Committee notes, if the amounts spent are converted to '1987' prices the actual increase in spending is less than £0.5m out of a total R&D budget of £114.5m. The Committee concludes that it is 'not convinced that MAFF have taken seriously their new responsibility' (para 4.52, p.36).

This may be thought to be a harsh judgement on the changes that could reasonably be effected over a five-year period during which considerable energy had to be devoted to coping with the decline in the level of government support and trying to establish a new *modus vivendi* with the private sector. Nonetheless, the thinking and medium-term planning of MAFF do not yet seem to have taken on board the sea-change occurring outside the agricultural establishment over the future purpose of the industry and the kind of research needed to support it. With 'green' and 'consumer' issues rising up the political agenda, MAFF is bound to come under increased pressure to fund out of its diminishing budget 'public good' research, particularly relating to consumer protection. The need to do so is made more urgent by the privatisation of parts of its current programme, either by direct transfer to the private sector or indirectly as research institutions seek desperately to keep their research teams together by making their work more attractive to funding by private sector clients.

An assessment

The chapter has focused on recent trends in the organisation and funding of R&D as a critical input to technological change, emphasising the different interests involved. Drawing on recent experience from the US and the UK, it has described how the private sector has increasingly taken – or, in some cases, been impelled to take – the lead. This process has been hastened by the reduced commitment of government to agricultural R&D since the 1970s and its attempts to involve private sector funds in public programmes where the research was judged to be 'near market'. At the same time, the declining economic importance of agriculture in the food chain and the reduced political influence in government of the farming lobby have threatened to marginalise the role of agricultural interests in the setting of research agendas. Moreover, these shifts are taking place against a background of increasingly vocal and articulate protest from consumer and environmental interests, raising new questions about the regulatory stance of government. But before reviewing these tendencies it is necessary to place the significance of technological change in perspective.

Technological change neither exists in a social vacuum nor does it determine the pattern of socio-economic change. As Heffernan (1986, p. 199) argues:

> Unlocking new knowledge and information may make possible certain outcomes, but many other factors, such as governmental farm programs and taxation policies, interact to produce particular social outcomes.

He goes on to make the point (p.218) that:

> . . . agricultural research is not unique in the way it operates. It simply reflects the larger social, political and economic system.

Not only does this statement draw attention to the ideology and style of economic management of the current administrations in the US and UK, and therefore to the scale and objectives of public investment in agricultural R&D, but also to the changing significance of agriculture in public affairs.

When food security was regarded as a priority and agriculture the foundation of the rural economy, the agricultural establishment always felt able to reach an accommodation of sorts with the state concerning its primary goal – food production. As these conditions have receded, this all-dominating purpose of agriculture, and especially how it is to be achieved, have been increasingly questioned, and uncertainty over the content of farm policy has increased. The immediate response of agricultural interests has been to seek traditional solutions to what are now much broader questions. In the UK, this is reflected, for example, in their support for the *status quo* over the funding of agricultural R&D (see, for example, evidence of the National Farmers' Union to the House of Lords, 1988). In essence, the Union prefers the present situation, which in the past they have criticised for being too divorced from the practicalities of farming, to one dominated by off-farm, private sector, industrial interests. Elsewhere, farming interests have lobbied vigorously to ensure that changes in policy designed to maintain the rural economy and environment have been channelled through them (see, for example, the cases of the Less Favoured Areas policy – MacEwen and Sinclair, 1983; the alternative land-use debate – Cox *et al.*, 1987; and farm diversification — Gasson, 1988). At best, this is a holding operation sustained by history and the large sums of money that are still allocated to agricultural price support; it disguises the long-term inherent weakness of the agricultural economic and political position, including its more specific role in influencing the nature of spending on R&D.

In spite of their particular historical and institutional differences, the two national case studies illustrate a number of common themes. The research programmes in both countries still give primacy to solving technical questions related to market competitiveness, but while the farming community still demands research and extension on issues related to their immediate needs, the more powerful agribusiness interests are pressing for the conduct of basic, generic science capable of international application. This is partly because their technical needs have changed with the greatest potential for market advance arising no longer from the established products of the bio-chemical and mechanical revolutions but increasingly from developments in biotechnology. It is also partly the result of government seeking to reduce its involvement in R&D. Gaps in the research effort threaten to appear for two main reasons.

(1)   On the basis of evidence drawn from the US, and in spite of their promotion of basic science, agribusiness, and its increasingly common pharmaceutical partners, will not step in to replace lost public funds unless they can either guarantee proprietorial control over the work or buy its findings cheaply via consultancy. If neither is possible, and if the area of work is of immediate commercial interest, private firms conduct the research themselves. The concern must be that in the absence of firm regulatory controls over the introduction of new technologies, these private sector strategies will not form an adequate substitute for public sector research as there will be a reduction in the degree of actual or potential public accountability, as well as in the flow of scientific information. While the government can decide what *not* to fund in the area of 'near market research', it is the private sector that will decide what reseach *is* done. This will increase the influence of short-term market considerations over the direction of R&D.

(2) Attempts to determine quantitatively the costs and benefits of public spending on agricultural R&D, and through them to conduct 'rational' research planning exercises, given the ever-widening goals for the industry and the coarseness of the techniques available, are so open to alternative interpretation as to represent, at best, no more than crude guidelines. Efforts to deploy them either for the purposes of deciding whether public funding is in aggregate too low, or which particular projects should be supported and which rejected, invariably weight the analysis in favour of the quantifiable, however spurious the figures. As a result, even under the changed social and political conditions of the 1990s (as reflected in the arguments contained in Pearce *et al.*, 1989, for example), it is unlikely that the social and environmental consequences of cost-cutting technologies will attract the comprehensive and politically powerful treatment they deserve.

It is, therefore, the *deployment* of such techniques by those making up the policy community, and not the techniques themselves, that should be commanding our attention. Traditionally, this community has consisted almost exclusively of economic or producer interests, including those research scientists who have benefited from this perspective, working in association with central government. Those representing consumer or environmental groups have been largely ignored, a fact that is clearly demonstrated by the membership of the Ministry of Agriculture's advisory groups listed in the White Paper *Food Safety: Protecting the Consumer* (MAFF, 1989). The composition of interests in the policy community seems certain to change, but, as the House of Lords Select Committee (1988) makes clear, in its view considerable inertia exists within the present system. Where consumer interests come into conflict with those of capital, change is likely to be slow and dictated by the interests of capital unless government is prepared to place its full weight behind a new set of priorities. In both the US and the UK, the current administrations are naturally inclined not to intervene while government action itself is compromised by the need to represent both producer and consumer interests at the same time. In the case of the UK, the present government is committed, in principle and practice, to de-regulation and the freer operation of markets. It is, however, confronted by a major contradiction each time it seeks to respond to consumer interests for political reasons while protecting capital for ideological reasons. The compromise most readily adopted is to introduce new forms of regulation which remain weak through poor enforcement and a continued emphasis upon voluntarism and guidance as opposed to statutory mechanisms.

It is impossible to articulate here the full extent of this tension but on present trends it can only become more widespread. The manner of its treatment to date can be illustrated through a couple of examples. Broadly speaking, the state's response to environmental concerns in the agricultural field has been to keep controls on farmers to a minimum, to make compliance voluntary and to offer compensation. It has, therefore, protected the immediate interests of farming capitals, and especially their private property rights, largely at the taxpayer's expense. The 'polluter pays' principle has been inverted. This approach is reflected in, for example, the treatment of wildlife habitat protection under the 1981 Wildlife and Countryside Act and related legislation (for discussion see Cox *et al.*, 1986; 1988), and in the compensation to be offered to farmers in Nitrate Sensitive Areas for loss of production. A similar position is evident in the case of food safety. The Government's White Paper on food safety, which foreshadowed the Food Bill introduced in the 1989–90 parliamentary session, is long on intent but short on action, especially when judged in the light of recent outbreaks of salmonella, botulism and listeria (MAFF, 1989). Although acknowledging the need to protect the consumer, it is a complacent document, placing an unhealthy trust in existing regulatory structures and modern methods of food production. It chooses to emphasise the 'new products, more convenience and important economic advantages' (p. 36) arising from technological advance, and the scientific qualifications of those on its advisory committees, rather than to address directly consumer concerns and the reasons why these concerns are being so forcefully articulated now. Ultimately, it places its faith in the market and consumer sovereignty to ensure the supply of healthy food.

It is the conjunction of these two forces, one political and the other economic, that is creating a new set of conditions for the funding and evaluation of agricultural R&D. In their simplest terms, these forces consist of an ideologically-driven emphasis on privatisation and reduced public expenditure, and revolutionary technological changes recasting the economic relations between the agriculture, food and pharmaceutical industries. They raise important questions about the effectiveness of state regulatory structures (Tait: chapter 8) and the ability of social scientific analysis to evaluate patterns of change and the interests they serve. They direct attention to issues concerning democratic rights under increasing corporate power, seeming to contradict the state's rhetoric about pluralistic entrepreneurialism, and the need to contest what is meant by 'efficiency' in the evaluation of both publicly-funded R&D programmes as well as in the application of new technologies to agriculture itself. To ensure greater foresight and protection of the public good, there is a crying need to evaluate the social and environmental consequences of R&D programmes and the distribution of their economic benefits *before* they are enacted. As Friedland (1984) has so cogently argued, there is an urgent requirement for 'anticipatory' social impact analysis with social scientists taking a pro-active rather than a reactive stance towards the development of new technologies and the R&D programmes which sustain them. But his proposal is dependent upon the programmes being open to independent scrutiny and that demands more, not less, research conducted in the public sector. When all is said and done, however 'undemocratic' the public sector may be in this field, greater opportunities exist to make it more accountable to a wider range of consumer interests than obtain in the private sector. But were its 'R&D function' to be reduced to a purely regulatory role it would always be open to the charge of being negative or obstructionist. To be an effective regulator, it has to retain its own independent capacity to innovate.

References

Beradi, G. M. and Geisler, C. C. (eds) (1984) *The Social Consequences of New Agricultural Technologies*, Rural Studies Series. Boulder, US, Westview Press.

Bonnen, J. T. (1983) Historical sources of US agricultural productivity: Implications for R&D policy and social science research, *American Journal of Agricultural Economics* 65, 958-966.

Browne, W. P. (1987) An emerging opposition? Agricultural interests and federal research policy, in Hadwiger, D. F. and Browne, W. P. (eds) *Public Policy and Agricultural Technology: Adversity despite Achievement*. London, Macmillan.

Browne, W. P. (1989) Access and influence in agriculture and rural affairs: Congressional staff and lobbyist perceptions of organized interests, *Rural Sociology*, 54, 365-381.

Busch, L. and Lacey, W. B. (1983) *Science, Agriculture, and the Politics of Research*. Boulder, US, Westview Press.

Buttel, F. H. (1986) Biotechnology and agricultural research policy: emergent issues, in Dahlberg, K. (ed) *op. cit.*

Buttel, F. H. (1989) Social science research on biotechnology and agriculture: a critique, *The Rural Sociologist* 9, 5-15.

Buttel, F. H. and Busch, L. (1988) The public agricultural research system at the crossroads, *Agricultural History* 62, 292-312.

Cannon, G. (1987) *The Politics of Food*. London, Century.

Carson, R. L. (1962) *Silent Spring*. Boston, Houghton Mifflin.

Cochrane, W. W. (1958) *Farm Prices: Myth and Reality*. Minnesota, University of Minnesota Press.

Cochrane, W. W. (1979) *The Development of American Agriculture: A Historical Analysis*. Minnesota, University of Minnesota Press.

Countryside Commission (1986) *Monitoring Landscape Change*. Unpublished Report, The Commission, Cheltenham.

Cox, G., Lowe, P. and Winter, M. (1986) From state direction to self-regulation: the historical development of corporatism in British agriculture, *Policy and Politics* 14, 457-490.

Cox, G., Flynn, A., Lowe, P. and Winter, M. (1987) *Alternative Uses of Agricultural Land in England and Wales*, IIUG rep 87-16, Research Unit Environment and Policy. Berlin, International Institute for Environment and Society.

Cox, G., Lowe, P. and Winter, M. (1988) Private rights and public responsibilities: the prospects for agricultural and environmental controls, *Journal of Rural Studies* 4, 323-337.

Curry, J. and Kenney, M. (1990) Land grant university-industry relationships in biotechnology: a comparison with the non LGU universities, *Rural Sociology*, 55 (forthcoming).

Dahlberg, K. A. (ed) (1986) *New Directions for Agriculture and Agricultural Research*. New Jersey, Rowman & Allenheld.

Danbom, D. B. (1986) Publicly sponsored agricultural research in the United States from an historical perspective, in Dahlberg, K. A. (ed) *op. cit.*

Dexter, K. (1977) The impact of technology on the political economy of agriculture, *Journal of Agricultural Economics* 28, 211–221.

Eldon, J. (1988) Agricultural change, conservation and the role of advisers, *ECOS* 9 (4), 14–20.

Friedland, W. H. (1984) Commodity systems analysis: an approach to the sociology of agriculture, *Research in Rural Sociology and Development,* 1, 221–235.

Friedland, W. H., Barton, A. E. and Thomas, R. J. (1981) *Manufacturing Green Gold: Capital, Labor, and Technology in the Lettuce Industry*. New York, Cambridge University Press.

Gasson, R. (1988) Farm diversification and rural development, *Journal of Agricultural Economics* 39, 175–182.

Gillespie, G. W. Jnr. and Buttel, F. H. (1989) Farmer ambivalence toward agricultural research: an empirical assessment, *Rural Sociology*, 54, 382–408.

Goodman, D., Sorj, B. and Wilkinson, J. (1987) *From Farming to Biotechnology: A Theory of Agro-Industrial Development*. Oxford, Blackwell.

Goss, K. F., Rodefeld, R. D. and Buttel, F. H. (1980) The political economy of class structure in US agriculture: a theoretical outline, in Buttel, F. H. and Newby, H. (eds), *The Rural Sociology of the Advanced Societies: Critical Perspectives*, 83–132, Montclair, NJ, Allenheld, Osmun.

Hadwiger, D. F. and Browne, W. P. (eds) (1987) *Public Policy and Agricultural Technology: Adversity despite Achievement*. London, Macmillan.

Harvey, D. W. (1987) *The Future of the Agricultural and Food System*, EPARD Working Paper No. 1. Reading, University of Reading.

Harvey, D. W. (1988) Research priorities in agriculture, *Journal of Agricultural Economics* 39, 81–89.

Heffernan, W. D. (1986) Review and evaluation of social externalities, in Dahlberg, K.A. *op. cit.*, 199–220.

Hightower, J. (1973) *Hard Tomatoes, Hard Times*, Cambridge, Mass, Schenkman.

Holmes, C. J. (1988) Science and the farmer: the development of the Agricultural Advisory Service in England and Wales, 1900–1939, *Agricultural History Review* 36, 77–86.

House of Lords (1984) *Agricultural and Environmental Research*, Select Committee on Science and Technology, 272-I. London, HMSO.

House of Lords (1988) *Agricultural and Food Research*, Select Committee on Science and Technology, 13-I. London, HMSO.

Kloppenburg, J. R. (1988) *The First Seed: The Political Economy of Plant Biotechnology, 1492–2000*. Cambridge, Cambridge University Press.

Kloppenburg, J.R. and Buttel, F.H. (1987) Two blades of grass: the contradictions of agricultural research as state intervention, *Research in Political Sociology*, 3, 111-135.

Lang, T. and Wiggins, P. (1985) The industrialization of the UK food system: from production to consumption, in Healey, M.J. and Ilbery, B.W. (eds) *The Industrialization of the Countryside*, 45-56, Norwich, Geo Books.

Lowe, P., Bradley, T. and Wright, S. (eds) (1986) *Deprivation and Welfare in Rural Areas*. Norwich, Geo Books.

MacEwen, M. and Sinclair, G. (1983) *New Life for the Hills*. London, Council for the National Parks.

MAFF (Ministry of Agriculture, Fisheries and Food) (1975) *Food from our own Resources*, Cmnd. 6020. London, HMSO.

MAFF, (1989) *Food Safety: Protecting the Consumer*, CM 372. London, HMSO.

Manchester, A.C. (1985) *Agriculture's Links with US and World Economies*, Agriculture Information Bulletin No. 496. Washington DC, USDA.

Marcus, A.I. (1987) Constituents and constituencies: An overview of the history of public agricultural research institutions in America, in Hadwiger, D.F. and Browne, W.P. (eds) *op. cit.*, 15-30.

Marsden, T.K., Whatmore, S. and Munton, R.J.C. (1990) The role of banking capital in British food production, in Marsden, T.K. and Little, J.K. (eds) *Perspectives on the Food System*. London, Gower.

Munton, R.J.C., Whatmore, S.J. and Marsden, T.K. (1989) Part-time farming and its implications for the rural landscape: a preliminary analysis, *Environment and Planning A* 21, 523-536.

National Research Council (1972) *Report of the Committee on Research Advisory to the US Department of Agriculture*. Washington DC, National Academy of Sciences.

Newby, H., (1985) *Green and Pleasant Land? Social Change in Rural England* (2nd edition). London, Wildwood House.

Newby, H. and Utting, P. (1984) Agribusiness in the United Kingdom: social and political implications, in Beradi, G. and Geisler, C.C. (eds) *op. cit.*, 265-289.

Pearce, D., Markandya, A. and Barbier, E.B. (1989) *Blueprint for a Green Economy*. London, Earthscan Publications.

Rasmussen, W.D. (1987) Public experimentation and innovation: An effective past but an uncertain future, *American Journal of Agricultural Economics* 69, 890-898.

Rockfeller Foundation (1982) *Science for Agriculture: Report of a Workshop on Critical Issues in American Agriculture*. New York, The Rockefeller Foundation.

Rothamsted Agricultural Experimental Research Station (1989) *Who pays for Rothamsted?* Harpenden, RAERS.

Ruttan, V.W. (1982) *Agricultural Research Policy*. Minneapolis, University of Minnesota Press.

Smith, W. (1984) The vortex model and the changing agricultural landscape of Quebec, *Canadian Geographer* 28, 358-372.

Thirtle, C. and Bottomley, P. (1988) Is publicly funded agricultural research excessive?, *Journal of Agricultural Economics* 39, 99–112

Ward, N. (forthcoming) A preliminary analysis of the UK food chain, *Food Policy*.

Wise, W. (1986) The calculations of rates of return on agricultural research from production functions, *Journal of Agricultural Economics*, 38, 151–161.

CHAPTER 6

Patterns of Research and Innovation in the Modern Agro-Food System

David Goodman and John Wilkinson

Introduction

The literature on innovation in agriculture is dominated by two approaches: the induced innovation model and what might broadly be termed a political economy or 'institutional' analysis. The former transposes the theoretical principles of neo-classical economics to agriculture, which is conceptualised as an industrial sector, where the basic lines of research and the diffusion of new technologies are determined by factor price differentials. Deviations from Pareto efficiency conditions arising from market imperfections will distort research decisions and technological choices, leading to welfare losses for society at large. Agriculture is portrayed as a highly competitive 'industry' in which price-taking, atomistic family producers are represented as typical capitalist firms. However, the issue of why it is only in agriculture that processes of concentration have been too weak to generate characteristic oligopolistic structures is not addressed. The political economy approach, on the other hand, places the market within a power structure analysis of economic change and technical progress. The abstraction of factors of production is replaced by the concept of social actors, which allows a more nuanced interpretation of innovation trajectories. It is also able to capture the heterogeneity of agricultural production structures, which has persisted throughout the process of modernisation.

In the political economy approach, relative factor prices depend on the balance of forces between specific economic interest groups. In an institutional context where economic power is unequally distributed, technological innovation is one of the stratagems used to restructure markets and gain competitive advantage. There is therefore no primordial allocation of factors of production reflecting real relative scarcity against which the 'efficiency' of research decisions and technological choice can be judged. Trajectories of technical change, it is argued, are historically and socially derived, and not the product of the 'invisible hand' of the market and the putative neutrality of scientific advance (Busch *et al.*, 1989).

However, while the political economy approach is proposed as an alternative to the neo-classical model of induced innovation, it shares similar presuppositions. Indeed, in some respects, it offers a mirror image, simply inverting the analysis so that market distortions and imperfections arising from economic power and its correlates become the norm rather than 'deviations' from an optimal position. Innovation then becomes an endogenous process in which intrasectoral determinants are uppermost. In relation to agriculture, this analysis is applicable to sectors dominated by powerful corporatist producer groups, including those based on natural monopoly, as in the case of certain plantation crops. Such an approach has also been extended to upstream agro-industrial sectors producing inputs for agricultural markets or which use agricultural crops as industrial inputs.

On the other hand, the induced innovation model is more appropriate to sectors of atomistic competition producing generic, homogeneous commodities, and where macro-economic variables consequently are likely to be more significant. In this sense, innovation is exogenous in that producers respond to relative factor prices which are determined by economy-wide factor endowments. The conventional treatment of technological innovation in agriculture thus comprises two competing but complementary models, whose relevance depends on the market structure of the sector in question. Insofar as atomistic structures are prevalent, the political economy approach serves mainly to qualify the induced innovation model rather than offering a truly alternative analysis.

In this chapter, we argue that both these approaches provide an inadequate framework for the analysis of the agro-food system. This is now entering a period of rapid change and structural reorganisation as advances in biotechnologies extend industrial control over fundamental biological processes. These innovations, which coincide with OECD agricultural surpluses and an increasingly demand-led food system, are creating tensions between major sectors as farm groups and agri-business redefine their strategies. In the following discussion, we examine emerging patterns of innovation in the agro-food system, the response of leading actors, and possible consequences at the international level.

An alternative point of departure

The crucial limitation of the models outlined above is that the standard *industrial* analysis of innovation is quite inappropriate for agriculture. The agro-food system is not readily assimilable to industry. This is because the biological production/consumption cycle underpinning this system presents unique problems for industrial organisation. The centrality of biological processes, and the constraints these have created to industrial innovation, have imparted singular characteristics to the industrialisation of agriculture and food production and to rural social structures. What is lacking is an overall framework which situates the different actors within the specific dynamics of agricultural modernisation. An essential first step is to bring biological processes to the centre of the perspective.

In earlier work, we have analysed the emergence of the agricultural inputs and processing industries as the result of the progressive but discontinuous industrialisation of agriculture (Goodman, Sorj and Wilkinson, 1987).

> Unable to subsume the rural production process *in toto*, selected rural activities have become sectors of accumulation for different fractions of industrial capital. As elements of the rural production process become amenable to industrial reproduction, they are appropriated by industrial capitals and *reincorporated* in agriculture as inputs or produced means of production. (*Ibid*, p. 7)

The key point here is that the industrialisation of agriculture has resulted from the industrial appropriation of *discrete* activities, in contrast to the unified transformation of the production process in domestic and rural handicrafts sectors, which gave free rein to the forces of concentration.

> These partial and historically discontinuous appropriations of rural production define the origins of agro-industrial capitals and the 'complex' of equipment, processing, seeds, and agro-chemical sectors. (*Ibid*, p. 7)

Agro-industry and the downstream industrial food system therefore provide the appropriate vantage points for analysing technological innovation in agriculture.

Once individual rural activities are appropriated as the result of technological innovation, with animal power being replaced by tractors and manure by synthetic chemicals, for example, the industrial sectors established then become *autonomous* sources of innovation. Pressures emanating from these agro-industrial sectors thus may lead to public policy measures which modify relative factor prices to favour the new industrial markets. In this case, mechanisation may occur in contexts of abundant and cheap rural labour – a typical situation in developing countries. Since R&D has occurred outside agriculture, the agro-industrial 'complex' has developed by historical accretion, adding new sectors as innovations are introduced for diffusion among agricultural producers. Moreover, the productive unit which was to become the object of the dominant agro-industrial model was not the typical capitalist firm but, on the one hand, the non-capitalised family farmer of the American Mid-West or the Japanese paddy-fields and, on the other, the modernising *latifundio* in Latin America.

The difficulty of developing technologies to appropriate the biological processes of agriculture (photosynthesis, species diversity, gestation, etc), which would convert it into a branch of industry, led historically to two relatively independent lines of mechanical and chemical innovation. Before the advent of hybrid seeds in the 1930s, these developments gave rise to two separate agro-industrial structures tied respectively to mechanical and automotive engineering and the heavy chemicals industry. This *fragmentation* of the innovation process, whose origins and dynamic lie outside agricultural production itself, has been responsible for the accumulation of ecological problems which, in their turn, are now redefining research agendas.

Although industrial appropriation successfully broke down the 'closed circuit' of the sustainable, self-sufficient *pre-industrial* production process associated with the mixed farm (Thompson, 1968), the technological 'revolution' which occurred in the nineteenth century was incomplete and the key biological processes continued to resist innovation, at least until the introduction of hybrid seeds after 1920. As a result, modern industrial agriculture is characterised by an anarchic production process in which industrial capitals pursue independent R&D strategies to promote sales of their inputs, disregarding their impact on the productive base of the system as a whole, i.e. the rural environment.

The stimulus to biological innovation in agriculture is not dependent only on an expansion of demand and the corresponding need to increase productivity. Unlike requirements in industry, innovation is a permanent necessity in order to adapt crop varieties to constantly changing environmental pressures, which otherwise would reduce current yield levels. The knowledge required for such innovation, however,

> ... can only be obtained by experiment, and by such and so long continued experiment as to place it beyond the power of individuals or ordinary voluntary associations. (OTA, 1981)

From an early stage, therefore, the State has assumed a central role in the direct promotion of innovation in agriculture through basic and applied research, the introduction of new varieties, and the development of new products. The processing industry also has contributed to the diffusion of biological innovations by promoting varieties suited to specific processing requirements.

Three basic factors have therefore been responsible for the *sui generis* dynamic of innovation in agriculture. On-farm research and development has been inhibited by the character of the historically dominant production unit – the non-capitalised family farm. Industrial innovation has been based on the fragmentation of the agricultural production process via partial industrial appropriation of rural activities. Finally, the State traditionally has been responsible for innovations in the biological sphere since these were simultaneously non-appropriable by industry and beyond the possibilities of atomistic non-capitalised agricultural production units.

This role was performed in the United States, for example, by the public land grant universities and state agricultural experiment stations, and this decentralised system was mainly responsible for the development and early diffusion of hybrid corn in the 1920s and 1930s. The task of gaining greater control over the biological determinants of agricultural productivity fell to the public system because private capitals lacked effective mechanisms, whether biological or legal, to appropriate the genetic information embodied in improved plant varieties as private property. In open-pollinated varieties, this information essentially is a public good since farmers can, if necessary, create their own seed stocks (Berlan and Lewontin, 1986). Once the focus of crop improvement research shifted towards hybrid varieties, however, farmers effectively lost the alternative of open-pollination since the yields from seeds harvested from these varieties were 20 per cent to 40 per cent lower than the hybrid itself. 'For all practical purposes, such a loss of yield amounts to biological sterility' (*Ibid*, p. 787). Furthermore, hybrid seeds provided the mechanism to integrate farmers into intensive crop management systems whose development was dictated by agro-industrial innovation. This 'locking-in' effect was achieved by a process of technological convergence in which the seed was adapted to the machine and chemical inputs, restricting the range of technological choice open to producers operating in competitive markets.

The development of hybrid seeds held out the promise of property rights to improved varieties, and the corresponding opportunity to earn economic rents from investment in crop improvement. In the case of corn, it was necessary first to select and test varieties adapted to highly specific local ecological systems. This varietal specificity of hybrid corn was admirably suited to the decentralised US public research system, whose principal strength lies in diffusing applied, locally adapted technologies (Buttel and Busch, 1988). Private seed companies lobbied strongly for the reorientation of corn improvement research to hybrids but, once these were well-established, they campaigned successfully to restrict public sector development of commercial hybrid corn lines. As a result, private R&D expenditure became an effective barrier to entry to the seed industry. These biological and institutional constraints subsequently acquired formal legal standing with the passage of plant breeders' rights legislation in 1970. As we see below, modern plant biotechnologies are provoking further shifts in the institutional division of labour between public and private research and renewing debates over intellectual property rights.

The current context of innovation in the agro-food system

We have seen that the inability to industrialise the biological production process conferred a major role on the public sector in the generation and diffusion of innovations. In the food industry, a similar lack of technological command over biological parameters has also lent distinctive characteristics to its development. Industrialisation of the downstream food system has been premised on processing agricultural commodities as if they were inorganic inputs, attempting to assimilate the food industry to patterns of non-food manufacturing. In recent years, fractionation methods drawn from the petrochemical industries, which reduce crops to their constituent chemical components, have become the norm. This ability to manipulate the basic constituents of food to create reconstituted foods and new products, including convenience foods, is complemented by the use of chemical additives. These are used to facilitate industrial processing, extend shelf-life and restore colour, flavour and texture lost in manufacture. However, this highly industrialised, mass production model of food processing reflected patterns of food consumption in which quantity, low prices and availability were prime considerations. These dictated a 'pile it high and sell it cheap' strategy of food processing and retail distribution.

In the 1980s, however, two major developments, one on the supply side and the other on the demand side, have radically altered the context of innovation in all sectors of the agro-food system. The first is the ability to engineer and programme living organisms for economic objectives, which marks a fundamental change in the technological frontiers of the food system. Secondly, the increasing pressures to adopt environmentally-friendly patterns of production and consumption at a societal level are paralleled by the shift towards more selective, health-conscious and additive-free regimes of individual food consumption. Both of these developments challenge the previous industrial model of agriculture and food processing. Moreover, these innovative pressures from the demand side coincide with the stagnation of traditional mass production food markets and structural over-production in agriculture.

What are the consequences of these developments for the institutional structures of innovation consolidated in the post-war organisation of the agro-food system? As with the earlier technological transfer of chemical and mechanical innovations, the new biotechnologies emerged outside the food industry. The major advances which established the commercial potential of genetic engineering occurred in the universities and gave rise initially to a new biotechnology industry of small, specialised science-intensive firms. This emergence of a *separate* embryonic industrial structure reflected the generic character of the new biotechnologies, potentially applicable to a wide range of economic activities.

However, biotechnology R&D capacity in this nascent industry has increasingly been taken over, directly or through a series of contractual devices, by the chemical-pharmaceutical complex. These acquisitions and 'strategic alliances' reflect in part an impasse in innovations *via* chemical synthesis. This path of research is failing to meet demands in the health sector, while new synthetic drugs are submitted to long and costly procedures to obtain approval from health authorities. In addition, traditional chemical processing technologies and products are being challenged by more rigorous environmental controls. As a result, rather than being presented primarily as *sectoral* innovations for the agro-food and health sectors, biotechnologies are becoming integrated within the economic system as innovations which potentially transcend the limits of an industrialisation model centred on non-organic, non-renewable resources. The technological capacity to manipulate the genetic code to produce entirely new products, from drugs and foods to biodegradable materials, and to engineer micro-organisms into an energy saving/waste recycling production force, prefigures a new bio-industrial paradigm.

The potential significance of biotechnologies for the economic system can be gauged from the mounting pressures to devise a new juridical framework for their development. Prior advances in the manipulation of nature through the development of hybrids and improved varieties also led to demands for industrial property protection. In this case, however, the redefinition of public and private spheres was limited to the economic sectors directly involved in plant improvement work. Now, the global significance of biotechnologies conferred by their generic characteristics is reflected in demands to allow the generalised patentability of all genetically-engineered living organisms whatever the source.

Alternatively, of course, these developments can be interpreted as the final, subjugation of living material to the dominant pattern of industrial development. Just as organic raw materials are processed using technologies derived from petrochemical engineering, now life forms will be isolated from their eco-systems and reduced to simple instruments or products of industrial production. The same processes therefore can be viewed from diametrically opposed standpoints – as the reversal or reorientation of the inherited industrial model in favour of a more sustainable, environmentally-friendly development or as the further extension of the dominant industrial paradigm to incorporate the engineering of living organisms.

It is perhaps not surprising, therefore, that consumers regard biotechnologies with great ambivalence. Certainly in the shift towards a more demand-targeted, less supply-driven production model the consumer emerges as an important influence on the rhythm and direction of innovation. This is particularly true of the food industry, as we see below. For the ecological activist, biotechnology may constitute a morally indefensible interference in the natural environment. Yet, in the main, consumer perceptions are likely to be determined by the use to which biotechnologies are put (see Tait: chapter 8). In the production of new vaccines or therapeutic drugs against cancer or AIDS, genetic engineered products probably will be adopted in direct response to their efficiency. A similar reaction is likely to anti-pollution and waste-recycling applications. On the other hand, the introduction of new biotechnological products in agriculture has met with opposition on health, safety and economic grounds, which has already slowed and may eventually block their diffusion, as in the case of ice-minus bacteria and BST.

We are not dealing, therefore, as was true with hybrid seeds, with an innovation confined to the agro-food industry. On the contrary, biotechnologies represent a strategic group of technologies in the restructuring of global economic relations. By the same token, the redefinition of public and private spheres in the generation of biotechnology innovations is a global concern. The different sectors of the agro-food industry thus will be forced to relate to these more general developments.

The position of the agro-food industry

That biotechnologies did not develop within the agro-food system is hardly surprising. We have previously noted that innovations in agriculture have primarily been exogenous, either emerging from within the public sector or the upstream agro-industrial branches. Food processing industries in turn have not shown high rates of endogenous innovation. Until the recent absorption of engineering methods developed in petrochemicals and pharmaceuticals, innovation in food processing mainly involved the mechanisation and scaling-up of techniques whose rudiments had been known for many years. It is thus tempting to conclude that the food industry can continue to apply its traditional passive 'user' strategy in relation to biotechnology. Such a view underestimates the wide-ranging impact biotechnologies will have on the food system.

Before biotechnologies, innovation in the downstream food industries had only a peripheral impact on the agro-food system's basic substratum: agricultural production. The inability to transform radically the essential characteristics of its organic agricultural feedstocks, exacerbated by the physiological requirements of human food consumption, has resulted in a pattern of innovation based on a strategy of attrition in which specific elements (secondary features) are replaced by chemical additives and substitutes. Nevertheless, this strategy has not disturbed the centrality of the agricultural product and the food system continues to be organised around specific commodities, forming specialised agro-food chains. Indeed, the principal organisational shifts in the food system in the past have arisen from new technologies which exploited the intrinsic natural qualities of the agricultural product. For example, the substitution of vegetable for animal oils.

Biotechnologies now threaten to *implode* the long-standing organisation of the food system around specialised commodity chains by their ability to transfer genes across species barriers and adapt agricultural products for non-traditional markets. There is the capacity simultaneously to relocate agricultural production in factories and industrial production in fields.

The historical rigidity of the agro-food system, the legacy of its biological production/consumption cycle, has led to the identification of major industrial groups with specific locations in the downstream food chain – primary processing, secondary intermediates, final products, etc. The potential and challenge of biotechnologies thus vary in accordance with the position of the leading firms in the overall structure. For food manufacturers, for example, the increasing identification by consumers of 'food' with 'nutrition' is opening up markets for new product lines, including bio-industrial fermentation products. However, a passive 'user' strategy is likely to be ineffective as chemical and pharmaceutical companies use biotechnologies to become established in these expanding, high value added markets. Food firms accordingly will have to develop autonomous R&D capacity, either in-house or via contract arrangements, if they are to harness biotechnologies to their industrial strategies.

Agri-biotechnologies also present a complex mixture of challenge and opportunity for agro-industrial firms. These include higher-yielding crop varieties, more productive livestock, the selective adaptation of crops to processing requirements, new sources of feedstocks for traditional and emerging industries, and more sustainable crop management systems. Yet agriculture, potentially a major area of biotechnological innovation, is subject to comprehensive state support and regulation. Public policy, therefore, will be a key factor in determining how biotechnologies are applied in the current context of agricultural over-production and stagnant markets for staple foods. This may have the effect of inhibiting innovation through the prohibitive pricing of raw material feedstocks or production controls (as with the EC's isoglucose production quota) or, alternatively, may direct innovation towards certain strategic goals, such as oilseed import substitution in the EC or ecologically sustainable farming practices.

New patterns of innovation

The traditional organisation of the food system around specific crops and product complexes is thus being undermined by changing technologies and shifting demand patterns. But these same trends also generate countervailing tendencies, creating tensions between rival models and trajectories of the agro-food system. Such conflicts spring from the generic characteristics of biotechnologies in extending industrial control over biological processes. Thus biotechnologies will strengthen the 'fractionation/reconstitution' food industry model by increasing the interchangeability of agricultural raw materials, leading towards a generic biomass inputs sector. Advances in bio-catalytic fermentation already have established a new secondary intermediates sector, which reinforces this trajectory, as we see below.

On the other hand, shifts in consumer preferences towards fresh produce and whole foods buttress the competitiveness of agriculture as a diversified production system supplying highly specific products. While organic farming systems may appropriate advances in biotechnology to achieve greater control over eco-systems, these techniques may be applied more directly to grains and livestock in order to modify fat/protein content in line with perceived consumer demand. Such applications would have the support of the large multiples in the increasingly dominant retailing sector. Farm commodity lobbies and primary processing interests on the other hand seek to mobilise public support for import substitution policies and campaign to divert traditional agricultural products to non-food uses, such as fuel and chemicals, in their efforts to maintain the integrity of agro-industrial commodity chains.

However, the very versatility of biotechnologies in facilitating diversification means that individual product complexes, such as cereals and sugar, are inevitably brought into conflict. These conflicts are symptomatic of new patterns of integration between agriculture and industry which are far removed from the constrained, chain-like rigidities of the past. Nevertheless, at this initial stage of the structuring process, the future organisation of the agro-food system can only be dimly perceived. Much will depend on how biotechnologies are integrated into the strategies of the leading actors, as well as trends in consumer demand. Here we try to identify recent patterns of innovation which illustrate new trajectories in the re-organisation of this system.

New intermediates

The efficiency of biocatalytic fermentation, an ancient method of food and drink production, promises to be enhanced in several ways by genetic engineering. First, it can increase the productivity of micro-organisms used directly in food manufacturing, either as active processing agents or as a source of compounds and secondary intermediates, such as amino acids, vitamins, flavourants and other additives (OTA, 1981). As well as raising the efficiency of industrial fermentation technologies, genetic engineering can be used to extend the range of possible feedstocks that can be converted by micro-organisms into food products. The greater efficiency and versatility of fermentation technologies has given rise to a new secondary processing or intermediates industry whose feedstocks include agricultural crops, biomass and hydrocarbons. The two leading products of this new sector, microbial single cell protein (SCP) and high fructose corn syrups (HFCS), exemplify the potential restructuring effects of biotechnologies.

SCP can be cultured on a variety of feedstocks, which includes starch, methane, ethanol, biomass, and effluent waste streams. Commercial initiatives using hydrocarbon feedstock were taken by Shell, British Petroleum and ICI in the late 1960s but, following the OPEC price increases of the 1970s, only ICI continued in production, manufacturing 'Pruteen' as a high protein additive for animal feed. The process engineering expertise acquired by ICI has been used to launch a new protein-rich food ingredient, myco-protein. This product, which is sold under the trade name 'Quorn' by a joint venture between ICI and Rank Hovis McDougall, reputedly has textural and other functional qualities which make it suitable for the production of meat analogues. Currently it is the main ingredient of a 'savoury pie' marketed by J. Sainsbury. Myco-protein is a micro-fungus produced by continuous fermentation on a glucose substrate, usually wheat or corn starch, but the starch feedstock can be obtained from virtually any carbohydrate.

Myco-protein illustrates several aspects of the process of bio-industrialisation into which the agro-food system is inexorably being drawn. First, possible myco-protein feedstocks transcend any single food chain or product complex, reducing the specificity of individual agricultural crops. Equally, the market diversification created by SCP production implies much stiffer competition between the various feedstock sources. Secondly, the industrial fermentation technology used to produce myco-protein takes cheaper carbohydrates and converts them into high grade protein, presenting a direct challenge to livestock products. Furthermore, many animal products run counter to current dietary recommendations, whereas 'Quorn' is low in calories, high in fibre content and cholesterol free. Finally, biotechnological engineering know-how has given ICI a platform for entry into high value-added food markets, where health criteria are uppermost. The reduction of barriers between food manufacturing and the chemical industry, with its strong pharmacological R&D base, and the opportunities for mergers and joint ventures, as in the case of 'Quorn', very much represent the wave of the future.

A second product of the new intermediate inputs sector, high fructose corn syrups (HFCS), can be regarded as part of an essentially defensive strategy to maintain existing agro-industry linkages. HFCS, together with gluten meal, corn oil and ethanol, are products of the corn wet milling industry, whose development is central to the diversification strategy of the US grains complex. This industry currently absorbs some 10–15 per cent of US corn production. HFCS are products of a recent process innovation, immobilised enzyme technology, whose efficiency was increased significantly by genetically engineered improvements in glucoamylase enzymes to raise the fructose content. HFCS have made serious inroads into markets for sucrose syrups, notably in soft drinks, which is the largest single outlet for HFCS. Similar substitution effects between cane and beet sugars and corn sweeteners have been inhibited in Europe following the introduction of an EC regulation in 1977 which established an isoglucose production quota of 200,000 tons.

This type of by-product diversification essentially is a 'beggar thy neighbour' strategy insofar as new markets are created at the expense of other product complexes. It also contributes to the long-term tendency of biotechnology to reduce all field crops and biomass to the status of generic intermediates. Significantly, carbohydrates rather than corn, wheat or sugar are the basic feedstock of the new intermediates industry.

The recent diversification of Tate & Lyle illustrates some of these points. Initially, this company sought to diversify within its traditional commodity base by increasing R&D in sucro-chemistry and developing a sugar-based industrial sweetener, *sucralose*, to compete with HFCS. It also has continued to increase its sugar-refining capacity by take-overs, notably of the US firm. Amstar, in 1988. However, the new, *generic* character of the world sweetener industry was given explicit confirmation when Tate & Lyle acquired Staley Continental, one of the leading US producers of HFCS, in April 1988. In addition to its own sucro-chemistry research, Tate & Lyle now has access to Staley R&D experience in starch chemistry, which is leading to the development of new speciality starches used in the paper, packaging and newsprint industries. The cross-cutting nature of these new technologies and their impact on industry demarcation lines again is evident. The Staley acquisition also allowed Tate & Lyle to raise its existing holding in CST, a major European group in cereal sweeteners and starch production, from one-third to two-thirds.

Ferruzzi, Europe's largest cereal trader and sugar processor, had in fact followed this diversification path a year earlier, acquiring the European starch and glucose interests of the US firm, Corn Products International, the world's foremost starch producer, in 1987. However, Ferruzzi has broken the mould as a primary processor by its recent acquisition of the chemicals and pharmaceuticals group, Montedison, which in 1986 had itself taken control of Fermenta, the Swedish pharmaceutical and biotechnology company. Ferruzzi now is in a position to exploit the synergies between its agricultural production and processing interests (cereals, sugar, starch, ethanol), its holdings in the plant biotechnology and seed industry, and agro-chemicals. In Europe, Ferruzzi is the archetype of the new bio-industrial, company.

The diversification strategies of primary processor and producer interests also have led to the expansion of ethanol production from corn in the US and sugar in developing countries, notably in Brazil with its Proalcool programme. These state-subsidised initiatives are intended primarily as alternative outlets for traditional crops in excess supply, but they also foreshadow the potential rise of a new food-chemicals-energy complex using renewable feedstocks. Some observers suggest that this prospect will be advanced by the effect of plant biotechnologies on crop yields, depressing the relative price of agricultural raw materials, and by their capacity to 'design' crops with the functional properties required by processing industries (Cormack, 1987). In 1986 the European Farming Union (COPA) and the European Federation of Chemical Manufacturers (CEFIC) lobbied successfully for a new EC regulation which modifies the production refund mechanism of the Community cereal regime to ensure that sugar and starch inputs utilised in the chemical industry and other non-food uses are available at world price levels. The possibility of extending this mechanism to oils and fats from agricultural feedstocks are now being explored.

> This regulation opens the door for the development of a new, non-food agriculture, and heralds a constructive new alliance between farming and biotechnology. (Cormack, 1987, p. 10).

Such an alliance, however, will have to overcome the strains of increasing competition between traditional product complexes, clearly indicated by the initial mobilisation of the European Association of Corn Starch Producers (AAM) against the European Council's Sugar regulation. In Europe, Ferruzzi presents itself as a symbol of such a new alliance in which a polyvalent agriculture is closely integrated into the reseach and product development activities of a diversified processing sector. Shifts in agricultural strategies can also be seen in the co-operative sector. In France, in the Lorraine valley, for example, the co-operatives have opted for an industrial rather than an agro-food strategy for the region's agriculture. When, as in this case, the stimulus to innovation comes from the agricultural sector, novel institutional arrangements are required. The programme to produce lactoserum sub-products for industrial use therefore has led to the formation of a consortium between the co-operatives, specialised biotechnology firms, regional industrialists, and the University Biotechnology Institute. Regional growth strategies have a similar dynamic. In the case of Picardy, the product specificities of the region's agriculture have been subsumed within the Glucides Development Centre (Centre de Valorisation des Glucides), which groups together the region's major agricultural associations, agro-industries and university departments.

New agriculture-industry relations are therefore emerging which reflect processes of positive adjustment rather than defensive reactions of sectoral interests. The European Commission has contributed to this development by resisting pressures to establish a broad ethanol programme or to undertake an animal feeds import substitution programme based on support for amino-acids R&D. Instead, the series of research funding programmes which have emerged from the Commission's Biotechnology Concertation Unit (BAP, ELATRE, ECLAIRE) have placed emphasis on the development of non-traditional, high value agricultural and agro-industrial products.

As these emerging patterns of innovation and industrial re-organisation demonstrate, biotechnologies are radically transforming downstream production processes which determine how agricultural crops are integrated into food manufacturing. The diversification strategies pursued by traditional product complexes or previously highly specialised firms, such as Tate & Lyle or Ferruzzi, are themselves testimony to the strength of the new technological forces at work, creating new by-products and entirely new sectors. As this process of implosion removes long-standing barriers, the agro-food system gradually will merge with the chemical and pharmaceutical industries to form a 'bio-industrial processing complex'.

Plant biotechnologies and agro-chemicals

Recent acquisitions of seed firms and plant genetic research companies by large chemical and pharmaceutical corporations represent a further important dimension of the restructuring of the agro-food system by bio-technologies. As we see below, these take-overs are accompanied by varying patterns of R&D organisation. This acquisition strategy recognises that the seed is central to the marketing of the new plant biotechnologies. Indeed, newly-established biotechnology research firms, such as Calgene and Plant Genetics, also have acquired seed companies for distribution purposes. In addition, as in the earlier case of hybrids, control over the technology incorporated in the seed can be used to extend markets for inorganic agro-chemicals. Alternatively, such firms will be well-positioned if research into biological nitrogen fixation and biological pest- and disease-resistance proves commercially exploitable.

The defensive characteristics of these acquisitions are well documented, especially the possibility of developing plant varieties that are resistant to proprietary agro-chemicals, thereby increasing their sales. A precautionary motive also appears to be a factor in the acquisition of seed and plant genetic firms since multinational agro-chemical companies obtain scarce plant biotechnological R&D capacity and can step up their involvement if the rate of innovation accelerates and generates commercial products. Such long-term considerations undoubtedly offer some explanation for these acquisitions since profitability levels in the seed industry are notoriously low. Indeed, some insiders privately doubt that the multinationals will see a return on their investment.

Nevertheless, whether for precautionary reasons or otherwise, there has been a competitive scramble to take over seed companies. For example, ICI embarked on this course in 1985 when it acquired Garst Seeds and further acquisitions, including Sinclair McGill and Société Européenne de Semences (SES), have since taken it into the top ten world seed producers, joining its major multinational competitors, such as Monsanto, Ciba-Geigy, Shell and Sandoz. Unilever has followed this example by purchasing the Plant Breeding Institute at Cambridge after its privatisation by the British government in 1988. The restructuring of the seed industry has been accompanied by a parallel round of take-overs in agro-chemicals, raising concentration levels in this industry. Again using ICI as an example, in June 1987 it acquired Stauffer Chemicals, taking ICI to third place in world agro-chemical sales behind Bayer and Ciba-Geigy. This acquisition drew the comment that 'For ICI and its rivals, the aim is to create an agricultural package reaching from fertilisers through pesticides to the plant itself, which can be tailor-made through genetic manipulation to fit the maker's system and no one else's' (Lex, Financial Times, 13 June 1987). While that still remains a long-term prospect, major chemical and pharmaceutical firms are aware of the restructuring potential of plant biotechnologies, and hence the need to establish a general competence in the main fields of application, particularly if these are the companies' core business sectors.

Food manufacturing

We have suggested that the final food sector increasingly has become demand-orientated, prompting firms to move towards more dynamic higher value-added product lines to counter the general stagnation of markets for mass produced foods. One important dimension of this change is the closer identification of food with 'nutrition' and 'health', which confers qualities more usually associated with pharmaceuticals than food products. Growing attention is devoted to the constituents of food (calories, proteins, cholesterol, fibre content, etc) and to the inputs used in processing. This changing conception of food has been met by advances in fractionation/reconstitution methods and the growth of the new intermediates sector to supply 'natural' food additives and bio-industrial foods, such as myco-protein. With the slow growth of total food consumption, the capacity to respond to changing demand patterns is an important source of competitive advantage, which favours larger science-based companies in an industry traditionally known for its low ratio of research expenditure to turnover.

The blurring of divisions between food, new intermediate inputs, especially organoleptic substances, and pharmaceutical products can also be seen in the entry of large food companies, such as Nestlé and Unilever, into health products, cosmetics and perfumes. On the demand side, the cosmetics industry also has experienced the same shift in consumer attitudes as food manufacturing to give preference to biological rather than chemical inputs. This sector therefore is an inviting target for agro-food firms with a scientific base in biotechnology, particularly since it involves a move into a high value product sector. Such moves by final food manufacturers into non-food sectors are in response to scientific/technological and final demand synergies. Fermentation food firms, such as Kirin and Bass, also are diversifying into pharmaceuticals. A related trend is the development of transgenic animals to supply medical products. Researchers at the Institute of Animal Physiology in Edinburgh, for example, have transferred new genetic material into sheep which produce valuable molecules in their milk for use in the pharmaceutical industry.

These patterns of innovation in food manufacturing again emphasise how the new biotechnology-centred research base is integrating this sector into a wider bio-industrial system, where distinctions between food and non-food sectors become progressively blurred. As this new technological base restructures the agro-food system, breaking down historical barriers of specialisation, it is falling under the domination of chemical and pharmaceutical companies, a process especially evident in the downstream food sectors. The enhanced importance of R&D, a relatively neglected activity in the food industry, is the main vehicle of this growing ascendancy as advances in industrial microbiology increase the transferability of both feedstocks and process engineering between the different segments of the new bio-industry.

Public and private spheres in biotechnology R&D

The development of 'the toolkit' of genetic engineering, which permitted the commercial exploitation of advances in molecular genetics, occurred in the early 1970s when such research was overwhelmingly concentrated in the universities. As industrial corporations became aware of its potential, these origins of commercial biotechnologies had a profound effect on the structure of the nascent biotechnology industry. The initial firms in this industry, especially in the United States, were small, specialised research companies, frequently established by university researchers, whose heavy R&D financing needs and the lengthy gap between laboratory trials and marketable products made it difficult to resist linkages with larger corporations. As we have seen, these corporations have strategic reasons for gaining access to biotechnology R&D, whether actively to extend their core businesses or to retain a 'window' on a new field of innovation.

The modes of entry used by large multinational chemical and pharmaceutical companies vary but principally they reflect the financial weakness of the new biotechnology research firms and their limited manufacturing facilities and marketing networks. These modes include outright acquisition of genetics research companies, equity participation, the formation of joint ventures and limited R&D partnerships, investment via private venture capital firms, funding university contract research, and creation of in-house R&D capacity (Goodman, Sorj and Wilkinson, 1987). A number of companies have adopted these strategies concurrently. Since the October 1987 stock market crash, 'strategic alliances' between large corporations and small biotechnology firms have been more widely used as a mechanism for financing R&D . These patterns characterise all the main fields of biotechnology – agriculture, food, chemicals, therapeutics, environmental protection – and not just plant biotechnologies on which we are focusing.

> The evidence that the logic of biotechnological innovation...is shifting the centre of gravity overwhelmingly in favour of multinational and 'Fortune 500' corporations is inescapable....The large corporations...now dominate commercial biotechnology and, increasingly, the direction of fundamental research. This domination...extends across the board in the biosciences...(*Ibid*, p. 110)

In a recent paper, Walker (1989) identifies some striking differences in the integration of agri-biotechnology into corporate strategies in Europe and the United States. The agri-biotechnology sector in the US, as in other segments of the industry there, is characterised by numerous small specialist start-up companies, although several major US corporations, such as Monsanto and Du Pont, have strong in-house R&D facilities. However, the start-up firms possess only a limited capacity to fund long-term R&D independently and to distribute new products as innovations reach the market place. Large European corporations have exploited these structural weaknesses to take over agri-biotechnology firms and seed companies and to establish strategic alliances, which give access to on-going R&D via contract research and marketing franchises. Recent alliances include Ciba Geigy/Agri-Diagnostics, Rhone-Poulenc/Calgene and Roussel Uclaf/Calgene. This ease of entry to US biotechnology R&D has allowed European and Japanese corporations to diversify their interests with a relatively limited expenditure, raising fears in the United States that technological leadership in second generation products and processes will be lost (Burrill, 1989; Dibner, 1989). Strategic alliances have increased since 'Black Monday' in October 1987, which reduced the availability of capital for US start-up firms, and European corporations have seized the opportunity to become important financiers of US biotechnology R&D.

At the same time, Western Europe has impressive public sector research institutions in agri-biotechnology and national governments actively promote public-private sector R&D links, as we have seen. Walker (1989) argues that this state-of-the-art research capacity is complemented by the overwhelming weight of large companies in the European agri-biotechnology sector.

> This lack of start-ups should not be seen as a weakness, rather a strength: external companies have limited access to European expertise, as most of it is jealously guarded by its large corporate owners. These corporations represent powerful players. They include Bayer, Ciba Geigy and ICI, the world's three largest agri-chemical companies...large agribusiness corporations such as Unilever and Nestlé, and major chemical companies, such as Rhone-Poulenc, Montedison, Shell, Hoechst and Enichem. (*Ibid*, p. 123)

These same corporations, as noted previously, have led successive waves of acquisitions in the seed industry. Although the top dozen companies, all multinationals, currently control only 13 per cent of the US$26 billion world commercial seed market, Kidd (1987, p. 8) believes that

...by the year 2000 between 10–20 multinational-owned seed and plant biotechnology companies will dominate the most profitable, research-intensive segments of the seed trade.

Walker (1989) suggests that the agro-chemical-seed nexus created by European companies has given them the lead in agri-biotechnology, which is being explicitly applied to increase their competitiveness in these core businesses. In contrast, plant biotechnologies in the United States are seen more as an investment opportunity for start-up firms and venture capitalists, while the large chemical companies oscillate between strong in-house R&D capacity (Monsanto) and reliance on contract research and licensing agreements, as in the case of American Cyanamid (Walker, 1989).

The rise to pre-eminence of multinational corporations has been associated with significant changes in the dividing line separating public and private research (Munton, Marsden and Whatmore: chapter 5). This is exemplified by the extensive and varied corporate-university links, including contract research and the formation of research 'clubs' and consortia embracing private industry, universities and public research institutes. In OECD countries, such institutional mechanisms play a major part in the science and technology policies of governments anxious not to fall behind in the race to develop commercial technologies. For example, in the early 1980s, the British Technology Group, formerly the National Research Development Corporation, set up two commercial companies, Celltech and the Agricultural Genetics Company (AGC), to commercialise public sector research and to manage contract research. Celltech and the AGC were given first refusal to all biotechnological research undertaken by the Medical Research Council and six leading centres of the Agricultural and Food Research Council, respectively. Shareholders in the AGC include Ultramar, Ciba-Geigy, Eli Lilly and venture capital groups, such as the Rothschild Trust's Biotechnology Investments. By establishing joint ventures with Celltech or the AGC to develop and market selected product or process innovations, industrial companies can secure access to biotechnology research expertise for a relatively modest outlay.

In plant biotechnologies, there is widespread concern that the activities of large corporations will eclipse the public research system in the development of new varieties, even when this capacity is not crippled, as in the British case, by expenditure cuts, closures and privatisation. In the United States, Kenney and colleagues (1983, p. 486) argue that

> ...the high capital intensity of biotechnology-related plant breeding will render public breeding technologically antiquated *vis-à-vis* its more adequately funded counterpart in the private sector.

Private firms will increasingly dictate the research agenda on the frontiers of plant breeding, and hence the future applications of plant biotechnologies, whether to 'patch-up' the present agro-chemical model, to support more sustainable systems or to give weight to Third World priorities, such as improving crop yields in resource-poor environments (Redclift: chapter 4).

The growing strength of large industrial corporations in plant biotechnologies and the seed industry has brought vigorous demands that patent protection be extended to plant varieties developed by genetic engineering. Companies meanwhile are exploring the advantages of trade secret protection as an alternative to patenting in view of the present confused state of international patent legislation. These pressures, which reflect the different ethos of public and private research, have led one director of an international agricultural research centre to lament 'the growing secrecy attached to biotechnological research because of commercial considerations' (Swaminathan, 1982, p. 39). Farmers similarly will feel more vulnerable as private companies consolidate their control over varietal improvement. The transfer mechanisms which are used to disseminate the new plant biotechnologies to the Third World clearly will depend on how this control is exercised and the institutional arrangements in force to protect intellectual property.

In this respect, very significant differences in organisational forms of technology transfer inevitably will emerge for the new plant biotechnologies compared with the earlier innovations of the Green Revolution. The latter originated in the public research system in the United States and were disseminated internationally through the multilaterally-funded CGIAR system of international agricultural research centres (IARCs) and their national counterparts in the developing countries. The diffusion of the US technology model, adapting plant breeding techniques to tropical and sub-tropical environments, was achieved by replicating the corresponding institutional model, based on public research and extension systems. The increasing control and internalisation of pure science research and applied plant breeding by large industrial corporations, epitomised by changing public-private sector relations and new complementary institutional mechanisms, suggest that the transfer of plant biotechnologies will be dictated primarily by commercial interest. These changes will lead to pressure for the re-definition of the IARC system, including demands that basic research and the breeding of finished varieties be left to the private sector, confining the IARCs increasingly to the diffusion process and the collection and conservation of germ plasm. In this context, developments in patenting policy and the current GATT discussions on intellectual property rights assume great significance.

Concern about obstacles to technology transfer in the intensely competitive, increasingly commercial world of biotechnology is a major factor underlying the UNIDO initiative to establish an International Centre for Genetic Engineering and Biotechnology. Although seen as a positive step by Third World governments to counter efforts by OECD states and multinational corporations to restrict the transfer of biotechnologies, some observers doubt that the new centre can repeat the role played by the IARCs in the Green Revolution (Busch and Lacy, 1986). There also is scepticism that developing countries have the resources, scientific cadres and infrastructure of equipment supply companies necessary to sustain an independent research effort that can keep pace with innovation in OECD countries. Even in relation to tissue culture technologies, let alone genetic engineering, Busch and Lacy (1986, p. 20) argue that

> Only a handful of developing countries will be able to afford to create a critical mass of scientists in this area.

Given the enormous potential of plant biotechnologies to redefine comparative advantage in agriculture, for example, through import substitution in temperate OECD countries or by *in vitro* production, the organisational forms of technology transfer will have a considerable impact on economic growth and welfare in developing countries. As in the case of information technologies, it is not surprising that leading developing countries, notably Brazil and India, are pursuing policies to overcome perceived constraints on the international transfer of biotechnologies.

Conclusion

This discussion has examined the tensions and possible trajectories of the agro-food system created by current trends in research and innovation. Biotechnologies are the critical catalytic force in this transformation, which is redefining the agriculture-food-industry nexus. The potential of biotechnologies to transcend species barriers is accompanied by a related capacity to overcome industrial barriers to entry between hitherto separate sectors. We have seen that transnational chemical and pharmaceutical firms now dominate biotechnology research on a global scale and increasingly are involved in producing intermediate and final products for the food industry. Concomitantly, leading food processors are diversifying into non-food outlets for agricultural produce. These developments foreshadow the growth of a generic bio-industry based on inputs and technologies equally applicable to food and non-food products (Wilkinson, 1987).

An important corollary is that the relative exclusiveness of different eco-systems, which historically has often imparted geographical specificity to agro-industrial organisation, also is threatened by biotechnologies. The current structural reorganisation of agriculture-industry relations therefore also implies a global geographical realignment as, for example, between temperate and tropical agriculture. This redefinition of the international division of labour is not reducible to a shift in North-South relations but rather corresponds to the rise of new strategic actors and new centres of demand in Europe, Japan, and middle-income, newly industrialising countries. Their emergence challenges US hegemony and points towards a more pluralistic organisation of the global food system.

We would argue, therefore, that the analysis of innovation patterns and the strategies of transnational firms must be situated within a systemic view of the global transformations in agricultural production and food consumption. In the changing mode of integration of agriculture into industrial production, characterised by a new technological paradigm and new consumption patterns, the distinction between food and non-food agricultural products is rapidly losing its relevance. Current analytical models, whether based on the agro-industrial complex or food system approaches, no longer capture the dynamic behind the restructuring now underway.

References

Berlan, J-P, and Lewontin, R. (1986) Breeders' rights and patenting life forms, *Nature*, 322, 28 August, 785–88.

Burrill, G. S. (1989) Biotechnology – a worldwide perspective, *BIOTECH '89* (Pinner, UK, Blenheim Online Ltd), 1–6.

Busch, L. and Lacy, W. B. (1986) Biotechnology: its potential impact on interrelationships among agriculture, industry and society. Paper presented at the Symposium on Biotechnology and the Food Supply, The Food and Nutrition Board, National Research Council.

Busch, L., Bonnano, A. and Lacy, W. B. (1989) Science, technology, and the restructuring of agriculture, *Sociologia Ruralis*, Vol. 29 (2), 118–130.

Buttel, F. H. and Busch, L. (1988) The public research system at the crossroads, *Agricultural History*, Vol. 62 (2), 303–24.

Cormack, C. A. (1987) New EEC legislation on agricultural raw materials for biotechnology, *BIOTECH '87* (Pinner, UK, Online Publications), 9–14.

Dibner, M. (1989) Biotechnology in the United States and Japan: strategies and trends, *BIOTECH '89* (Pinner, UK, Blenheim Online Ltd), 7–13.

Goodman, D., Sorj, B. and Wilkinson, J. (1987) *From Farming to Biotechnology*. Oxford, Blackwells.

Kenney, M., Kloppenburg, Jr., J., Buttel, F. H. and Cowan, J. T. (1983) Genetic engineering and agriculture: socioeconomic aspects of biotechnology R and D in developed and developing countries, *BIOTECH '83* (Northwood, UK, Online Publications), 475–89.

Kidd, G. H. (1987) Macroeconomics of seed and plant biotechnology in the 1990s *BIOTECH '87* (Pinner, UK, Online Publications), 1–8.

Office of Technology Assessment (OTA) (1981) *Impacts of Applied Genetics*. Washington, DC, US Congress.

Swaminathan , M. S. (1982) Perspectives in biotechnology research from the point of view of developing countries, in *Priorities in Biotechnology Research for International Development*. Washington DC, National Research Council.

Thompson, F. M. L. (1968) The second agricultural revolution, *Economic History Review*, Vol. 21 (1).

Walker, A. (1989) Europe steals the lead in plant biotechnology, *BIOTECH '89* (Pinner, UK, Blenheim Online Publications), 121–128.

Wilkinson, J. (1987) *Europe within the World Food system: Biotechnologies and New Strategic Options*. FAST Exploratory Dossier, DGXII/122/87-EN. Brussels, Commission of the European Communities.

CHAPTER 7

New Technologies in the Agro-Food System and US-EC Trade Relations

W. Jos Byman

Introduction

New technologies, especially biotechnologies, are confidently expected to provide solutions for many of the problems of contemporary agriculture, such as overproduction and environmental pollution. Efforts are made, therefore, to be the first to apply them and to come out of the technology race as the most competitive producer. At the same time these technologies are changing the whole structure of the production and processing of agricultural products, accelerating the internationalisation of the agro-food system[1] and transforming the traditional relationship between farmers and agribusiness. Established agricultural policy, which is based on that relationship, is seriously challenged, too. The eventual outcome of this process of restructuring is hard to predict, but some key trends can be distinguished, not least in relation to international trade.

World agricultural production increased substantially during the 1970s, but international trade in farm products expanded even more rapidly. In the 1980s, the rapid trade growth faltered, while production and productivity continued to grow apace. The result was serious overproduction in some major exporting countries, particularly the United States. But while the US share of world agricultural exports decreased in the 1980s, competitors like the European Community (EC), Argentina and Canada actually expanded their share. A serious domestic farm crisis together with this loss of world market share revived the traditional aversion in the US against the Common Agricultural Policy (CAP) of the European Community. The policy – at one and the same time protectionist and expansionist – was portrayed as a major cause of American agricultural trade problems. The US took several steps to show its contempt for the CAP, both unilaterally and by way of complaints to the GATT dispute settlement panels, but with little success. For the US, with its large trade deficit, agricultural exports will continue to be very important for the economy as a whole, while in the EC, the change from being a net-importer to a net-exporter has led to the formulation of a more explicit export policy. Continued conflict seems inevitable, and new technologies are likely to cause a further strain on this trade relationship, as self-sufficiency is enhanced, interchangeability of agricultural products is increased, and agricultural and industrial products are substituted.

This chapter will assess the impact of new technologies on the agro-food system in the US and the EC and the consequences for the trade relationship between them. First, the structural changes taking place in the agricultural sector are discussed. As agriculture is just one part of the larger agro-food system, the characteristics of this system are then described, and the place of new technologies, particularly biotechnologies, in its different parts is assessed. The consequences are then considered for the structure of the agro-food system and for agricultural policy. Finally, we turn to the internationalisation of agriculture and the future of US-EC trade conflicts.

Structural change and the policy crisis in agriculture

During the last 50 years, the agricultural sector has gone through a series of structural changes. The most important and most striking development has been the reduction in labour input. In 1960 5.46 million people were employed in US agriculture (8.3% of total civilian employment); by 1985 the number had declined to 3.18 million (3.0% of total civilian employment). In the EC this decline was even more dramatic: from 18.89 million (18.4%) in 1960 to 7.67 million (7.2%) in 1985 (Newman *et al.*, 1987).

A decline in the agricultural workforce was necessary for the expansion of industrial production. In post-war Europe this transfer of labour from agriculture to manufacturing was promoted by government policies, with productivity growth in agriculture being a major determinant of the growth of the economy as a whole. Application of new technologies greatly increased land and labour productivity. In particular the mechanisation of agriculture in the 1940s, 1950s and 1960s and the large scale use of chemicals from the 1950s onward greatly enhanced agricultural production on a fixed land base.

One of the most characteristic features of the changing structure of agricultural production has been the trend towards larger but fewer farms: their numbers have rapidly declined since the 1940s, both in the US and the EC. Although this trend has slowed down since the 1970s, there is every reason to expect it to continue in the coming decades. Of course there are considerable differences between the structure of agricultural production in the US and the EC, and even within the EC between northern and southern member states. But, in general, the trend toward an enlargement of farms can be seen everywhere. In the US the number of farms reached a peak of about 6.8 million in 1935; by 1982 it had fallen to approximately 2.2 million (US Congress, 1986).

Projections of structural change in US agriculture to the year 2000 show a further decline, to just 1.2 million. These projections indicate a bimodal distribution of the remaining farms – a large proportion of small and part-time farmers, an increasing proportion of large farms, and a sharply declining number of moderate-sized units (US Congress, 1986). The financial outlook for the last group – the typical American family farm – remains gloomy. An important implication is the further concentration of the income to the farming sector. Between 1969 and 1982 the share of total farm income going to large farms grew steadily from 51 to 84 per cent. If this trend continues, over 90 per cent of net farm income will be earned by farms with sales over $200,000 by the year 2000. By that year the 50,000 largest farms (sales over $500,000) will probably produce 75 per cent of all farm products.

Conceivably, a decline in the number of farmers might ease the trade conflicts between the US and the EC, if pressures from farming interest groups on national policy makers were to diminish accordingly. As the number of farmers decreases, however, total production will not necessarily diminish. Such overproduction leads not only to international conflicts but also to environmental and social problems within the major producing countries. Indeed, the structural crisis in agriculture has provoked a policy crisis, as solutions to these problems cannot easily be found. A major aspect of this crisis is the high cost of agricultural policies (Goodman and Redclift, 1989).

Both in the US and the EC the costs of agricultural policy rapidly increased in the 1980s. Between 1982 and 1987 government outlays for agriculture more than doubled on both sides of the Atlantic, from around £12 billion to more than $25 billion (Newman, *et al.*, 1987). Since income is guaranteed by minimum prices or by deficiency payments, falling market prices have led to higher government payments. The faster growth of production over demand, moreover, results in high costs for the storage of surpluses and for export subsidies.

Although US outlays were considerably lower than EC payments during the 1970s, in recent years they have converged. There is, however, a difference in the kind of payments. About two-thirds of US expenditure is on grains, with an additional 9 per cent on dairy. In contrast, the EC spends only 15 per cent of its agricultural outlays on grains but 40 per cent on beef and dairy products. Export refunds cost the EC $5.1 billion in 1985 rising to $8.5 billion in 1986 (Newman *et al.*, 1987, p. 52). A 30 per cent fall in the value of the dollar and lower world market prices, resulting from lower US loan rates and the US Export Enhancement Program (EEP), contributed substantially to these costs.

The high budgetary costs of agricultural support programmes have led to serious criticism of the financial viability of current agricultural policy from other sectors of the economy and from politicians of all parties. With pressures generally to curb budget deficits, agricultural policy cannot escape cuts in its outlays. In the EC the ever growing cost of the CAP is straining the development of other sectors where common policies need to be designed and implemented. In the US the outlays for agriculture have come under severe scrutiny from those concerned about the huge budget deficit. Likewise, in the EC steps have recently been taken to restrict the growing costs of agricultural policy. In November 1987 the US Congress and the Administration reached agreement on a reduction of the budget deficit: outlays for agriculture were to be cut by $2 billion. In the EC, the European Council (bringing together the government leaders of member states) reached agreement on a package of measures to restrict the cost of the CAP in order to overcome the financial problems of the EC.

Still these measures are only minor steps in solving the major problems of agriculture, both at the farm level and at the policy-making level. Other solutions are expected to come from technological development and from trade liberalisation. To understand why these routes are being promoted, we must first describe the agro-food system, in the context of which the interests that promote rapid technological development and free trade can be distinguished.

The agro-food system

Changes in production practices brought about by technological change, though often introduced to cut costs, have led nevertheless to increased production expenses as a proportion of gross farm income. In the 1940s, roughly 50 per cent of gross farm income was allocated to purchases of livestock, feed, seed, fertilisers, depreciation, hired labour, repairs, taxes, interest on farm mortgage debt, and rent to landlords. In the 1970s, farmers spent nearly 70 per cent of their gross income on these items (ERS/USDA 1986). A growing inputs supplying industry was the major recipient of this spending. That and the other industries in the agro-food system have grown, both in absolute and relative terms, with farming itself taking a decreasing share. In 1982, farming in the US accounted for only about 11 per cent of the agro-food system's contribution to GNP (Penn, 1985).

This increasing integration of farming into the economy as a whole means that factors affecting the costs of inputs greatly affect net farm income. It also means that the inputs and processing industry have an interest in the continuing expansion of agricultural production. Growth in the inputs industry, for example, can only be realised if the farmer expands his production by using more inputs, or if he uses more sophisticated inputs.

Other factors also encourage expansion (Hoogh, 1987). First, the condition of perfect competition in agricultural production makes farmers very susceptible to new production techniques that lower production costs and enhance productivity, even if this leads to oversupply at the aggregate level. With its extensive research and development in productivity increasing technology, the inputs industry has a large stimulating effect on agricultural production. Secondly, the farmers themselves are a powerful group who have used their influence to obtain favourable agricultural policies. The main mechanism in these policies is income support by way of price guarantees, but such price support is unable to avoid oversupply, and increases rather than diminishes market instability. Thirdly, the food processing industry is becoming highly concentrated, and, in a context of inelastic demand, uses its economic power to market ever new food products manufactured from an abundant supply of raw materials. Fourthly, the public agencies, in particular the national departments of agriculture, have always favoured production and productivity growth. Through agricultural research and extension, all kinds of infrastructural provisions and tax policy, national governments have many instruments by which to foster domestic agricultural production. Departments of agriculture in most industrialised countries are, indeed, 'captive' agencies of the farming lobby.

This agro-industrial complex is not homogeneous. Already the farm sector and agricultural policy are in crisis. New technologies will not only reinforce these crises but will also alter the relationships between the different sectors of the agro-food system. And of all the new high technologies that are being developed, biotechnology will have the most far-reaching effect on the agro-food system, its individual sectors and the links between them (Goodman and Wilkinson: chapter 6).

With biotechnology one of the new 'core' technologies, the so-called technology race among industrialised countries (Tulder and Junne, 1988) will inevitably also encompass the agro-food system (and therefore agriculture). In this race each country stimulates its 'national' industries through specific industrial and technology policies, and considerable subsidies are often given to promising high technology industries. These new technologies are heralded as the solutions to all kinds of problems, related to the growth model that dominated the post-war period of rapid economic expansion. Since the 1970s, the model has been in crisis, beset by so-called control problems (Roobeek, 1986), including rising wages, a decline in productivity growth, overcapacity and overproduction, and environmental pollution. The new technologies are expected to provide answers to all these problems. At the same time, however, they help undermine the current structure of economic and political relations, and while not the prime cause of structural change, they do accelerate the process (Roobeek, 1986). Indeed, despite the fact that technological change has been a major factor in agriculture's oversupply problems, it is now being blithely suggested that new technologies can correct these very problems.

The impact of new technologies on different sectors of the agro-food system

Farming

The impact of biotechnologies on structural change is most obvious in the farming sector itself. According to Buttel (1986) the new biotechnologies will deepen the pattern of structural change in US agriculture, owing to three main factors.

(1) The new biotechnologies will, on the whole, be relatively capital intensive, meaning that they will be made available to farmers as relatively expensive proprietary inputs, which will be most readily afforded by larger operators.

(2)   Biotechnologies will tend to be very management-intensive: farmers with specialised operations and with superior management ability and access to information and data processing will be able to utilise them most effectively.

(3)   The new biotechnologies will tend to increase output and will, like most earlier new technologies, tend to result in a downward pressure on commodity prices.

Change in the structure of agricultural production will continue, in much the same direction, towards a bimodal model with many very small sub-commercial part-time farmers on one side and very big family proprietorships on the other. Large corporations will probably remain detached from the direct production of most agricultural products. After all, they control the input and processing phases of the agro-food system, and, as Buttel has commented, 'the way to make money in agriculture will continue to be selling inputs to and merchandising the output from farmers, rather than farming itself' (1986, p. 21). While farming will thus remain largely the preserve of family producers, their increasingly dependent position within the agro-food system makes them vulnerable to technological change in other parts of the system.

The input sector

On the input side the most interesting development is the integration of the seed industry in multinational (petro)chemical and pharmaceutical companies brought about by a number of factors (Buttel *et al.*, 1984). One is the traditionally close relationship between the agro-chemical and seed industries. Seedsmen, with their more valuable crops, use fertilisers, pesticides and fungicides in the production process with a greater intensity than does the average farmer: chemicals have been seen as a solution to problems that were regarded as insoluble by plant breeders. A second factor is that the distribution and sales channels for fertilisers, pesticides and herbicides are much the same as those for seeds; and close cooperation between the seed and chemical industries increases distribution efficiency. A third, and very important, reason is the development of new biotechnologies.

The importance of the agricultural market for biotechnology – 25 to 40 per cent of total sales by the year 2000 (Ayers and Greer, 1984) – has been recognised by petro chemical and pharmaceutical companies. The chemical industry was particularly looking for new ways to make profits, with established markets for bulk chemical products becoming stagnant. In order to obtain the necessary know-how, leading chemical companies have taken over or established a close relationship (via venture capital) with small biotechnology research firms (mainly in the US) or have themselves set up biotechnology research units (in Europe). To improve their access to and control over the agricultural market they have also acquired seed firms. This process of integration has been fostered by the strong financial position of the chemical industry on the one hand and the need of the seed business, on the other, for strong financial backing to pursue expensive biotechnology research.

With the development and application of biotechnology the boundaries between chemical and biological inputs in agriculture are dissolving. A company supplying both seed and pesticides can link these products in such a way that the farmer who buys the seed also has to buy a particular pesticide. Input industries will thus sell seed and chemicals packages to farmers. The link between seed and pesticide, established in the seed breeding stage, is of strategic importance for the chemical industry, because the patents of most of the major agro-chemicals will expire in a few years. As other companies can then provide these products, the original suppliers are looking for new ways to make money with their old products, and a proprietary combination of chemicals and seeds is seen to offer one such opportunity (Ruivenkamp, 1987).

This link does not always lead to the most socially and environmentally favourable solutions. While biotechnology holds the prospect of using fewer chemicals because it can make plants more resistant to pests, the current orientation of research could lead to more, not less use of agro-chemicals. In the US, for example, the biotechnology firm Calgene is doing research on herbicide resistance in tobacco. The goal is to make tobacco and other commercial crops fully resistant to the herbicide Roundup, produced by Monsanto, to allow farmers to spray any amount of it on their fields. The Belgian biotechnology firm Plant Genetic Systems is following the same path, trying to make plants resistant to the often used herbicide Basta, produced by the German chemical company Hoechst.

The food industry

The food industry is the traditional processor of farm products. Therefore the relationship between the farmer and the food industry has always been very close. Many food manufacturing industries were originally set up as co-operatives by farmers. The starting point in the relationship traditionally was the farmer. This means that the food industry was processing what the farmer produced, instead of the farmer producing what the food industry demanded. This relationship is now changing, with biotechnologies speeding up and shaping this change.

Together with information technology and membrane technology (new materials), applications of biotechnology will structurally change the food processing industry itself. The industry is the oldest and largest applier of biotechnology. In the production of staple foods like bread and cheese, micro-organisms such as yeast and lactic acid bacteria have been used for centuries, as far back as the ancient Egyptians. Their discovery, of course, was a matter of trial and error.

A characteristic of the new biotechnology, however, is the ability to manipulate micro-organisms to improve their performance. In this way production processes can be better controlled and thus become more efficient and cheaper. Also a whole range of new products can be designed and manufactured by way of biotechnology. The significance for the food industry can be gauged from the fact that virtually all of the world's top fifty food firms are now involved in biotechnology research.

Wilkinson (1987, p. 21) stresses five characteristics that together make biotechnologies the strategic technologies for the future of the agro-food system:

(i) biotechnologies will increasingly redefine existing purification, extraction, filtration and preservation technologies;
(ii) they facilitate and accelerate the move to automated production;
(iii) they break down the integrated chain of production uniting specific agricultural inputs with final food products;
(iv) they open the perspective for the assimilation of food production within broader industrial structures defined by common technology and inputs (e.g. biomass/hydrocarbon, fermentation/bioreactor);
(v) they represent at the level of production process an appropriate response to new patterns of demand which view food increasingly as nutrition, itself a reflection of the societal impact of advances in the life sciences.

Characteristics (iii) and (iv) will be discussed in more detail below. They cannot, in any case, be viewed independently from developments in the chemical industry, to which we now turn.

The chemical industry

The chemical industry – taken to include petrochemicals and pharmaceuticals as well as other chemicals – is of strategic importance for the agro-food system. As Figure 7.1 shows, the chemical industry has traditionally held strong relationships with the different industries in the agro-food system. In the inputs sector it provides agro-chemicals, energy and fertilisers. Veterinary health products as well as additives for animal feed are supplied to the farming sector. The primary processing industry provides feedstocks to the (bio)chemical industry. And in the final food production stage, the chemical industry supplies additives and vitamins.

Figure 7.1 The role of the chemical industry in the agro-food system

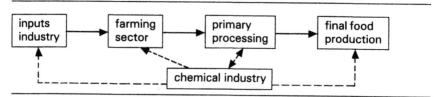

Although most food manufacturing companies are now engaged in biotechnology research, most of the new biotechnologies are and will be developed in the chemical industry and in small biotechnology research companies. Because the latter depend on the former for upscaling and marketing of their inventions, it is the chemical industry which is of most interest (Wilkinson, 1987).

In the petrochemical industry it was the development of bioproteins – Single Cell Proteins (SCP) – on the one hand and biomass on the other hand that first led this industry into biotechnology. Bioproteins can be seen as an attempt to valorise existing petrochemical raw materials through the development of co-products. Biomass was seen as an alternative energy feedstock, which becomes important with depleting or more expensive fossil energy sources. Although the production of bioproteins and the transformation of biomass is only taking place in pilot plants, their commercial possibilites and strategic significance for technology development are both very important. Nowadays, biomass is not only considered important as an alternative energy source, but also as an alternative feedstock for the production of chemicals.

The shift from bulk to speciality chemicals and the diversification of inputs have, likewise, coincided with a move into biotechnologies. Although in some parts of the chemical industry biotechnology has been used for a long time (biochemical industry), the prospect of a larger range of raw materials (both biomass and energy feedstocks) and the production of speciality chemicals by way of tissue and cell culture have opened the way to new production processes and new products, and therefore new opportunities for growth and profit. The production of intermediates by way of biotechnology processes is a very important growth sector. Examples are biopolymers for biodegradable plastics and amino acids for food and feed production.

In the pharmaceutical industry, biotechnology will provide substitutes for increasingly scarce animal and plant raw material and will be a source of new products: for example, interferon, diagnostic kits.

In the petrochemical, chemical and pharmaceutical industries, in short,

> Biotechnology becomes a component of industrial strategy respectively with regard to valorisation/substitution of raw materials, production of intermediates, and the production of new products. While fermentation/bioreactor technology is common to all, specialised expertise in microbial and plant biology corresponds to the petrochemicals strategy, enzyme technology to that of chemicals and genetic engineering in the case of pharmaceuticals. (Wilkinson, 1987, p. 24)

Biotechnology in the agro-food system as a whole and the implications for agricultural policy

Not only are new product and production processes being developed across the agro-food system, but as biotechnologies in the various sectors of the system become of strategic importance, the relationships between sectors are changing fundamentally. It becomes increasingly difficult to distinguish between different stages of production of the constituents that make up the final food or chemical product. At the industry level, these different stages can more easily be integrated in the same company.

The relationship between the chemical and the food industry is being qualitatively modified with the introduction of biotechnology. Since the basic technology is the same for both industries, it is of strategic importance for companies in both sectors to become involved in the other sector as well.

At the same time, the position of the farming sector in the agro-food system is no longer clear. Farm products are used as feedstocks for the chemical industry, as biomass for the petrochemical industry (bio-ethanol), and as raw material for the primary processing part of the food industry. The farming sector is thus getting squeezed between the inputs and processing sectors. On the one hand, the incorporation of the seed business within the chemical industry transforms farming itself into a downstream activity (Kloppenburg, 1988). On the other hand, the traditional relationship between agriculture and the food industry, where the latter was buyer and processor of the products of the former, will be changed into a relationship where the farmer produces what the (primary) processing industry demands. If the inputs supplying sector and the processing sector of the agro-food system become incorporated in one company, which is increasingly happening, the farmer completely loses his independence, becoming little more than an extension of the chemical/food industry.

The interchangeability of all kinds of agricultural products at the level of primary processing, particularly of different sources of carbohydrates like starch and sugar, but also vegetable oils, will increase the competition between farmers from different regions, and different countries. If agricultural products are used as a feedstock in the (bio)chemical industry, no longer is the type of carbohydrate so important, only the price of the raw material. Besides, former farm products can now be manufactured industrially, by way of cell and tissue cultures in bioreactors. Certain low volume/high price products are already being produced along this biotechnology route. Although this is not a large market, it is a highly profitable and still growing market, and, as we have seen before, of strategic importance for further technological development.

Ruivenkamp (1984, 1989) has described these structural changes in the agro-food system from the perspective of traditional agricultural production. He distinguishes three restructuring processes.

(1) First, there is the separation of agricultural production from its natural environment, as the development of new plant and animal species adapted to formerly adverse natural conditions becomes possible through genetic engineering techniques. Agricultural production in non-traditional locations can lead to both increased self-sufficiency and increased trade. In particular, if harvesting a crop is labour intensive, it may become profitable to shift production to regions of low labour costs.

(2) Second, there is the separation of food production from agricultural production, as food is no longer considered essentially to be processed agricultural products, but to be nutrition. Therefore food products are constituted from different components either of agricultural origin or

from the chemical industry. Basic constituents like carbohydrates, proteins and fats are supplemented with flavours, colours, preservatives and, to give a healthy character, with vitamins.

(3) Third, there is the separation of agricultural products from their intrinsic qualities, as such products are split up into their basic components, like proteins, carbohydrates and fats, which are then combined in different qualities and quantities, together with additives, to create food products.

A clear example of the interchangeability of agricultural products, and the effects on national and international agricultural production and trade, is the competition between different sweeteners (Ruivenkamp, 1986). In the 1970s, the development of specific enzymes made possible the large scale production of high fructose corn syrup (HFCS), a starch based sweetener, made from corn. The substitution of sugar by HFCS in the soft drink industry was encouraged by a US policy of high sugar prices. Because of a growing supply of sugar and HFCS, US import quotas have continuously been modified downwards, and, together with the surplus production in the EC, they have had a far-reaching impact on traditional sugar cane producing regions such as the Caribbean and the Philippines.

For the production of HFCS different sources of starch can be used: corn starch or potato starch. But what is more important is that sugar and HFCS are becoming competitors in the food industry. Therefore, sugar farmers and corn farmers, both nationally and internationally, also become competitors. Recently, these farmers have encountered a third competitor: the biochemical industry producing synthetic sweeteners, in particular aspartame.

As we have seen, agricultural policy is already facing major challenges: including financial problems because of overproduction, environmental problems and falling incomes for many farmers. On top of these come the changes in the agro-food system, induced by biotechnology and other new technologies. This raises the spectre of what future there is for national agricultural policy as an independent field of policy making.

With decreasing numbers of farmers and heightened competition between those who remain, their political power can be expected to diminish in the long run. Because of a legacy of established institutional relationships and policy processes, however, farmers have more power than one would expect on the basis of their current numbers and contribution to GNP. But this cannot continue indefinitely and in the future farmers will have less influence on the policies that affect them directly. The other industries of the agro-food system will achieve more influence. As these industries increasingly exercise strategic control over the whole chain of production, they want commensurate political power. As the traditional relationship between farmers and agro-food industry loosens due to the interchangeability of raw materials in the processing phase, and as the coalition of interests behind the expansionist model falls apart, the struggle between farmers and manufacturing industries over agricultural policy will become increasingly unequal.

As international competition forces agro-food industries to buy their raw materials as cheaply as possible, they try to influence agricultural policy in the direction of lower agricultural prices. Both the US and the EC are, indeed, following such a course. In the EC, however, price levels are still far above those on the world market. Therefore some (bio)chemical industries have threatened to leave the EC if raw material prices are not lowered for them, because they have to compete with industries outside the EC that do have access to much cheaper raw materials. The European Commission has complied with some of these demands, and has made available sugar and starch, major feedstocks for the biochemical industry, against world market prices. The main reason for the Commission to subsidise such supplies was to keep the industries which use new biotechnologies in their operations inside the EC. Given the importance of these high technologies in the international technology race it is considered of crucial importance to have them developed and applied within the Community. Of course, the cost of this measure was relatively low, since the raw materials involved are in surplus in the EC, and the Commission would otherwise have had to pay much more for intervention storage or for export restitutions to dispose of them outside the Community. But the trend toward complying with demands from the agro-food industry, that are not necessarily favourable for farmers, is of significance.

This example of providing concessionary cheap raw materials for the biotechnology industry shows that agricultural interests must increasingly be weighed against manufacturing and technology interests. Biotechnology is considered such an important new technology for the future economic prosperity of the EC that any obstacles to its development and application must be demolished. We might say that agricultural policy is thus increasingly becoming part of an overall industrial policy. The European Community has, indeed, stressed the promotion of biotechnology for agro-industrial development (Commission, 1986 and 1988). In the proposals for the Council of Ministers, the Commission identifies which technologies should be promoted (and subsidised) for which sectors of the agro-food system. The emphasis is on the food and biochemical industry that will use old and new raw materials from agriculture. The assumption is that agricultural production must be adjusted to the technological interests of the chemical/food complex.

A main focus of research, it is argued, should be the animal feed industry and the enhancement of self-sufficiency in certain oilseed products. The EC is a major importer of vegetable oils, used in the food and chemical industries, and of oilseeds, used in the animal feed industry. Biotechnology research projects are therefore targeted at enhancing the quality and output of European oilseed production. In the chemical industry, the use of European vegetable oils can greatly be expanded if the right kind of fats are produced in oilseed crops. The compound feed industry is a major processor of protein from oilseeds, mainly soya. Here the research is targeted at adjusting soya varieties to Western European climates. Spain, in particular, has the right climate for greatly expanding soya production. Another focus of EC biotechnology research is enhancing the content of the right amino acids in European grain varieties. An important example is the content of lysine, a necessary amino acid for animal feed, in rye. If this content can be enlarged, fewer proteins for animal feed have to be imported.

All these research efforts are aimed at diminishing the import of agricultural products in the EC. This, of course, will have important implications for the USA as the largest exporter of agricultural products to the EC. Already, European grain farmers have lobbied for restrictions on the import of grain substitutes. If, however, the price of EC grain products is lowered, which is a major policy objective of the Commission, and the protein content of European grain varieties can be suitably enhanced, the imports will no longer be needed. Such substitution of EC products for imported products will lead to further conflicts with the US, which sees a major export market threatened. As a quarter of the total US soy bean crop is exported to the EC, and other markets are not easily found, the US will not take this loss of exports lightly: undoubtedly, it will add to the already difficult transatlantic relationship over agricultural trade.

The internationalisation of agriculture and US-EC trade conflicts

In the 1950s and 1960s agricultural trade was a residue of national agricultural policies, to support farm income and to dispose of incidental surpluses, in particular by way of food aid. By the 1970s, however, a change of policy had taken place in the US. A 1970 Presidential Commission (the Williams Commission), set up to recommend means of correcting US export decline, suggested expansion of exports in two sectors: agriculture and electronics (Cathie, 1985). This policy was helped substantially by a rapid price increase for agricultural products on the world market after 1972. US farm exports grew from $7.3 billion in 1970 to more than $41.2 billion in 1980 (McCalla and Learn, 1985).

The increase in US agricultural exports, both in value and in volume, was part of and facilitated by an unprecedented growth of agricultural trade. The volume of world agricultural trade grew from 285 million tonnes in 1970 to 518 million tonnes in 1981. Demand from developing countries and centrally planned ones provided for the bulk of this increase. The combination of rapid population growth and strong economic growth in many developing countries expanded demand for food faster than domestic agricultural production. This trend had become apparent in the 1960s, but it became more pronounced in the 1970s. In the early 1970s the Soviet Union also became a major player in the world market for grains when it began to use imports to offset its internal production shortfalls: a policy change to enlarge the internal supply of meat necessitated the import of feed grains. Other centrally planned economies followed a similar course. This combination of world events, together with a modest decline in total world output of grains in 1972/73, resulted in a sharp increase in the volume of trade and huge rises in the prices of most traded agricultural products.

Government policies greatly encouraged the expansion of production and trade. As we have seen, the US government made export earnings a major goal of agricultural policy, and farmers were recommended to plant every acre they could. The high inflation of the period meant that real interest rates were low, and many farmers were persuaded to borrow money, buy more land and expand their output. Between 1971 and 1975 the US grain area expanded by some 8 million hectares, or about 10 per cent (Brown, 1987).

In the EC, technological change together with the workings of the CAP have led to ever increasing production. High internal prices, prohibitive import barriers and unlimited intervention buying prompted EC farmers to produce any amount they could. As long as this output could be sold on the internal market no major problems for outside competitors arose. During the 1970s, however, the internal market became saturated. As self-sufficiency rates surpassed 100 per cent, export to markets outside the EC became necessary. Since the EC internal prices were higher than world market prices, export restitutions were needed to bridge the price gap. As exports were still limited in the 1970s, and price differences were rather small, the cost of export subsidies was relatively low. Moreover, because the world demand for agricultural products was still growing, there was room on the world market for every exporting country.

With the integration of agriculture into the international economy, its vulnerability to changes in that economy increased, as became clear in the 1980s. Changes in monetary policy in the US, debt crisis in the developing countries, worldwide recession, and changing demand for agricultural products all had their effect on the prosperity of the farm sector.

To halt the downward slide of the dollar and to fight inflation, the US Federal Reserve changed its monetary policy in 1980. Restricted money supply and high interest rates successfully reduced inflation rates and rapidly raised the value of the dollar against other major currencies. For the US farm community this monetary policy was a disaster. The investments farmers had made during the 1970s suddenly became serious financial liabilities, as interest rates soared to 20 per cent. With the high value of the dollar American products lost their international competitiveness. The most severe crisis in agriculture since the 1930s was the result.

The high value of the dollar was not the only reason for the loss of export markets. US monetary policy, together with a worldwide recession in the beginning of the 1980s, likewise contributed to the debt crisis in developing countries. These countries, particularly in Latin America, were forced to lower their imports and to expand their exports in order to earn more foreign exchange to pay interest on their debt. For US agricultural trade, this meant not only less export to these countries, but also more competition on the world market. Brazil and Argentina expanded their production and export of soy beans and wheat respectively, both major US export products. Traditional importing countries, such as China, India and Saudi Arabia, greatly raised their self-sufficiency rates for grains. In the 1970s they had imported large quantitites of grains, mainly from the US, but in the 1980s some of them became exporters themselves.

As we have seen, the EC developed into a net exporter of many agricultural products in the 1970s. In the early 1980s because of the high value of the dollar, it further increased its share of the world market. Many economists and politicians disapproved of the use of export subsidies to discharge the EC's oversupply. However, the financial costs were not yet high enough to enforce a change in policy. This occurred only when the dollar came down again in 1985, and the costs of export restitution soared, causing great financial problems for the EC. Yet it took another three years, till February 1988, before the EC reached agreement on restrictions on grain production.

Right from its inauguration the Reagan Administration had condemned the Common Agricultural Policy (CAP) of the EC, in particular its trade provisions. As the farm crisis became more severe in 1984 and 1985, the US began to adopt a more aggressive stance towards the EC. Julien (1987) gives a chronology of the different phases of the resulting trade conflict. It started in 1981/82 with official US Administration statements attacking the basic principles and mechanisms of the CAP. US Secretary of Agriculture, John Block, a pronounced advocate of free trade, expressed his disapproval of the CAP on several occasions. In 1982/83 the US took several complaints about EC trade practices to the GATT for dispute settlement. These complaints concerned export restitution on wheat, wheat flour, pasta and poultry; production subsidies on raisins and canned fruit; and preferential tariffs on citrus from developing countries in North Africa and the Middle East. In 1983 the US decided to start using export subsidies itself to turn the tables on the EC. In the words of one commentator.

> The decision to subsidise the sale of 1 million tons of wheat flour to Egypt came as the unsurprising conclusion of a long period of verbal exchanges. (Butler, 1986, p. 125)

In 1985 the US announced the so-called BICEPS export programme under which bonuses from government stocks were to be added to otherwise commercial deals. In this way the government could dispose of a part of its large surplus stocks, and the overall price of the export commodity could be lowered. The programme was specifically targeted at traditional EC markets, such as the countries of North Africa, and was part of the Export Enhancement Program (EEP) of the 1985 Food Security Act. Another major provision of the Act to win back export markets was a reduction of loan rates. For rice, cotton and corn, special policy measures were taken in order to expand exports by lowering minimum prices to world market levels.

New GATT panels were installed in 1986 to discuss US complaints concerning citrus and pasta. The same year saw the outbreak of a major conflict over the enlargement of the EC and the consequences for US exports of feed grains and oilseeds to Spain and Portugal. This last conflict was the most serious so far, and brought the US and EC very close to an all-out trade war. Both trading blocks had prepared a list of retaliatory measures for restricting bilateral trade, but managed to patch up an agreement in January 1987, just two days before the deadline set by the US.

In the new round of GATT trade negotiations, which started in September

1986 and is due to end in December 1990, agricultural trade is one of the main issues. The US was a strong supporter of incorporating this topic in the Uruguay round, allying itself with the Cairns group of countries heavily dependent on agricultural exports (including Australia, Brazil, Canada, Colombia, Chile, the Philippines, Hungary, Indonesia, Malaysia, New Zealand, Thailand and Uruguay) which have challenged the agricultural protectionism of the EC and Japan. These talks have temporarily eased the trade conflicts. While negotiations are going on, no party wants to jeopardise the continuation of the discussion by taking unilateral measures. However, there still exist some serious disputes concerning, for example, US meat exports to the EC; EC proposals to limit the import of grain substitutes, such as corn gluten from the US; and US exports of soy beans to the EC, which are under constant pressure from the expansion of EC oilseed production, promoted by large subsidies to oilseed producers and processing industries.

US agricultural exports are very vulnerable to EC decisions to restrict imports, taken in order to promote self-sufficiency or to encourage (with or without sanctions) the substitution of EC products for imported products. The EC is still the largest US export market, with an annual agricultural trade surplus for the US of $2.5 billion and with specific products very dependent on the EC market. As mentioned above, 25 per cent of all US soy bean production is exported to the EC and for corn gluten the figure is even higher. Corn gluten is a by-product in the production of HFCS and bio-ethanol from corn. The export to the EC is a major factor in the profitability of HFCS production. If the EC is lost as an export market, the US balance of payments would be hit twice: with lost export earnings and increased sugar imports. Not only are corn farmers strongly opposed to EC import restrictions, therefore, but the US Administration also has a strong interest in this transatlantic trade, which underpins its own promotion of the production of bio-ethanol. Since the production of bio-ethanol, which is promoted for environmental and energy reasons and to support the further development of appropriate technology, is only viable with subsidies, every dollar that is earned with the export of the corn gluten means less subsidy.

The option of trade liberalisation, proposed by the Reagan Administration, is being pursued by the Bush Administration and is supported by the internationally oriented agro-food industries in the US, the EC and other major exporting countries. These industries have a clear interest in the expansion of agricultural production and trade, and wish to exploit technological developments to their advantage. Since internal markets are saturated, the only way to expand is by liberalising worldwide trade in agricultural products, and restructuring existing relations within the agro-food system. The development of new technologies has given agro-food industries an additional reason to promote free trade. The increasing interchangeability of agricultural products as raw materials for the primary processing industry, made possible by biotechnology, encourages these industries to lobby for unrestricted trade in their sources of biomass.

The expectations, particularly in the US, of a favourable outcome to the current round of GATT negotiations are very high. If no satisfactory agreement can be reached, however, the frustration will be equally high and protectionist measures may be taken unilaterally. A major difficulty is the incorporation, in the talks, of national agricultural policy measures. Previous discussions on agricultural trade dealt only with specific trade measures. Agricultural trade policy, however, cannot be separated from agricultural policy in general. The trade provisions are directly related to other provisions of national farm policy. Without discussing these national policies, no major improvement of world agricultural trade can be reached. But their inclusion in talks about international trade make the negotiations very difficult and the outcome quite uncertain.

While searching for adjustments of internal policy, the negotiators have to take into account the same aspects of agricultural policy making that have also led to the trade conflicts: internal institutional rigidities; the strength of agricultural fundamentalism, particularly in the EC; the position and influence of interest groups, not only farmers' organisations but also agro-industrial groups, particularly in the US; and, last but not least, a solution for the farm crisis.

Conclusions

The most direct effect of new technologies on the trade relationship between the US and the EC is the increasing self-sufficiency of the Community. The adaptation of plant varieties to European climates, and the enhancement of the quality of the protein content of certain grain varieties will make the import of large quantities of agricultural products obsolete. As the US is the major supplier of these products, the development and application of biotechnologies will have a profound impact on US exports to the EC. With the integration of Spain and Portugal into the EC, the climatic variety and therefore the possiblities of producing all kinds of agricultural raw materials inside the EC, have greatly increased.

Reduction of imports will come not only from the improvement of European plant varieties with regard to their protein and oil contents, but also from the interchangeability of different agricultural products thus allowing greater use of locally produced raw materials. This is particularly the case for different sources of carbohydrates (starch, sugar) and vegetable oils (soya oil, olive oil). Here again the effect on US exports to the EC will be negative.

A third development in the primary processing of agricultural products into raw materials for the food industry and biochemical industries is total crop use. Economising on raw materials can thus be achieved as every component of the farm product is being used. This concept of total crop harvesting is being developed by researchers in Denmark and other EC countries, with support from the Commission of the EC (Rexen and Munck, 1984).

The importance of biotechnology in the technology race between industrialised countries causes national (or EC) governments to defend and promote its development, for instance through financial assistance to precompetitive research. Protection of national 'high tech' industry is also part of this strategy, and the EC has made clear its wish to foster the biochemical industry within the Community. As most new biotechnologies are being developed by agro-industries, these sectors are considered of vital interest, both in the EC and in the US.

With the further integration of agriculture in the chemical/food complex, it is no longer sufficient to look only at agricultural policies for an explanation of EC-US trade conflicts. If the interests of farmers and other industries of the agro-food system no longer coincide, industry will exert more influence on the making of agricultural (trade) policy. As agricultural policy increasingly becomes part of a larger industrial policy, developments in the total agro-food system, and its effects on national policy, must be assessed. An example is the EC ban on hormones, and the resulting import restriction on meat from animals treated with hormones. The US pharmaceutical industry exerted substantial pressure on the Administration to keep the EC from implementing this policy measure (Financial Times, July 7, 1987). The animal health sector is the fastest growing biotechnology market in agriculture. This high value/high technology industry has relatively few transatlantic connections, while government involvement is extensive, but consumer concern is strong and can be an issue of considerable political mobilisation. Therefore the potential for further conflict certainly exists in this sector.

For the future of the EC-US trade relationship we must look at developments in the agro-food system, in particular in the chemical and food industries. Both 'in-house' research and development in biotechnology and the supply of cheap agricultural raw materials are of strategic importance for these industries. In looking at the food industry it is useful to distinguish between primary processing and final food production. The companies engaged in the latter have a more global scope, since there is no direct relationship with farmers supplying raw materials. The European food company Unilever is a good example and is an exponent of a free-trade oriented food industry.

The primary processing industry, which gets its raw materials directly from the farming sector and supplies the final food and biochemical industries, has a stronger relationship with the national or regional agricultural sector. Therefore, at a policy level this industry is the first target of agro-industrial stimulation. The production of bio-ethanol is a clear example of regional agricultural interests connected with certain primary processing industries and enjoying government support. There are strong pressures from the industry (for instance Ferruzzi in Europe, and Archer Daniels Midland in the US) together with (certain) farming interest groups for further support of the production of bio-ethanol, either from corn (in the US) or from sugar or surplus cereals (in the EC). Even if this process is not yet economically viable, strong pressures exist to foster the industry.

The close relationship between primary processing (and trade in these products) and farmers can still work out in two separate ways. In the US the orientation is primarily towards export and free trade. Biotechnologies are therefore being developed to lower production costs, to increase international competitiveness. In the EC, however, stimulation of biotechnology is aimed at promoting self-sufficiency and substitution of domestic surplus products for imported products. Given these opposite policy orientations for trade and technology, the threat of further Atlantic trade conflicts is still very real.

Note

1. The agro-food system encompasses all the industries engaged in the production of food products. Within this system four sectors can be distinguished:
   - the industries which supply the inputs for the farming sector, like agro chemicals, seed, and equipment;
   - the farming sector itself;
   - the primary processing industry;
   - the final food industry.

References

Ayers, J. H. and Greer, J. D. (1984) *Biotechnology in Agriculture. Advances in Commercial and Plant Production Technology*, Business Intelligence Program, Report no. 707. Menlo Park, California, SRI International.

Brown, L. R. (1987) Sustaining World Agriculture, in Brown L.R. *State of the World 1987* (A World Watch Institute Report on Progress Toward a Sustainable Society). New York/London, Norton.

Butler, N. (1986) *The International Grain Trade: Problems and Prospects*. London/Sydney, Croom Helm (for the Royal Institute of International Affairs, London).

Buttel, F.H., Cowan, J.T. Kenney, M. and Kloppenburg Jr., J. (1984) Biotechnology in Agriculture: The Political Economy of Agribusiness Reorganization and Industry-University Relationships. *Research in Rural Sociology and Development*, vol. 1, 315–348.

Buttel, F.H. (1986) *Agricultural Research and Farm Structural Change: Bovine Growth Hormone and Beyond*, mimeo.

Cathie, J. (1985) US and EEC Agricultural Trade Policies. A long-run view of the present conflict, *Food Policy*, February, vol. 10, no. 1, 14–18.

Commission of the European Communities (1986) *Biotechnology in the Community: Stimulation of Agro-Industrial Development* (COM (86) 221), Brussels, CEC.

Commission of the European Communities (1988) *Commission proposal for a first multi-annual programme (1988–1993) for Biotechnology-Based Agro-Industrial Research and Technological Development*, (COM (87) 667), Brussels, CEC.

ERS/USDA (1986) *Embargoes, Surplus Disposal, and U.S. Agriculture*, (Agricultural Economic Report no. 564). Washington, DC, Economic Research Service, US Department of Agriculture.

166

Goodman, D. and Redclift, M. (eds) (1989) *The International Farm Crisis*. London, Macmillan.

Hoogh, J. de (1987) Agricultural Policies in Industrial Countries and their Effect on the Third World. A critical view on comparative-static analysis of a dynamic process, *Tijdschrift voor Sociaalwetenschappelijk onderzoek naar de Landbouw (TSL)*, vol. 2, no. 1, 68–81.

Julien, B. (1987) Policy Conflict between the U.S. and the E.C, in Wesley, E. and Peterson, F. (eds) *U.S. and European Community Agriculture: Changing Policies and Conflicts over Trade*. Faculty Paper Series, FP87–13. College Station, Texas, Department of Agricultural Economics, Texas A&M University, 17–22.

Kloppenburg Jr J. (1988) *First the Seed. the Political Economy of Plant Biotechnology, 1492–2000*. Cambridge, Cambridge University Press.

McCalla, A. F. and Learn, E. W. (1985) Public Policies for Food, Agriculture, and Resources. Retrospect and Prospect, in Price (1985) *op cit.*, 1–22.

Newman, M., Fulton, T. and Glaser, L. (1987) *A Comparison of Agriculture in the United States and the European Community*, Foreign Agricultural Economic Report no. 233. Washington, DC, Economic Research Service, US Department of Agriculture.

Penn, J. B. (1985) The Agricultural and Rural Economy. Profile, Current Issues, and Policy Implications, in Price (1985), *op. cit.*, 23–46.

Price, K. A., (ed) (1985) *The Dilemmas of Choice* (The National Center for Food and Agricultural Policy, Annual Policy Review 1985). Washington, DC, Resources for the Future.

Rexen, F. and Munck, L. (1984) *Cereal Crops for Industrial Use in Europe*, Report prepared for The Commission of the European Communities, EUR 9617 EN. Copenhagen, Carlsberg Research Laboratory.

Roobeek, A. J. M. (1986) *The Crisis in Fordism and the Rise of a new Technological System. The Social-Political Dynamism of the International Race in Technology and the Shape of a Post-Fordist Society*, Research Memorandum no. 8602. Amsterdam, Department of Economics, University of Amsterdam.

Ruivenkamp, G (1984) *Biotechnology: The Production of New Relations within the Agro-Industrial Chain of Production*, Contribution to the Conference of the World Assembly, Rome, November 12–15, 1984. Amsterdam; Department of International Relations, University of Amsterdam.

Ruivenkamp, G. (1986) The Impact of Biotechnology on International Development: Competition between Sugar and New Sweeteners, *viertel jahresbericht – Problems of International Cooperation*, no. 103, März 1986, 89–101.

Ruivenkamp, G. (1987) Shell en Biotechnologie, in Hendriks, F. (ed.) *Shell*. Utrecht, Van Arkel, 245–278.

Ruivenkamp, G. (1989) *De invoering van biotechnologie in de agro-industriële produktieketen. De overgang naar een nieuwe arbeidsorganisatie*. Utrecht, Uitgeverij Jan van Arkel.

Tulder, R. van and Junne, G. (1988) *European Multinationals in Core Technologies*. Chichester, Sussex, Wiley.

US Congress, Office of Technology Assessment (1986) *Technology, Public Policy and the Changing Structure of American Agriculture* (OTA-F-285). Washington, DC, US Government Printing Office.

Wilkinson, J. (1987) *Europe within the World Food System: Biotechnology and New Strategic Options* FAST Exploratory Dossier (FAST – DG XII/122/87-EN). Brussels, Commission of the European Communities.

CHAPTER 8

Environmental Risks and the Regulation of Biotechnology*

Joyce Tait

Introduction

'New biotechnology', dating from the early 1970s, was made possible by a range of developments in the understanding of genetic processes and in the manipulation and culture of cells, culminating most dramatically in the ability to engineer new genetic material and hence alter the nature or quantity of specific chemicals produced by cells. Thus,

> for the first time, man can go beyond working within the bounds of nature and can manipulate those bounds. (Sharp, 1985)

Genetic engineering opens up the possibility of creating new forms of life, tailored to meet specific human needs. However, its application on a large scale requires a wide range of other advances in the manipulation of cells and cell components and in the storage, organisation and retrieval of information. Each such development could, in isolation, have a major influence on our exploitation of natural resources. Viewed as a whole, they have the potential to create a revolution whose impact could dwarf that of the earlier 'green revolution'. Within twenty years it may be possible to produce virtually unlimited quantities of:

- products never before available;
- products that are currently in short supply;

---

*Based on a paper, 'Biotechnology: Interactions between Technology, Environment and Society', prepared for the EC MONITOR/FAST Programme 1989-90, Synthesis Report No.1 Project: Biosphere and the Economy, DGXII/H/3, March 1990.

168

- products that cost substantially less than those made by existing methods;
- products that are safer than those now available;
- products made with raw materials that are more plentiful and less expensive than those now used (OTA, 1984, p. 65).

Figure 8.1 Interaction between industry, government and public opinion in the development of biotechnology

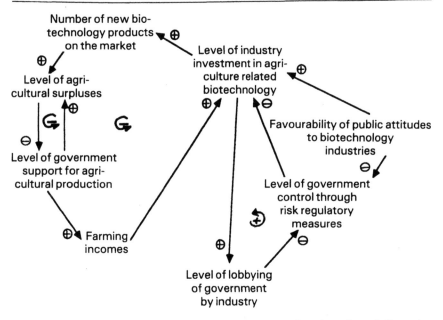

In the above causal loop diagram, the following conventions have been followed:

(i)   arrows should be read as 'causes', 'influences' or 'effects';

(ii) a positive sign attached to an arrow indicates a direct relationship between the two variables involved;

(iii) a negative sign attached to an arrow indicates a reciprocal relationship between the two variables involved, i.e. as one increases, the other decreases, and vice versa;

(iv) positive or negative feedback is indicated by the sign in the centre of a loop, enclosed in a circular arrow.

Indeed, biotechnology is seen by some theorists as the harbinger of the next long wave economic cycle now being entered by western societies (Freeman *et al.*, 1982; Thompson, 1986). Even those who are sceptical about this theory would agree that the range of potential applications of biotechnology in many fields of human activity creates ' . . . a powerful tool for renewal of the economic base of contemporary society' (Commission of the European Communities, 1984, p. 10).

However, this technological optimism is counterbalanced, in many quarters, by misgivings about the safety of some new developments and about their potential social impact, as well as by scepticism about some of the claims being made. This is particularly true of the agriculture-related developments which are the subject of this chapter. The outcome, over the next ten or twenty years, will depend on:

(1) the level of investment by industry in different types of innovation;
(2) the nature and level of government support policies for agriculture;
(3) the evolution of national and international risk-regulatory systems; and
(4) the favourability or otherwise of public attitudes.

Each of these factors interacts strongly with all the others, as indicated in Figure 8.1. In the resulting system, perturbations in any one factor will have a major effect on the others, through a complex system of feedback loops determining the level of industry investment in agriculture-related biotechnology. This chapter will examine these interactions and the consequences for the progress of the biotechnology industry, examining successively, the nature of new biotechnology developments, their potential social and environmental impacts, the assessment of the risks involved and the popular response. The final section will then assess the interactions among the various interests identified.

Overview of new biotechnology developments relevant to agriculture

Plant breeding and crop development

Developments in plant breeding are among some of the most dramatic and revolutionary in the new biotechnology armoury. The ability to isolate the gene responsible for the production of a specific chemical or property, and to transfer it to the chromosomes of another, different species (recombinant DNA technology) is rapidly becoming commonplace. Persuading some genes to express the desired property in the new species is proving more complex and is the main stumbling block to further developments in many areas.

On the other hand, once a genetically-desirable plant variety has been found occurring naturally, or induced in a laboratory, micro-propagation techniques are now halving the time taken to bring it to the market place (Giles, 1985). Such techniques are financially viable for the horticultural market, with its insatiable demand for new, exotic varieties at high prices, or where there are problems of virus disease transmission in seed (e.g. potatoes), or difficulties in multiplying crops from seed (e.g. banana and oil palm).

The ability to fix nitrogen directly from the air, reducing the need for fertiliser inputs, is one of the properties scientists are seeking to transfer.

Currently micro-organisms such as *Rhizobium* can carry out this function only in symbiotic association with legumes (Johnston *et al.*, 1985). The genes necessary for nitrogen fixation and for nodulation in the host plant have been identified, and have been transferred to non-leguminous species, but achieving the aim of, for example, breeding a cereal crop that fixes nitrogen from the air does not seem likely in the immediate future (Mantegazzini, 1986, p. 71). More promising developments in the shorter term may be: the use of nitrogen fixing bacteria such as *Azosporillium*, isolated from the root zones of many grasses (Elmerich *et al.*, 1985) or algae (OTA, 1984, p. 182); using genetic manipulation techniques to improve the efficiency of *Rhizobia* and to improve their compatibility with leguminous host plants; and improving nitrogen uptake and its incorporation into the tissues of cereal plants by increasing the activity of the relevant plant enzyme (Mantegazzini, 1986, p. 72).

Rapid progress is now being made in identifying other potentially beneficial interactions between plants and micro-organisms, in addition to the fixation of nitrogen. The most widely publicised example is the discovery that frost damage on many plants can be caused by strains of *Pseudomonas syringae* and *Erwinia herbicola* that initiate the formation of ice crystals. Strains lacking this feature ('ice minus') have been developed, with a view to using them to replace the wild micro-organisms on crops and protect them from frost damage. After many delays, a commercial product 'Frostban' has been field-tested in California (Krimsky and Plough, 1988). Progress is also being made in the understanding of microbial interactions that promote plant growth, either by facilitating the uptake of nutrients from the soil, or by the secretion of specific growth-promoting chemicals (OTA, 1984, p. 184).

The efforts of conventional plant breeding programmes to develop varieties with pest and disease resistance or improved yield will be considerably speeded up by new biotechnology techniques such as micro-propagation. Genetic manipulation will also remove the randomness and uncertainty of the older methods. Major foci of attention are the provision of a better ratio of harvestable yield to total plant matter, breeding for stress resistance (e.g. drought tolerance) (OTA, 1984, p. 186), breeding cereal crops with improved amino acid content in the grain (Miflin *et al.*, 1985) and the removal of toxins from potentially useful crop plants such as lupin (Allen, 1985). It has been estimated that the retail value of plants bred by new bio-technology techniques will be equivalent to about a third of the value of all the seed currently planted by 2005 (Kidd, 1985, quoted in Sargeant, 1985).

Many naturally occurring microbes have the ability to control insects, plant diseases and weeds and some have been used in place of pesticides in the past. Biotechnology companies are capitalising on their improved ability to culture such organisms in marketable quantities. More sophisticated developments are: to encode the gene responsible for producing the relevant toxin into the genetic material of the plant itself, as has been done for the insecticidal *Bacillus thuringiensis* (BT) toxin in several crop species; or to change the spectrum of activity of the relevant microbe or toxin by genetic manipulation (Lisansky, 1985; New Scientist, 17 April 1986, p. 18). In another advanced example, Monsanto has developed a genetically enhanced form of the soil bacterium *Pseudomonas fluorescens*, encoding DNA from *B. thuringiensis* to manufacture a toxin lethal to soil pests. Among the earliest successes of biotechnology has been the development of crop plant varieties that can flourish in the presence of normally lethal levels of certain herbicides.

Animal breeding and health

Research and development on animals of agricultural significance is also experiencing a range of advances leading to improved nutritional efficiency, animal health and productivity, increased reproductive capacity, more rapid development of improved genetic stock, the genetic manipulation of animals to produce non-food commodities, such as drugs, and improved and cheaper sources of feed.

Vaccine development is one of the furthest advanced sectors in animal biotechnology. It has proved attractive to small biotechnology companies, because the regulatory requirements are less stringent than for human medical specialities and because the market for a single vaccine is often small enough to avoid attracting competition from the multinationals. Vaccines for the prevention of colibacillosis scours in piglets and calves, developed using gene-splicing technology, are already on the market, and others are being developed for foot and mouth disease and infectious bronchitis virus in poultry. A wider range of micro-organisms is also being exploited to produce new antibiotics for the control of animal diseases (Armstrong, 1985).

In the past, improvements in the breeding stock of farm animals have been dominated by the male of the species. No matter how desirable the characteristics of a female, the limited number of reproductive cycles in a lifetime dictated the number of offspring that an animal could produce. The new techniques of super-ovulation, embryo transfer and cloning are already having a significant impact on the rate at which desirable characteristics in a breed can be multiplied (Polge, 1985). It is also possible to engineer specific genes, e.g. to induce the animal to secrete higher levels of growth hormone (Steane, 1985), or to increase wool growth in sheep (Armstrong, 1985).

A range of interesting possibilities is being created by various manipulations of growth hormone levels in animals to increase their feed conversion. Daily injections of growth hormone such as bovine somatotrophin, produced using recombinant DNA technology, can increase the milk yield of lactating cows by up to 40 per cent. Administering growth hormone to young animals increases the daily live-weight gain, often with an increase in the protein content of meat at the expense of fat. Similar effects can be achieved by auto-immunisation of animals against the hormone somatostatin which is antagonistic to growth hormone resulting, in lambs, in a 20 per cent reduction in rearing time to slaughter and a 27 per cent improvement in feed utilisation (Spencer, 1985). Interest is also being shown in the manipulation of the microbial population of the rumen in cattle and sheep to improve the efficiency of feed conversion (Armstrong, 1985).

Advances are also being made in the development of totally new animal feeds and in improving the nutritive value of low quality feeds. In the latter case, enzymes are being developed to improve the digestibility of straw (Wallace *et al.*, 1983). New sources of protein for animal feed, based on microbial fermentation of a range of substrates, such as methanol or starch, have already been marketed, the best known being ICI's 'Pruteen'. Recombinant DNA technology is being used to improve the efficiency of the fermentation process (Armstrong, 1985).

Industrial developments

Biotechnology is, in addition, opening up novel uses for agricultural products, making feasible the industrial production of traditionally agricultural commodities, and introducing new methods of producing fine and commodity chemicals in agricultural systems.

A major development has been the ability to fix enzymes on a substrate, thus facilitating their use on a commercial scale (Marstrand, 1981). Enzymes are already used in the US to produce high fructose corn syrup (HFCS) as a sweetener for the catering industry, and in 1980 this process saved the US $1.3 billion in sugar imports. Likewise, the gene responsible for the production of rennet has been cloned so that calf rennet, an enzyme used in cheese making, can now be produced by microbial fermentation (OTA, 1984, p. 238-9).

A wide range of raw materials for the food, toiletries and detergent industries, traditionally agricultural in origin, can now be produced by microbial or enzyme fermentation, e.g. bulk chemicals such as alcohols and fatty acids, xanthan gum thickener, speciality proteins and polypeptides, and many flavouring agents. These may be produced from a variety of substrates. Single cell protein, for example, used as an animal feed and potentially as a supplement for the human diet, can be produced from carbon dioxide, methane, methanol, ethanol, sugars, petroleum hydrocarbons or some industrial or agricultural wastes. In general, such products are not yet cheap enough to compete with traditional food sources, but biotechnology could increase the efficiency of the production process.

As biotechnology is used to exploit natural products in increasingly sophisticated ways, new and traditional crops will be grown for the specific purpose of providing feedstock or finished products for the chemical industry, such as enzymes for industrial biotechnology processes (Eades, 1986). The production of pharmaceuticals from plants and animals will become increasingly common. Evening primrose crops are already grown on a small scale for this purpose, and Monsanto in the US has grown petunias containing the genetic sequence for human chorionic gonadotrophin, which is used as a drug in the treatment of infertility. 'Transgenic' animals have been bred in the UK to produce milk containing pharmaceuticals. For example, one of the blood clotting factors needed by haemophiliacs can be produced in a form free from possible contamination by the AIDS virus

Figure 8.2 The Impact of New Biotechnology Developments on Rural Land Use

Development	Likely timescale of implementation	Effect on agric. productivity	Effect on land use
(i) PLANT BREEDING AND CROP DEVELOPMENT			
(a) Micropropagation	Already in use commercially	To speed up the implementation of other developments	Land releasing
(b) Nitrogen fixation			
– within non-leguminous plant tissues	Extremely long-term	Input-saving	Land releasing
– by free living soil bacteria	2000*	Input-saving	Land releasing
– improving fertiliser uptake by cereal plants	1995*	Input-saving	Land releasing
– improving the efficiency of nitrogen fixation within legumes	1995*	Input-saving	Land releasing
(c) Harnessing microbial-plant interactions			
– frost protection	Under development	Loss avoidance	Land releasing
– growth promotion	Under development	Increased productivity	Land releasing
(d) Extensions of classical plant breeding			
– insect and disease resistance in plants	1995	Loss avoidance & input saving	Land releasing
– improved stress resistance	1995	Increased productivity	Land releasing
(e) New developments in crop protection			
– biological control agents	1995*	Input-saving	Land releasing
– herbicide resistance	1990*	Improved efficiency	Land releasing

(ii) ANIMAL BREEDING AND HEALTH

(a)	Disease control	1990*	Increased productivity	Land releasing
(b)	Reproduction	1990–95*	Increased productivity	Land releasing
(c)	Feed conversion	1990*	Increased productivity	Land releasing
(d)	Developments in animal feeds	1995*	Use of crop wastes or non-crop products	Land releasing

(iii) INDUSTRIAL DEVELOPMENTS

(a)	Enzyme technology			
	– high fructose corn syrup	Already in use	—	Land releasing
	– rennet production	Already in use	—	Neutral
(b)	Microbial production processes			
	– food production from non-agricultural substrates, e.g. single cell protein	Already in use		Land releasing
	– food production from agricultural substrates	Already in use		Neutral
(c)	New sources of industrial feedstock			
	– from plants	Already in use on a small scale	—	Land using
	– from animals	Already in use on a small scale	—	Land using
	– energy cropping	Already feasible (timing of implementation dependent on oil prices)	—	Land using

*See North (1986)

(Independent, 21 December 1986). On a much larger scale, it is possible to produce many commodity chemicals from biomass feedstock such as starch and cellulose, rather than non-renewable resources such as petroleum. Biotechnology could also improve the efficiency of fuel extraction from crops grown specifically for this purpose, or from crop wastes.

The social and policy relationships surrounding new biotechnology developments

It is obvious that the new developments summarised above have the potential to create major changes to agricultural systems and patterns of rural land use over the next twenty years. Predicting future developments in such a rapidly advancing field is bound to be highly speculative, but the guess-work can be more intelligent given a better understanding of some relevant features of the major industries concerned, agriculture, food and biotechnology.

The agricultural context

The agricultural context within which this putative revolution would take place is one where productivity has already increased to unprecedented levels, through the combined effects of technology and policies designed to support agricultural prices. Indeed, conventional plant breeding methods, more optimal use of fertiliser and better pest and disease control, even in the absence of any of the more speculative biotechnology developments, are likely to sustain cereal yield increases at a rate of approximately 2 per cent per annum until around the year 2005 (North, 1986). These high levels of production, however, have become an embarrassment to governments in Europe and North America and a variety of policy instruments have been introduced to reduce food surpluses to more manageable proportions.

As long as large food surpluses continue to exist, and continue to be unacceptable, biotechnology seems likely to exacerbate the problem. As summarised in Figure 8.2, many developments could further increase the productivity of agricultural land. North (1986) has estimated that: the area of land needed to grow cereal crops in Britain could fall from 3.87 million hectares in 1985 to between 1.75 and 2 million hectares in 2015; and if the demand for dairy produce remains static, the number of cows plus replacements needed could fall from 4.1 million in 1985 to 2.1 million in 2015 (the associated grassland area dropping from 2.2 million hectares to 0.6 million hectares).

The market for the new biotechnology developments and products therefore seems likely to be a turbulent one and they will face a very different agricultural policy environment from that enjoyed by the innovations introduced over the past twenty years. These factors are probably already deterring biotechnology companies from expanding into agriculture. However, some new developments could create new uses for the land released from agriculture by higher levels of productivity.

Of the land using options indicated in Figure 8.2, energy cropping will not be commercially viable without substantial increases in the price of oil, an outcome which could be delayed by biotechnology developments in other commercial sectors leading to increased efficiency of extraction of oil reserves (Mantegazzini, 1986, p. 26). There is also the possibility of providing new sources of chemical industry feedstock from plants and animals. However, at present, these opportunities seem unlikely to take up large areas of land. Many of the products will be supplied to the low-volume, high-value fine chemicals industry. In the case of human blood clotting factors, for example, the world demand could be satisfied by one herd of cows or sheep. Feedstock for commodity chemicals production could use considerably more land than fine chemicals, but probably not enough to take up a significant proportion of that no longer needed. These land-using biotechnology options are also vulnerable to other feasible biotechnology developments, particularly the vat culture of chemicals by genetically-altered micro-organisms. The latter would give industry a more predictable quantity and quality of supply, more conveniently located, and land-based production could prove to be an interim measure, soon to give way to completely industrial production processes.

There appears to be no escape from the prediction that biotechnology is likely to release very large areas of land from agricultural production, to an extent that would dwarf present problems of re-structuring the economies of rural areas. However, the commercial viability of the new developments will depend on the existence of a healthy, thriving agricultural and food industry and this in turn will depend on the government policies adopted in the immediate future to manage the problems of over-supply. As the following section shows, the biotechnology industries themselves will have a powerful influence on these policies, helping to ensure a favourable commercial environment for their products.

The industrial context

Many of the multinational companies now investing heavily in biotechnology are the same companies that have supplied the inputs to today's increasingly efficient farming systems, e.g. American Cyanamid, Dow, DuPont, Monsanto, Shell, ICI, Hoechst, Bayer, Syntex. They are joined by a number of new biotechnology firms which are making an important contribution to innovation in animal and plant agriculture, although their long-term survival alongside the multinational giants is somewhat precarious. Many firms are also engaged in other areas of development, such as the food and drink industries, fine chemicals and bulk chemicals, fuel substitutes and waste management, all of which will have repercussions on agriculture and rural land use.

The aggregate equity investments in new biotechnology firms by established US companies in the period 1977–1983 was $372 million (OTA, 1984, p. 101), but since then, the growth of investment in small, new firms has tailed off, largely due to the greater, and less visible, in-house investment by multinational companies. By the end of this century, the projected world turnover for sales of products connected with biotechnology in agriculture and food processing is 100 billion ECU (Porceddu, 1986).

The history of the agrochemical and pharmaceutical industries is very relevant to the prospects for biotechnology. Since the late 1970s these industries have been entering the phase of development described as 'maturity' or 'stagnation'. As more drugs and pesticides were produced, the number of profitable potentially new markets declined.

Also, biologically active chemicals that were cheap to make and safe to people and the environment became increasingly difficult to find. This combination of market saturation and new product starvation has led to a very significant decline in the inflation-adjusted price of pesticides over recent years, making it increasingy difficult for companies to fund their costly research and development (R&D) programmes (Tait, 1981; Tait and Lane, 1987).

Faced with such a situation, a company has two choices: either abandon R&D and become a producer of chemical commodities with a low profit margin, or diversify into new business areas. A series of interviews with managers in the agrochemical industry has indicated a shift in attitude over the past thirteen years. In 1973 they were dismissive of the idea of any involvement with biological forms of pest control. They saw themselves as the elite of the chemical industry, and proud of it. Anything else was 'not their business' (Tait, unpublished data). According to the chairman of Monsanto in the USA, this was 'a glamour period for the chemical industry. We were high tech and we were the darlings of Wall Street' (Fernandez, 1985). But now 'We are overdue for another big splash of revolutionary change...Our creativity needs new outlets...Biotechnology will drive us into the next golden era...in the middle of the 1990s'. In 1983, interviews with UK agrochemcial industry managers indicated that they held similar views to Fernandez, and a primary personal and company objective was to be at the forefront of biotechnology (Tait, unpublished data). With such powerful commercial interests increasingly committed to them, new biotechnology developments may prove unstoppable (Metz, 1984).

An important aspect of the agrochemical industry's relationship to biotechnology is the purchase by multinationals of the majority of the independent plant breeding companies in Europe and the USA. When this began in the early 1970s, the aim was to begin 'breeding under a pesticide umbrella' (Tait, unpublished data). This meant that, instead of breeding primarily for pest or disease resistance as the independent companies had done, the aim of the new breeding programmes would be to maximise yields on the assumption that chemicals would be used to take care of pest and disease problems. The development of varieties with enhanced responses to chemicals is still a major objective of commercial plant breeders owned by agrochemical multinationals, as indicated by work being done on the breeding of crops with specific herbicide resistance genes. However, the situation is no longer as clear-cut as it was when these companies were first taken over. As indicated above, many of the new biotechnology developments could replace pesticides and fertilisers with more environmentally benign products.

The companies involved in biotechnology have, in the past, been major export-earners in Europe, the USA and Japan, and international competition is intensifying at government level in the race to develop new biotechnology industries. European biotechnology is generally seen as lagging behind that of the United States and Japan but making determined efforts to catch up (Narjes, 1986; Fasella, 1986). Governments therefore do not question the need to support biotechnology, complete with its heavy investment in agriculture-related developments, despite the fact that it is no longer politically fashionable to subsidise agriculture.

A variety of programmes is being set up to increase the effectiveness of government and EC-funded research and development, to encourage international co-operation within the EC, to encourage better collaboration between universities and industry and to ensure favourable pricing policies for chemical industry feedstock (Narjes, 1986; Sargeant, 1985).

Viehoff (1986) has drawn attention to the potentially damaging social and environmental impacts of biotechnology, and to the fact that

> Biotechnology will impose a restructuring of agricultural policy on a much broader scale and perhaps at a much faster speed than that acknowledged up to now.

Whether there will indeed be further biotechnology-induced increases in the amount of land lying 'idle' will depend not only on technical expertise, but also on the emerging balance of power between the agricultural and industrial lobbies (Bijman *et al.*, 1987). In Europe, increasingly, this balance is such as to suggest that, once they have appreciated the connection, governments will choose policies to deal with food surpluses that will not impede the development of biotechnology. Therefore, by implication, they will encourage the continuing intensification of agricultural production on an ever-diminishing land area. The resultant problems of rural social disruption and depopulation would, if this analysis is correct, have to be resolved by policies that do not involve the growing of crops for food, fuel or chemical feedstock.

Assessing the risks of biotechnology: scientific aspects

As Yoxen (1987) has pointed out, the future impact of biotechnology is highly sensitive to a number of political choices, some specific to biotechnology and some not, including, as discussed above, agricultural price supports and innovation and research policies. This section deals with the central positive feedback loop illustrated in Figure 8.1, involving the nature and extent of the risks posed by the new technology and government regulation of these risks, with particular emphasis on the environmental hazards arising from the release of genetically modified organisms (GMOs).

Reactive and pro-active approaches to risk regulation

When the multinationals that are now operating in the biotechnology area were developing drugs and pesticides in the 1950s, 60s and 70s, the climate of risk regulation was entirely *reactive*. New products were assumed to be harmless until proved conclusively to be otherwise. Once a hazard had been identified, regulations were put in place to ensure that new products developed subsequently did not pose the same set of risks. No organised attempt was made to anticipate previously unforeseen hazards. In the case of organochlorine pesticides, for example, a very convincing standard of proof of environmental damage was demanded before any action was taken to limit their use. (The resulting adverse publicity for the agrochemical industry is still affecting their public image over twenty years later.)

Prior to the experience with organchlorine pesticides, persistence in the environment was seen by decision makers in the agrochemical industry as an essential feature of any new pesticide. Any non-persistent pesticide would need to be applied more frequently than, for example, DDT and so would not be competitive with it in the market place. Following the proof of environmental damage resulting from organo-chlorine pesticides, and the setting up of regulatory systems to avoid similar damage from new pesticides, the perception of the value of this attribute was reversed and any chemicals which showed undue persistence were weeded out at an early stage in the R&D screening process.

Different environmental impacts emerged in subsequent generations of pesticides and were dealt with in a piecemeal fashion. For example, the organophosphorus insecticide, carbophenothion, which was introduced as a replacement for dieldrin seed dressings, proved to be selectively toxic to geese (Jennings *et al.*, 1975). As a result, in the UK, its use was restricted to regions of the country where over-wintering geese could not be harmed by it. In another series of incidents, the fungicides benomyl and thiophanate methyl were found to be lethal to earthworms (Stringer and Lyons, 1974). The response in this case was to question the agricultural value of earthworms, and no action was taken to restrict the use of the pesticides concerned.

These points serve to illustrate the main characteristics of a reactive system of risk regulation: the industry concerned, and its products, are controlled by a system set up *in response to* adverse impacts that have arisen in earlier generations of products. New products are screened to ensure that they do not give rise to any similar risks.

In the case of biotechnology, an attempt has been made to learn from the mistakes of the past, to move beyond the previous reactive approach to risk regulation and to set up a system that is pro-active. To quote from a major UK report on genetic engineering,

> As in the 1950s, the characteristics of products – whether chemicals then or organisms now – are better understood than the nature of their impacts on the environments in which they will be used. The opportunity exists to learn from the experiences and the predictions of the past in order to build environmental foresight into any necessary regulation of these new products. (Royal Commission on Environmental Pollution, 1989).

In the very earliest stages of research, as soon as it became clear that the creation of recombinant DNA was technically possible, a world-wide moratorium on this type of research was agreed voluntarily by the scientists concerned, who were working mainly in universities and government research laboratories, to allow time to assess the potential hazards resulting from the new techniques (Yoxen, 1983). The outcome of the debates initiated at this stage has been the setting up of regulations governing the level of *containment* required for organisms and procedures, presenting varying degrees of risk, at the laboratory and industrial scales (for example, Organisation for Economic Co-operation and Development, 1986; Health and Safety Executive, 1989).

A pro-active approach to risk regulation could therefore be defined as one where the industry concerned, and its products, are controlled by a system set up to avoid potential risks, identified as a result of thorough scientific scrutiny, undertaken *in advance* of the development or marketing of products. In the case of biotechnology, therefore, safety issues have become an integral part of the development of the *industry* concerned, as well as its products.

The pro-active approach has thus already been applied, with some success, to the earliest research stages of the new biotechnology industries. The main focus of attention has moved to potential commercial products now going through the various stages of R&D, with emphasis on the need for trials to ensure the safety of the product in use, and the avoidance of risk during the trial stages themselves.

This represents the first attempt to define and distinguish reactive and pro-active approaches to risk regulation. It is important that we begin to understand these differences, as a basis for the design of better approaches to environmental risk regulation. Otherwise there is a danger that, as suggested below, arguments will develop needlessly around false issues.

The pro-active approach presents two major challenges to the risk regulator. First, there are difficulties in attempting to predict, on a scientific basis, the nature and extent of future hazards and the likelihood of their occurrence: the human imagination can be boundlessly inventive; but we can also fail to see outcomes that are, with hindsight, blatantly obvious. The remainder of this section will discuss this aspect of pro-active risk regulation for biotechnology.

The second major challenge presented by the pro-active approach is the requirement for a public input to the risk regulatory process (Pollak, 1985). Openness, accountability and public acceptability are legitimate demands of such a process, but they are much more difficult to achieve where the products concerned do not yet exist. This aspect is dealt with in the next section.

The risks surrounding the release of GMOs

The *deliberate release* to the environment of a GMO has been described (Royal Commission on Environmental Pollution, 1989, para. 2.17) as

... use without provision for containment such as special procedures, equipment and installations or facilities that provide physical barriers to minimise the organism's spread (and that of its nucleic acid) to the environment.

With previous risky products such as pesticides, the trial period and subsequent monitoring have provided sufficient safeguard for the environment. With GMOs this is no longer the case – even a trial release could lead to uncontrollable multiplication, destruction of natural habitats and the transfer of novel genetic material among natural populations. In such cases, therefore, the earlier laboratory and production-oriented strategy of containment is not an option. Competitive pressures are demanding that regulatory systems should be developed very rapidly and that they should not inhibit legitimate and safe commercial developments.

The environmental risks arising from the release and use of GMOs in agriculture can be divided into two broad categories (Tait, 1989). *Direct risks* are those that are intrinsic to the product itself, for example, uncontrollable replication of novel species, disturbance of the natural equilibrium of habitats, transfer of novel genetic material among natural populations, or development of toxins in parts of plants destined for human consumption. *Indirect risks* are mediated through human behaviour and arise as a result of the way people treat or make use of the product, for example, risks that arise from carelessness, failure to observe regulations or misuse of products. The staff in charge of a trial release may fail to observe recommended precautions or, once the product is available commercially, a farmer may attempt to maintain a culture of a genetically manipulated micro-organism in order to avoid having to make repeat purchases, with unpredictable effects on its genetic characteristics and a greatly increased chance of the transfer of genetic material to other micro-organisms. Indirect risks can also arise from secondary effects such as over-use of herbicides by farmers growing herbicide-resistant crops.

The aim of an effective pro-active risk-regulatory system should be to eliminate any GMO that poses direct risk to the environment at the pre-commercial stage of development, as a result of experience during trial release. Considerable effort is currently being expended on the design of trial release programmes so as to maximise the probability of retaining control over GMOs at this stage of their development (Bishop *et al.*, 1988; National Research Council, 1989; Royal Commission on Environmental Pollution, 1989). Indirect risks are more difficult to guard against. They could arise in the pre-commercial stage of development from mistakes or misuse by the scientists or technologists handling the GMOs or, once a product is commercially available, from carelessness or deliberate misuse by farmers or others. Indirect risks are more likely to arise in a complacent system than in one which is vigilant. It would be a mistake to assume that products will be used as recommended, or to fail to monitor closely the observance of regulations. Also GMOs should, where possible, be designed to be 'foolproof'.

In the chemical industry, systematic approaches to safety, particularly in plant design, have been developed over the past twenty years. Given the close links between the chemical and biotechnology industries, it is not surprising to find that these approaches are being examined and adapted to improve the effectiveness of biotechnology safety systems.

Two such approaches in widespread use in the UK are HAZOP (Hazard and Operability Study), which is used to identify potential hazards, and HAZAN (Hazard Analysis), which attempts to apply quantitative methods to safety problems (Chemical Industries Association, 1989; Kletz, 1986). The Royal Commission on Environmental Pollution (1989, paras. 6.15–6.20) is currently developing a variant of the HAZOP technique in order to

> ... encourage people to think of possibilities that might not otherwise have been considered, to test to the limit all possible outcomes and to minimize chances of overlooking significant hazards.

The Royal Commission also makes the case for a substantially enhanced scientific base to underpin the release of GMOs to the environment.

The rapid rate of change in the science of genetic manipulation and the expanding number of opportunities for commercial exploitation do raise the prospect of new and unexpected safety issues. But the lack of an existing strong research base on the potential environmental impact of GMOs, coupled with the strong commercial pressures from industry for a more rapid appraisal of new products is, as discussed below, leading to pressures for the abandonment of attempts to develop a pro-active approach to risk regulation for biotechnology.

The field testing of GMOs

Several potential direct risks arising from the release of GMOs have been identified to date and proposals to ensure the safety of new products in field tests have been put forward in recent reports from the US National Research Council (1989), the UK Royal Commission on Environmental Pollution (1989), and a group of eminent US ecologists (Tiedje et al., 1989). The examples given relate mainly to new developments designed for use in agriculture but, at least as far as direct risks are concerned, the same principles will apply to products to be used in other areas of natural resource management, mineral extraction or waste disposal.

The US National Research Council (NRC) (1989) Report on the Field Testing of GMOs took as its remit 'to evaluate scientific information pertinent to making decisions about the introduction of genetically modified micro-organisms and plants into the environment... under field test conditions, but not large scale commercial applications'. The report also supports a statement by the National Academy of Sciences (NAS, 1987) that risk assessment of a GMO

> should be based on the nature of the organism and the environment into which it will be introduced, not on the method by which it was modified.

The NRC committee saw itself as attempting to determine a reasoned consensus about what scientific questions must be asked and how such questions can aid in the development of a soundly-based decision making process.

Overall, the tenor of its report is reassuring. It points out that, at least in the case of plants, there is past experience of confinement procedures to limit the genetic contamination of or by field plots, and that these methods will be equally applicable to GMOs. Confinement has been achieved by several means, in research and in commercial use:

- the choice of an isolated location;
- the use of border rows of plants to limit the exit or entry of insects or diseases;
- fencing to limit animal access;
- limitation of the size of the field plot;
- removing pollinating or other reproductive organs from plants;
- bagging flowers;
- adjusting the time of year plants are grown to avoid pests;
- use of dams, soil terraces or tillage practices, or the use of chemical or biological control agents for the control of insects or fungi;
- physical barriers and security against unauthorised entry;
- genetic modification of plants to induce sterility or to reduce the ability of the plant to survive or to escape predation;
- removal of organisms that are hosts for a pathogen or insect.

If these methods should fail to achieve containment, a variety of methods exists for destroying the unwanted plant material, such as burning, ploughing under or treatment with herbicides.

The NRC report concludes that 'crops modified by molecular or cellular methods should pose risks no different from those modified by classical genetic methods for similar traits'. The point is also made that, as the new genetic manipulation techniques are more specific in terms of what genes are being added, users of these methods will be more certain about the traits they introduce into plants. However, given the rapid rate of change in the science of genetic manipulation, it would be unwise to assume that this will continue to be the case in future.

Where crops have been genetically modified so as to introduce traits dissimilar to those with which we have past experience, the report recommends that careful evaluation in small-scale field tests will enable plants exhibiting undesirable phenotypes to be destroyed. The report considers the issue of enhanced weediness in genetically modified plants but concludes that the incidence of such traits in the past has been extremely low and has been controllable. Such problems as have occurred have affected managed ecosystems rather than natural ecosystems.

The conclusions reached about micro-organisms are similar to those outlined above regarding plants. For example the comparability of classical and molecular methods for genetically modifying micro-organisms, and the greater precision of the latter, are stressed. Once again it is emphasised that the key concern is not the method by which the micro-organism is modified, but rather such phenotypic properties as the potential for gene transfer, its competitiveness and, if applicable, its pathogenicity. Past experience with micro-organisms, such as biological control agents or those used for nitrogen fixation, is assumed to provide a relevant basis for the assessment of risk and, where uncertainties persist, it is concluded that these will be resolved scientifically as our knowledge of microbial ecology increases.

As regards the environment into which a micro-organism is to be released, the ease and reliability with which it can be confined are important considerations. It may also be desirable to mark the micro-organism so that it can be monitored after introduction or to make genetic modifications designed to limit its persistence and minimise the transfer of genetic material.

Whereas the NRC report states repeatedly that no distinction needs to be made between classical and molecular methods of genetic manipulation, the Royal Commission on Environmental Pollution begins its report by asking the question, 'What is different about genetic engineering?' (RCEP, 1989, paras. 2.9–2.11). It concludes that,

> Organisms derived by genetic engineering can contain genetic information and exhibit properties that have evolved in the context of an unrelated species. These organisms may be produced in days or weeks, rather than the years required for traditional breeding techniques or the millenia for evolution. They are products of the laboratory and may well contain combinations of genes that are extremely unlikely to have occurred in nature in situations where the organisms in question could multiply.

This difference in emphasis is sustained throughout the report. Thus, whereas the NRC report (1989, p. 66) draws comforting conclusions from our past experience of plant introductions to new environments, the Royal Commission lists a series of instances where the introduction of 'exotic' organisms has caused environmental degradation. These include the uncontrollable spread of *Rhododendron* and the introduction of Dutch elm disease in the UK, the Nile perch in Lake Victoria, the rabbit in Australia and the arrival of pine blister rust, which makes it impossible to grow five-needle pines in the UK. The report also quotes the case of an obscure and rare British grass, *Vulpia fasciculata*, which has become a major introduced weed in Australia, a change in status which could not have been predicted by a detailed study of its ecology in Britain.

The report also considers the environmental impact of introduced plants and animals, bred by classical techniques. These are seen as a closer potential analogy for the introduction of GMOs, and in general they are not perceived as posing any distinct environmental threat. However, even here, adverse impacts have arisen. Oilseed rape, for example, has colonised many roadside verges and field boundaries and is now a source of mixed pollen which could hamper attempts to introduce improved strains of the crop. The conclusion reached is that the comparison between the introduction of exotics, with their record of occasionally serious environmental consequences, and that of

GMOs, is relevant where the latter is released into an environment where it is not native. Even if the GMO were released into an environment where the unmodified organism occurred naturally, it would still be necessary to consider whether the genetic manipulation concerned might upset the ecological balance that previously limited the population growth of the organism.

The situation is further complicated by the existence of critical threshold densities for population survival. Below the critical density, populations will probably fail to survive, no matter what is done to try to save them. Above it, long-term survival is much more likely. This becomes a particularly relevant consideration when one is attempting to use the information from a trial release to predict the outcome of large scale and repeated applications of a commercial product.

The Royal Commission considered various risk assessment criteria from which one could deduce that the ability to predict the outcome of a release of a GMO would be greater if it were a modified version of an organism common to the locality of the release, if its behaviour in that environment were well understood, if the genetic modification were limited in scope, if the properties of the new genetic material and its interaction with the original organism were known, and if the total quantities to be released were not large (RCEP, 1989, para. 5.14).

The Royal Commission report is sceptical of claims that gene deletions should be considered safe and that GMOs will almost invariably be less fitted for survival than their naturally occurring counterparts: a deletion could profoundly alter the behaviour of an organism, and, after release, GMOs themselves may adapt in response to selection pressure.

The Royal Commission also identified the possibility of the transference of genetic material from a GMO to another organism (for example, by plasmid transfer between micro-organisms or via pollen) as a crucial consideration. This concern is particularly relevant to the development of herbicide resistant plants where there may be a risk that the trait of herbicide resistance could be transferred to neighbouring weeds. Some plant such as oilseed rape and oats already contain many of the genes necessary to confer 'weediness' and relatively small genetic changes could significantly alter their status. The same may be true of many wild plants whose behaviour is less well understood. Problems could also arise with the insertion into plants of the *Bacillus thuringiensis* gene coding for an insecticidal toxin, if it were spread to other plant species, affecting non-target insects or increasing the selection pressure for resistance to the toxin.

Based on such considerations, the Royal Commission (1989, para. 6.12) suggested that the following information should be supplied to any panel set up to grant permission for the release of GMOs:

Scientific criteria:
- description of the parent organism, any vector and the resultant GMO, including relevant biological and ecological information;
- description of the manipulation to produce the GMO, including its possible unwanted effects;

- potential environmental effects including information on any previous related releases;
- objectives of the release;
- location of the proposed release including relevant geographic and environmental information.

Criteria related to the fitness of the applicant:
- identity of personnel involved including qualifications and training;
- arrangements for the release including preparation of the site, timing of the release, method of the release and any subsequent dismantling or decontamination of the site;
- monitoring arrangements;
- contingency plans in case of unexpected events;
- results of prior local assessment and consultation.

The scientific criteria on this list can be seen as relevant to the direct risks arising from the release of GMOs, and the criteria related to the fitness of the applicant as relevant to the indirect risks.

The overall tenor of the Royal Commission report is much more cautious than that of the NRC. It acknowledges that GMOs raise issues which do not arise in other circumstances and, as our understanding of potential hazards is still very inadequate, GMOs need

> an extra degree of scrutiny by people with particular knowledge of their behaviour and the ability to judge their environmental impact and who may nor normally be involved in the product assessment process. (para. 6.5)

A recent comprehensive review paper by a group of US ecologists (Tiedje *et al.*, 1989) goes into more detail on the ecological aspects of risk regulation than the NRC and Royal Commission report. In deciding whether an organism needs careful scientific scrutiny before being released from containment, the paper proposes sets of criteria relating to the attributes, in turn, of the genetic alteration (e.g. low genetic stability); of the parent organism (e.g. pest status); of the engineered organism (e.g. increased fitness); and of the environment (e.g. the presence of selection pressure for the engineered trait). Where the organism or the relevant environment exhibit *any* of these attributes, a high level of scientific consideration should be required, thus triggering a need for regulation during the trial release stages of product development.

Product-based and process-based approaches to biotechnology regulation.

Superficially there would not appear to be a scientific consensus about the level of scrutiny required for the field testing and regulation of GMOs. Nevertheless, each of the above reports does claim to favour a product-based, rather than a process-based approach to biotechnology regulation – a distinction which calls for closer examination.

A *process-based approach* can be defined as one where: (i) all products

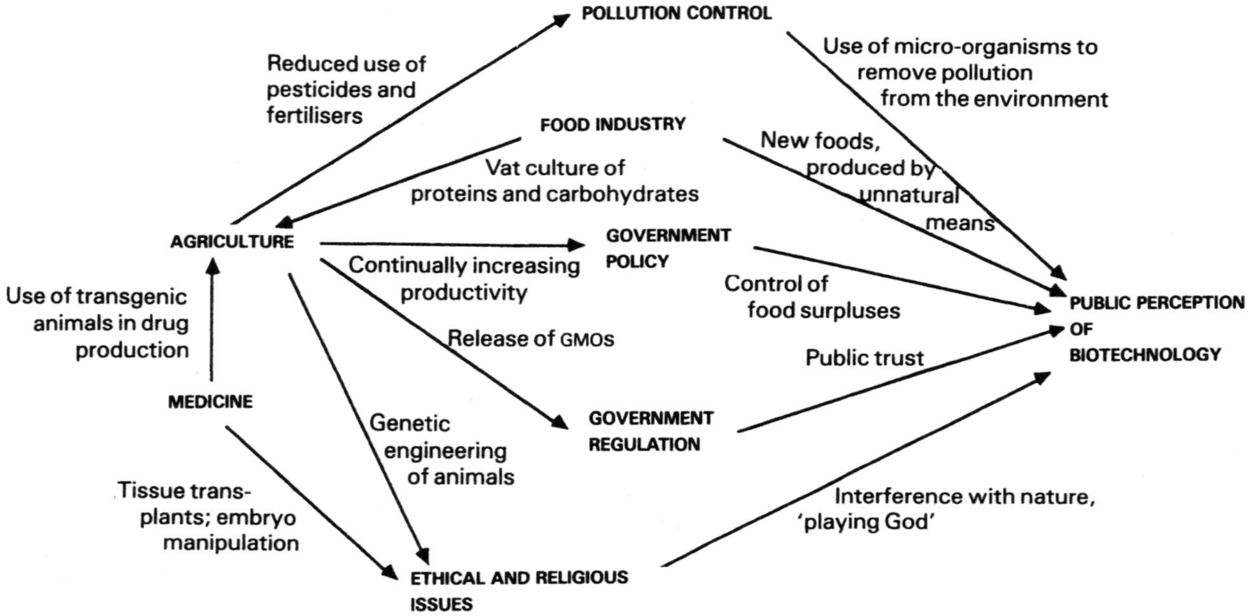

Figure 8.3 Issues affecting public perceptions of biotechnology

derived from the process of genetic manipulation, and designed to be released into the environment, are considered to have the potential to give rise to a unique range of environmental hazards, not possessed by previous generations of products; and (ii) we need to devise new types of environmental oversight and regulation to ensure that any products giving rise to such environmental hazards are excluded from further commercial development. A *product-based approach* is defined as one where: (i) it is assumed that GMOs do not present any unique environmental hazards arising from the process by which they were developed; and (ii) any environmental hazards that they do possess can be regulated effectively by the existing systems set up to deal with foods, drugs and pesticides. Based on these definitions, it follows that only the process-based approach is *proactive*, while the product-based approach implies a return to a *reactive* basis for risk regulatory decision making.

It would be useful in clarifying and advancing debate about the regulation of GMOs if there were general agreement on the nature and validity of these distinctions between product- and process-based approaches. However, although each of the above reports pays lip service to the adoption of product-based regulation only the NRC report *appears* to come close to favouring a genuinely product-based approach.

The product-based concept appears to have originated in the United States, partly as a result of fears that the emerging biotechnology industries would be stifled by draconian regulation. Fiskel and Covello (1986, p. xi), for example, refer to the formulation of a framework for the regulation of biotechnology that is directed at the product, and not the process of recombinant DNA, claiming the advantage that it would provide

> ... a measure of regulatory certainty for industry, permitting US industry to deal effectively with commercialisation and to promote increased competitiveness internationally.

Mantegazzini (1986, pp. 8–9), on the other hand, in a report prepared for the Commission of the European Communities, adopts a clearly process-based stance when commenting that:

> environmental regulations, as they stand now, were not designed to control the risks which could arise from accidental or deliberate release into the environment of new living organisms ... In some instances it may be possible to extend present legislation to cover various aspects of environmental concern. Nevertheless, the number of regulations to be amended and the inherent complexity and importance of biotechnology applications do not suggest that this piecemeal approach will provide complete, consistent and predictable legislation to ensure environmental protection and productive industrial growth.

The argument for a product-based approach within the United States appears to be largely uncontested. In Europe the situation is still fluid, with both cases being argued much more vigorously. However, the argument may be based more on rhetoric than on reason and scientific principle, and in practice there may be little difference between systems claiming to be product-based and those claiming to be process-based.

Risk perceptions in relation to biotechnology: human values

It is now widely regarded as legitimate that public attitudes should have some input to the risk regulatory process. However, this raises difficulties for pro-active risk regulation where the public may have little understanding of the nature of the products concerned or their likely benefits and risks and public attitudes will be labile and poorly defined (Tait, 1988a). In such cases, opinion tends to be led by public interest pressure groups, in competition with the public relations efforts of industry. Figure 8.3 indicates some of the biotechnology related issues that may contribute to the formation of public attitudes to biotechnology.

The companies working in the new biotechnology area, particularly on agriculture-related developments, are extremely wary about the impact of public attitudes on their industry. They have already seen serious delays in research and development, for example in California over the field testing of the 'ice minus' bacterium (Krimsky and Plough, 1988). Similar disruption and delays have been experienced in some European countries, particularly Denmark and West Germany; and there is considerable nervousness that adverse public attitudes, and disruptive public behaviour, will spread to other countries, like France, the Netherlands and the UK, where there has so far been little public protest.

Public opinion polls on biotechnology

In the United States, the Office of Technology Assessment has recently carried out a major survey of public perceptions of biotechnology (OTA, 1987). After some preliminary questions about the benefits and risks of science and technology, the survey dealt with the understanding of genetic engineering, the uses of biotechnology in agriculture and medicine and the regulation of its risks.

The report of this survey presents a picture of a public with mixed, and sometimes contradictory, feelings about biotechnology (Tait, 1988b). For example, only one in five Americans has heard of any potential dangers from genetically engineered products, but 52 per cent believed that they were at least somewhat likely to present a serious danger to people or the environment. At the same time, 66 per cent thought that genetic engineering would make life better for all people. Among the most commonly cited hazards of biotechnology were (in declining order of frequency): difficulty in controlling growth or spread; health hazards, harmful effects; creation of mutations, monsters; environmental harm, contamination; unforeseen, unintended consequences; creation of new bacteria, disease; and causing cancer. The fact that only 12 per cent could cite a specific hazard of bio-technology was regarded as reassuring for the American government.

However, if this 12 per cent were to become very vocal or active in their opposition to biotechnology they could have a very significant impact on public opinion, not least by mobilising the passive 52 per cent noted above.

The OTA report states (p.57) that, 'The public does not appear to be concerned about the morality of genetic engineering of plants and animals'. This conclusion is based on the findings that 68 per cent said that it was not morally wrong, and the 24 per cent who felt it was, had a lower educational attainment or greater religious commitment than the rest of the population. By comparison, only 52 per cent felt that it was not morally wrong to change the genetic make up of human cells, against 42 per cent who felt that this was wróng. Among those who had moral objections to genetic engineering, the report also states that religious issues did not seem to be paramount, since only 31 per cent explained their objections in terms of religious beliefs or God, while 35 per cent objected on the grounds that 'people shouldn't tamper with nature'.

A majority approved of the use of genetic engineering, in the absence of risks to people, for the following: new treatments for cancer (96%), new vaccines (91%), cures for human genetic diseases (87%), disease resistant crops (87%), frost resistant crops (85%), more productive farm animals (74%) and larger game fish (66%). The level of approval was thus highest for the uses with the most immediate human benefits. A majority of the population, indeed, was prepared to accept fairly high risks to the environment to gain the potential benefits of genetic engineering. Fifty five per cent would approve the use of an organism that would significantly increase farm production if the risks of losing some local species of plants or fish were 1:1000. If the risk was described as 'unknown but very remote', 45 per cent would still approve of its use. But only 42 per cent thought that commercial firms should be able to apply genetically engineered organisms on a large scale.

In relation to some of the apparent inconsistencies in the findings, the OTA report concluded:

> It is entirely possible to hold general preferences in the abstract that are inconsistent with specific preferences in concrete situations. While that does not mean that general preferences are not important or potentially influential, this survey consistently found genetic engineering much more popular when the public was queried in specific instances than in the abstract. (p. 83)

A similar survey of public perceptions of biotechnology was carried out recently in the UK by Research Surveys of Great Britain Ltd. (RSGB, 1988), on behalf of the Department of Trade and Industry. This investigated the awareness, understanding and level of interest in biotechnology, and its perceived benefits and risks over the next ten years. Unlike the OTA survey, genetic engineering was treated here as a separate issue from biotechnology, with questions asked about awareness, areas where research should continue and levels of confidence in safety control in relation to each issue.

Only 38 per cent of the British sample had heard of biotechnology compared with, for example 91 per cent for silicon chips, 77 per cent for nuclear physics or 60 per cent for fibre optics. The only scientific term on the list which fewer people had heard of was superconductivity, with 23 per cent. This is similar to the results of the OTA survey where 35 per cent had heard or read a 'lot' or 'a fair amount' about genetic engineering, and 63 per cent 'relatively little' or 'almost nothing'. In answer to an open-ended question about the meaning of biotechnology, most of those who were aware of the term were unable to give more than a vague answer, with medical or health-related applications predominating.

Interviewees were asked to respond to the following list of applications, indicating which they would associate with biotechnology (those items marked with an asterisk were assumed by those who drew up the questionnaire not be to associated with biotechnology):

- vaccines
- production of insulin/antibiotics
- organ transplants*
- fertility drugs*
- finding a cure for AIDs
- disease resistant crops
- human embryo transplants*
- cloning of animals/crops
- genetic engineering
- producing new foods/crops
- biological washing powders
- breakdown of oil slicks/waste
- natural food flavourings
- artificial limbs*
- making cheese.

The applications most frequently associated with biotechnology were the production of drugs such as vaccines and insulin/antibiotics. Those who were previously aware of biotechnology, and those who were more highly educated, had a stronger tendency to associate all the applications with it, including the items marked with an asterisk on the list. The survey report notes that one of the most commonplace applications of biotechnology was the one least likely to be associated with the subject – making cheese.

An interesting aspect of this survey was an attempt to illustrate the effect of provision of information on public opinion. Interviewees were asked whether they thought biotechnology would improve or harm the quality of life over the next ten years, and the question was repeated at three points during the interview, first at the beginning, the second time after interviewees had been shown the above list of applications and the third time after interviewees had been shown the same list, excluding the items marked with an asterisk. The result appeared to indicate very significantly that the more information people were given, the more likely they were to agree that biotechnology would improve the quality of life. However, it is important to note that people were only given information about potentially beneficial applications of biotechnology. Provision of information about its hazards would probably have had the reverse effect.

Respondents were asked to say whether genetic engineering research should continue in a range of areas, and the results indicate that there is concern about experimentation with animal cells and, to a lesser extent, about releasing genetically engineered micro-organisms. Genetic engineering involving human or animal cells for non-life saving reasons are the least acceptable, and medical applications the most acceptable. Thus the production from altered micro-organisms of drugs to treat chronic diseases such as cancer and heart disease was rated most highly (77%), followed closely by the alteration of human cells to prevent inherited diseases. There was little support (13%) for research to improve the level of intelligence that children would inherit. There was also relatively little support (24%) for changing the make-up of animal cells to breed more productive farm animals; but 41 per cent felt that releasing micro-organisms to control agricultural pests should continue; and 68 per cent approved of altering plant cells to produce disease resistant crops.

Confidence in the adequacy of safety controls was fairly evenly divided. For genetic engineering, 40 per cent were very confident or quite confident and 41 per cent were not very confident or not at all confident; similar results were found for biotechnology. Those who had little or no confidence in the control of biotechnology were less likely to see it as improving the quality of life, more likely to see it as harmful, and less likely to think that research should continue.

Opinion polls about risk perceptions obviously provide information that governments and companies value. Otherwise they would not continue to be funded. They can tell an industry whether it already has a serious public image problem, whether different sectors of the population have different perceptions and, if carried out regularly, whether perceptions are changing with time. However, there are pitfalls and often inadequacies in the interpretation of data from opinion polls, and they cannot provide much of the information on risk perceptions that is needed to support a pro-active approach to risk regulation.

One problem with opinion polls occurs particularly with a topic like biotechnology, where most people do not have a clear understanding of what it means, or a well-formulated set of opinions about it. In such circumstances, subtle changes in the wording of questions can result in apparently contradictory opinions or, as shown by the British example above, information or prompts provided in the course of a survey can lead to major, but probably unstable, changes of outlook.

In reality, the public is not an amorphous entity. It is made up of distinct but mobile groupings some of which have a greater role in opinion formation than others, and some of which are in a stronger position to take some form of action in relation to a particular issue than others. Without information on such factors, it is impossible to know what weight to give to some of the survey results. For example, 4 per cent of the 24 per cent in the OTA survey who opposed the creation of hybrid plants and animals on moral grounds did so out of opposition to scientific experimentation on animals. Animal liberation pressure groups are among the most militant in the UK and the US and, if this small fraction of the population was heavily represented in such groups, they could have an impact on the development of biotechnology quite out of proportion to their numbers.

Interest-based and value-based conflicts

The value of opinion polling is limited in that it cannot provide *detailed* information on the nature of perceptions about an issue, why they are favourable or adverse, whether these perceptions will remain latent or are likely to be translated into actions, and for which groups this is most likely to be the case.

It also does not indicate the extent to which opinions are motivated by concern for the interests of protagonists or by ethical and value-based considerations.

Conflicts of interest arise when a development will selectively and adversely affect the interests of one group of people, while benefiting other groups. In a *value conflict*, a development is opposed because it is regarded as intrinsically bad. The distinction is illustrated in the OTA survey results by two groups of respondents: the 32 per cent who were against field testing *in their own community* (an interest-based judgement); and the (probably overlapping) 20 per cent who would not approve of the field testing of GMOs *at all* (value-based judgement).

It is important to understand the extent to which interests and values are involved in any conflict, because tactics that will improve one may exacerbate the other. As summarised in Figure 8.4, a conflict of interest can sometimes be resolved simply by giving more or better information to change the public understanding of the potential impact on their interests. Where there is a genuine divergence of interests, the various parties can bargain with one another until a satisfactory settlement is reached. Conflicts of value, on the other hand, can be exacerbated by both tactics. Protagonists in a value conflict may only accept information that is in accordance with their beliefs, with everything else treated as propaganda and its source discredited. Attempts at bargaining to reach a settlement may be treated as bribery, the trading of principles for cash.

In any community of individuals who are concerned about an issue, for some their response will be interest-based, for some value-based and for others a mixture of the two. There will be a continuum of shades of attitude both between and within individuals and there is therefore a need to understand the extent to which an issue can be characterised as one type or the other, and the extent to which it is likely to change from one to the other. A switch from self-interested to principled opposition can occur relatively easily, catalysed, for example, by an incident which leads to a loss of public trust in regulators (see Figure 8.3); but achieving change in the reverse direction is often a difficult and slow process.

Pressure groups can be categorised on these dimensions in much the same

Figure 8.4 Conflicts over potentially hazardous activities in the biotechnology industries

INTEREST CONFLICTS	VALUE CONFLICTS
Based on self-interest of protagonists	Based on ethics or values of protagonists
Likely to be restricted to specific biotechnology developments	Likely to spread across all biotechnology developments
Likely to be location-or sector-specific	Likely to be organised nationally or internationally
Can usually be resolved by the provision of information or compensation, or by negotiation	Very difficult to resolve–information is viewed as propaganda, negotiation as betrayal, compensation as bribery

(*Source*: Tait, 1988a)

way as individuals. For example, private interest pressure groups such as trade associations in industry or lobbying organisations for the farming industry, are based on the shared *interests* of their members and will tend to react to issues accordingly. Public interest pressure groups such as Friends of the Earth or Greenpeace are organised around the shared *values* of their members. As illustrated in Figure 8.4, the response of such groups tends to spread conflicts over biotechnology to a wider range of developments, over a wider geographical area, and to make them more difficult to resolve.

Interactions between technology, environment and society

This chapter has attempted to explore some of the factors that will shape our technological, environmental and social futures, as they will be determined by new biotechnology developments in the agricultural and food sectors. Ultimately, all three will depend on the kinds of products industry chooses to develop, or is able to develop, and the level of investment in the industry and hence the number and variety of products available, as indicated by the central position of this variable in Figure 8.1.

What are the possible effects on agriculture?

The likely impacts on socio-economic systems of biotechnology innovations are represented by the negative feedback loop on the left hand side of Figure 8.1. Negative feedback leads to a position of overall stability, the equilibrium point in this case being dependent on such factors as the level of government support for agriculture, farming incomes and competition between companies. Industry is not, however, behaving passively in this situation. Where a 'market pull' for a new product does not exist, companies are engaging in 'technology push', putting up with longer product lead times and greater development costs in an attempt to move this feedback loop up to a new equilibrium point involving a higher level of overall activity.

There are strong indications that biotechnology is technically capable of leading to major increases in the efficiency of agricultural production and hence, if food surpluses are to be avoided, to very large reductions in the area of land given over to agriculture. Several factors, such as government regulation or adverse public opinion could inhibit this process, but it would be a mistake to underestimate the determination of the large multinational companies to succeed in this area.

If biotechnology leads to major reductions in the area of land under agriculture and hence to social upheaval in rural areas, analogous to that caused by the earlier green revolution in developing countries, this could well provoke social opposition to biotechnology (Kloppenburg, 1984; Viehoff, 1986). There is some evidence that such factors are already contributing to the resistance by the farming community to the introduction of bovine somatotrophin.

Will biotechnology change our relationship to nature?

There are two ways of looking at the question addressed in this section. On the one hand we can treat all agriculture as an essentially un-natural, industrial activity and attempt to minimise its environmental impact on the surrounding land areas. If biotechnology does enable us to make major improvements in agricultural productivity, the land released from agriculture will provide us with the best opportunity for decades to restore natural ecosystems on a large scale, and we increasingly have the scientific and management knowledge to enable us to do this (Tait *et al.*, 1988c). Biotechnology will, in addition, enable us to achieve these higher levels of productivity and, at the same time, to reduce the pollution and hence the impact of agriculture on the surrounding areas.

The other way of looking at this question is to regard agriculture as part of nature and to emphasise the extent to which it remains subject to natural forces. From this point of view, biotechnology is usually seen as driving agriculture onto a new technological treadmill and further away from long-term sustainability which is only achievable by working with nature rather than against it. It is, however, conceivable that biotechnology could come to be regarded as more 'biological' and hence more 'natural' than the previous generation of industrial inputs, pesticides and fertilisers. Whether this is the case will probably depend largely on the kinds of products industry chooses to concentrate on (either input saving, such as pest-resistant crops, or input-using, such as herbicide-resistant crops). Such factors are beginning to influence strategic decision making in companies but it is too early to predict the outcome.

Biotechnology is likely to increase the degree of polarisation between these two extreme viewpoints about our relationship to nature and therefore to increase the levels of conflict. For those who see agriculture as a largely industrial, un-natural activity, it will increase their sense of mastery over nature. For those who view agriculture as a benign harnessing of nature, biotechnology will be seen as an even greater threat to the system than the previous chemical revolution. Such factors underlie some of the conflicts already surfacing in several countries.

It is important that policy-makers should begin to appreciate the range and subtlety of the potential interactions in these areas. We need to consider whether nature would benefit more from a continued intensification of agriculture and a greatly increased area of land available for wildlife conservation or whether it would be better served by adopting less intensive agricultural systems over a wider land area. These options would lead to very different agricultural policies which would in turn affect strategic decision making in industry, as illustrated in Figure 8.1. An 'intensification' policy will encourage industry to develop products supporting increasingly industrialised agricultural systems; an 'extensification' policy will encourage industry to develop products supporting more 'natural', 'sustainable' agricultural systems.

How should we handle the environmental risks?

The relationships on the right hand side of Figure 8.1, centred on the government regulation of environmental risks, are currently a major focus of attention. The level of government control through regulatory measures is not normally a *variable*. Only at times such as the present, when regulatory systems for biotechnology are being developed, would it be so open to lobbying influences. In this instance, industry perceives that a high level of regulation will inhibit investment and is lobbying accordingly in an attempt to keep the positive feedback loop running so as to favour increasing investment. Some public interest groups who are antagonistic to biotechnology see the present situation as an opportunity to influence government decision making so as to exert a long term inhibitory influence on industrial investment in agriculture-related areas. The argument appears to be focusing on whether the regulatory systems adopted should be product-based or process-based.

It is usually assumed, somewhat simplistically, that industry and government are involved in risk regulation as a rational, scientific process and that public perceptions are the only area where values enter into the equation. However, the actions and statements of scientists, regulators and managers will be influenced by their own interests and values. It is possible that one reason for emphasising the lack of need for a process-based approach is to reassure the public that the products of biotechnology do not present any unique hazards not possessed by previous generations of agricultural inputs. However, as the analysis of public attitudes and responses showed, such arguments could back-fire. For example, if the public perceives the emphasis on product-based regulation as an abandonment of a pro-active approach to regulation this may diminish their trust of the regulators and of industry.

The consensus underlying the rhetoric here seems to be that the regulatory systems developed for GMOs should take account of the fact that products may present unique hazards to the environment which would not be expected to occur in non-genetically manipulated products, and that regulatory systems and field testing protocols will need to be specially adapted to guard against this. We may be able to relax some requirements once we have more experience in this area but given our present state of ignorance and the small amount of environmental research being carried out, relative to the amount of investment in a wide range of new products, it is better to err on the safe side.

How should we inform the public?

As the relationships on the right hand side of Figure 8.1 indicate, the eventual level of government control through risk-regulating measures will depend, among other things, on the balance of influences from industry and from the public, still to be resolved.

The initiative in public opinion-formation on the subject of biotechnology appears, in some countries at least, to have been taken by public interest pressure groups who are opposed, in principle, to biotechnology. The evidence from opinion polls conducted so far is that the public as a whole has yet to make up its mind about biotechnology and opinions are still quite labile. However, one seriously hazardous incident involving biotechnology could lead to rapid and adverse changes in this situation. The process of polarisation of public attitudes could take place quite rapidly, and would be very difficult to reverse, so it is very important to ensure that it does not happen needlessly.

There is no doubt that the public needs to be better informed about biotechnology, its benefits and its potential social and environmental impacts. However, it is difficult to attract the attention of a relatively uninterested public with anything other than sensationalism and most suggestions for public education involve a top-down flow of information to passive recipients. One way of arousing responsible interest is to provide greater opportunities for public comment and to involve the public to a greater extent in decision making.

The central role of industry

In Figure 8.1 the 'level of investment by industry' is treated as a single variable. However, different sectors of industry and different companies will, in fact, respond to the various influences in different ways. Up to a point, regulation *benefits* large multinational companies by acting as a barrier to entry to small new firms. There is considerable evidence that small biotechnology companies in the agriculture area are choosing not to develop products that involve the use of genetic manipulation because of fears that public pressures will persuade governments to impose excessively strict regulatory regimes. If this continues and small and medium-sized companies are forced out of this sector, there will be a major impact on the nature of the new biotechnology products brought to market. Many of the socially and environmentally useful new biotechnology products and developments are likely to be in 'niche markets' not big enough to be attractive to a multinational company. If there are no small companies operating in this sector, these products are unlikely to be developed. In this case it will be in society's interests, as well as the interest of industry, to avoid unnecessarily demanding regulatory regimes.

This chapter has shown how a wide range of interacting variables will work together to influence the level of industrial investment in new biotechnology products and hence the nature of our food and agricultural industries, the management of rural resources, our general approach to nature conservation and rural social structures.

There is a need for a similarly integrated approach to policy making so that agricultural and industrial support policies, risk regulatory systems, public information campaigns and nature conservation initiatives can all be developed in the full understanding of their mutual interactions.

References

Allen, Sir Geoffrey (1985) The Needs for the 1990s: Biotechnology, *Chemistry and Industry*, 23, 784-6.

Armstrong, D. G. (1985) The General Implications of Biotechnology in the Agricultural Industry, in (eds) Copping, L. G. and Rodgers, P. *Biotechnology and its Application to Agriculture*, Monograph no. 32. Croydon, British Crop Protection Council Publications, 3-11.

Bijman, J., van den Doel, K. and Junne, G. (1987) *The International Dimension of Biotechnology in Agriculture*. Dublin, European Foundation for the Improvement of Living and Working Conditions.

Bishop, D. H. L., Entwhistle, P. F., Cameron, I. R., Allen, C. J. and Possee R. D. (1988) Field Trials of Genetically Engineered Baculovirus Insecticides, in (eds) Sussman, M. *et al. The Release of Genetically Engineered Micro-organisms*. London, Academic Press, 143-179.

Chemical Industries Association (1989) *A Guide to Hazard and Operability Studies*. London, CIA Ltd.

Commission of the European Communities (1984) *Eurofutures: The Challenges of Innovation*. Forecasting and Assessment in Science and Technology (FAST), The Commission of the European Communities in association with the journal *Futures*. London, Butterworth & Co. Ltd., 199.

Eades, A. (1986) Chemical Industry will Pay Farmers to Grow Molecules, *Agricultural Supply Industry*, 16(12), 5.

Elmerich, C., Fogher, · C., Perroud, B. and Bozouklian, H. (1985) *Azosporillium*: a Potential Biofertilizer for Grasses, in (eds) Copping, L. G. and Rodgers, P. *Biotechnology and its Application to Agriculture*, Monograph no. 32. Croydon, British Crop Protection Council Publications. 121-6.

Fasella, P. (1986) The European Dimension for Biotechnology, in (ed) Davies, D. *Industrial Biotechnology in Europe: Issues for Public Policy*. London, Frances Pinter, 140-148.

Fernandez, L. (1985) Splashes and Ripples: the Chemical Industry in the New Millennium, *Chemistry and Industry*, 23, 787-9.

Fiskel, J. and Covello, V. T. (eds) (1986) *Biotechnology Risk Assessment: Issues and Methods for Environmental Introductions*. New York, Pergamon Press.

Freeman, C., Clark, J. and Strete, E. (1982) *Employment and Technical Innovation*. London, Frances Pinter.

Giles, K. L. (1985). Recent Advances in Commercial Micropropagation, in (eds) Copping, L. G. and Rodgers, P. *Biotechnology and its Application to Agriculture*, Monograph no. 32. Croydon, British Crop Protection Council Publications, 51-7.

Health and Safety Executive (HSE) (1989) *Genetic Manipulation Regulations 1989: Guidance on Regulations*. London, Her Majesty's Stationery Office.

Jennings, D. M. *et al.* (1975) Organophosphorus Poisoning: a Comparative Study of the Toxicity of Carbophenothion to the Canada Goose, the Pigeon and the Japanese Quail, *Pesticide Science*, 6, 245-257.

Johnston, A. W. B., Rossen, L., Shearman, C. M., Evans, I. and Downie, J. A. (1985), in (eds) Copping, L. G. and Rodgers, P. *Biotechnology and its Applications to Agriculture*, Monograph No. 32. Croydon, British Crop Protection Council Publications. 119-20.

Kletz, T. A. (1986) *HAZOP and HAZAN: Notes on the Identification and Assessment of Hazards*. Rugby, The Institution of Chemical Engineers.

Kloppenburg, J. (1984) The Social Impacts of Biogenetic Technology: Past and Future, in (eds) Berardi, G. M. and Geisler, C. C. *The Social Consequences and Challenges of New Agricultural Technologies*. Boulder, US, Westview Press, 291-321.

Krimsky, S. and Plough, A. (1988) *Environmental Hazards: Communicating Risks as a Social Process*. Dover, Mass, Auburn House Publishing Co, 75-129.

Lisansky, S. G. (1985). Microbial Insecticides. in (eds) Copping, L. G. and Rodgers, P. *Biotechnology and its Applications to Agriculture*, Monograph no. 32. Croydon, British Crop Protection Council Publications, 145-51.

Mantegazzini, M. C. (1986) *The Environmental Risks from Biotechnology*. London, Frances Pinter.

Marstrand, P. K. (1981) *Patterns of Change in Biotechnology*. SPRU Occasional Paper Series No. 15. Brighton, University of Sussex, Science Policy Research Unit.

Metz, G. (1984) Solving Structural Problems of the European Chemical Industry, *Chemistry and Industry*, 24, 871-7.

Miflin, B. J., Kreis, M., Bright, S. W. J. and Shewry, P. R. (1985) Improving the Amino Acid Content of Cereal Grains, in (eds) Copping, L. G. and Rodgers, P. *Biotechnology and its Application to Agriculture*, Monograph no. 32. Croydon, British Crop Protection Council Publications, 71-78.

Narjes, K. H. (1986) The European Commission's Strategy for Biotechnology, in (ed) Davies, D. *Industrial Biotechnology in Europe: Issues for Public Policy*. London, Frances Pinter, 123-133.

National Academy of Sciences (1987) *Introduction of Recombinant DNA-Engineered Organisms into the Environment: Key Issues.* Washington, DC, National Academy Press.

National Research Council (1989) *Field Testing Genetically Modified Organisms: Framework For Decisions.* Washington DC, National Academy Press.

North, J. J. (1986) Use and Management of the Land: Current and Future Trends, *1986 British Crop Protection Conference – Pests and Diseases.* Thornton Heath, BCPC Publications, 3–14.

Office of Technology Assessment (OTA) (1984) *Commercial Biotechnology: an International Analysis* (OTA-BA-218) Washington, DC, US Congress, Office of Technology Assessment.

Office of Technology Assessment (OTA) (1987) *New Developments in Biotechnology – Background Paper: Public Perceptions of Biotechnology* (OTA-BP-BA). Washington DC, US Government Printing Office.

Organisation for Economic Co-operation and Development (1986). *Recombinant DNA Safety Considerations.* Paris, OECD.

Polge, C. (1985) Artificial Breeding, in (eds) Copping, L. G. and Rodgers, P. *Biotechnology and its Application to Agriculture*, Monograph no. 32. Croydon, British Crop Protection Council Publications, 89–96.

Pollak, M. (1985) Public Participation, in (eds) Otway, H. and Peltu, M. *Regulating Industrial Risks: Science, Hazards and Public Protection.* London, Butterworths, 76–93.

Porceddu, E. (1986). Agriculture as a Customer and Supplier of Biotechnology, in (ed) Davies, D. *Industrial Biotechnology in Europe: Issues for Public Policy.* London, Frances Pinter, 83–96.

Research Surveys of Great Britain Ltd (1988) *Public Perceptions of Biotechnology: Interpretative Report* Ref 4780. RSGB.

Royal Commission on Environmental Pollution (1989). *Thirteenth Report: The Release of Genetically Engineered Organisms to the Environment* Cm 720. London, HMSO.

Sargeant, K. (1985) A European View of Biotechnology in Agriculture, in (eds) Copping, L. G. and Rodgers, P. *Biotechnology and its Application to Agriculture*, Monograph no. 32. Croydon, British Crop Protection Council Publications, 13–20.

Sharp, M. (1985). Biotechnology: Watching and Waiting, in (ed) Sharp, M. *Europe and the New Technologies.* London, Frances Pinter Ltd., 161–212.

Spencer, G. S. G. (1985) Future Prospects for Growth Promotion, *Span*, 27, 24–26.

Steane, D. E. (1985) Potential Benefits of Improved Breeding Programmes, in (eds) Copping, L. G. and Rodgers, P. *Biotechnology and its Application to Agriculture*, Monograph no. 32. Croydon, British Crop Protection Council Publications, 79–88.

Stringer, A. and Lyons, C. H. (1974) The Effect of Benomyl and Thiophanate Methyl on Earthworm Populations in Apple Orchards, *Pesticide Science*, 5, 189–196.

Tait, E. J. (1981) The Flow of Pesticides: Industrial and Farming Perspectives, in (eds) O'Riordan, T. and Turner, R. K. *Progress in Resource Management and Environmental Planning*, Vol. 3. Chichester, John Wiley & Sons, 219–250.

Tait, E.J. and Lane, A.B. (1987) Insecticide Production, Distribution and Use, in (eds) Tait, E. J. and Napompeth, B. *The Management of Pests and Pesticides: Farmers' Perceptions and Practices*. Boulder, US, Westview Press, 38–48.

Tait, J. (1988a) NIMBY and NIABY: Public Perception of Biotechnology, *International Industrial Biotechnology*, 8(6), 5–9.

Tait, J. (1988b) Public Perceptions of Biotechnology Hazards, *Journal of Chemical Technology and Biotechnology*, 43, 363–372.

Tait, J., Lane, A. and Carr, S. (1988c) *Practical Conservation: Site Assessment and Management Planning*. Sevenoaks, Hodder and Stoughton.

Tait, J. (1989) Pro-active Risk Regulation for Biotechnology Products. *Proceedings, International Seminar on the Safety of Agricultural Biotechnology*. Gent, Royal Flemish Society of Engineers, Antwerp, 32–43.

Thompson, S. (1986) Biotechnology – the Shape of Things to Come or False Promise?, *Futures*, August 1986, 514–525.

Tiedje, J. M., Colwell, R. K., Grossman, Y. L., Hodson, R. E., Lenski, R. E., Mack, R. N. and Regal, P.J. (1989) The Planned Introduction of Genetically Engineered Organisms: Ecological Considerations and Recommendations, *Ecology*, 70(2), 298–315.

Viehoff, P. J. (1986) Biotechnology and the Role of the European Parliament, in (ed) Davies, D. *Industrial Biotechnology in Europe: Issues for Public Policy*. London, Frances Pinter, 109–113.

Wallace, L., Paterson, A., McCarthy, A., Raeder, U., Ramsey, L., McDonald, M., Haylock, R., and Broda, P. (1983) The Problem of Lignin Degradation, in (eds) Phelps, C. F. and Clarke, P. H. *Biotechnology*. London, The Biochemical Society, 87–95.

Yoxen, E. (1983) *The Gene Business: Who Should Control Biotechnology?* London, Pan Books Ltd.

Yoxen, E. (1987). *The Impact of Biotechnology on Living and Working Conditions*. Dublin, The European Foundation for the Improvement of Living and Working Conditions.

For Product Safety Concerns and Information please contact our EU
representative GPSR@taylorandfrancis.com
Taylor & Francis Verlag GmbH, Kaufingerstraße 24, 80331 München, Germany

www.ingramcontent.com/pod-product-compliance
Ingram Content Group UK Ltd.
Pitfield, Milton Keynes, MK11 3LW, UK
UKHW021828240425
457818UK00006B/117